Social Capital in the Asia Pacific

Social capital is broadly conceptualised as consisting of resources and network ties embedded in the social structures and relationships that facilitate beneficial outcomes for the actors within those structures. Despite the number of research studies on social capital, there have been fewer attempts to examine social capital in the context of service-oriented firms, particularly in the Asia Pacific. This is surprising as the service industry plays an important role in the global services trade transactions and business activities. Social capital enables and maintains social relations for business transformation for service-oriented firms. Indeed, it would be unimaginable for any economic activity, particularly in service-oriented firms, to occur without social capital.

This examination of social capital in the Asia Pacific region provides the context for recognising the cultural, social and economic opportunities and challenges of several Asia Pacific countries that can potentially enrich our knowledge and understanding of the region. Contributions are drawn from cases based in Thailand, Indonesia, South Korea, China and Australia, for relevant application in the areas of social capital and service-oriented firms in the Asia Pacific.

This book was originally published as a special issue of the *Asia Pacific Business Review*.

Yuliani Suseno is with the School of Business and Law at Edith Cowan University, Joondalup, Australia. Her research interests are in the areas of social capital, international HRM, knowledge management and innovation.

Chris Rowley has affiliations with Kellogg College at the University of Oxford, UK; Cass Business School at the City University of London, UK; Griffith University, Nathan, Australia; and the Institute of Asia and Pacific Studies at Nottingham University, UK.

Social Capital in the Asia Pacific

Examples from the Services Industry

Edited by
Yuliani Suseno and Chris Rowley

Routledge
Taylor & Francis Group

LONDON AND NEW YORK

First published 2019
by Routledge
2 Park Square, Milton Park, Abingdon, Oxon, OX14 4RN, UK

and by Routledge
52 Vanderbilt Avenue, New York, NY 10017, USA

First issued in paperback 2020

Routledge is an imprint of the Taylor & Francis Group, an informa business

British Library Cataloguing-in-Publication Data
A catalogue record for this book is available from the British Library

ISBN 13: 978-0-367-58436-8 (pbk)
ISBN 13: 978-1-138-35294-0 (hbk)

Typeset in Myriad Pro
by codeMantra

Publisher's Note
The publisher accepts responsibility for any inconsistencies that may have arisen during the conversion of this book from journal articles to book chapters, namely the possible inclusion of journal terminology.

Disclaimer
Every effort has been made to contact copyright holders for their permission to reprint material in this book. The publishers would be grateful to hear from any copyright holder who is not here acknowledged and will undertake to rectify any errors or omissions in future editions of this book.

Contents

Citation Information

The chapters in this book were originally published in *Asia Pacific Business Review*, volume 24, issue 2 (April 2018). When citing this material, please use the original page numbering for each article, as follows:

Preface
Gordon Redding
Asia Pacific Business Review, volume 24, issue 2 (April 2018) p. 137

Introduction
Reflections on research on social capital and the services industry
Yuliani Suseno and Chris Rowley
Asia Pacific Business Review, volume 24, issue 2 (April 2018) pp. 138–149

Chapter 1
Spilling the social capital beans: a comparative case study of coffee service enterprises within Asia-Pacific
Aaron Tham, David Fleischman and Peter Jenner
Asia Pacific Business Review, volume 24, issue 2 (April 2018) pp. 150–173

Chapter 2
Disruptive innovation and the creation of social capital in Indonesia's urban communities
Yuliani Suseno
Asia Pacific Business Review, volume 24, issue 2 (April 2018) pp. 174–195

Chapter 3
Selling trust in cyber space: social networking service (SNS) providers and social capital amongst netizens in South Korea
Ingyu Oh, Wonho Jang and Sanghyeon Kim
Asia Pacific Business Review, volume 24, issue 2 (April 2018) pp. 196–211

Chapter 4
The effect of technology management capability on new product development in China's service-oriented manufacturing firms: a social capital perspective
Weiwei Wu, Yexin Liu and Tachia Chin
Asia Pacific Business Review, volume 24, issue 2 (April 2018) pp. 212–232

Chapter 5
Beyond 'know-what' and 'know-how' to 'know-who': enhancing human capital with social capital in an Australian start-up accelerator
Pi-Shen Seet, Janice Jones, Lloyd Oppelaar and Graciela Corral de Zubielqui
Asia Pacific Business Review, volume 24, issue 2 (April 2018) pp. 233–260

Conclusion
Future directions for research on social capital and the services industry
Yuliani Suseno and Chris Rowley
Asia Pacific Business Review, volume 24, issue 2 (April 2018) pp. 261–271

For any permission-related enquiries please visit:
http://www.tandfonline.com/page/help/permissions

Notes on Contributors

Tachia Chin is a Professor of Human Resource Management in the School of Management at Hangzhou Dianzi University, China.

David Fleischman, PhD, is a Lecturer in Marketing at the University of the Sunshine Coast, Australia. David's research focuses on value co-creation in services marketing, international higher education, community engagement and food marketing. His work has been published in several leading marketing journals and conferences.

Wonho Jang is a Professor of Sociology at the University of Seoul, South Korea. He received a PhD in Sociology from the University of Chicago, USA. His main research interests are urban sociology, social capital and popular culture.

Peter Jenner is a Lecturer in International Business at the University of the Sunshine Coast, Australia. Peter's research focuses on social entrepreneurship, social enterprise sustainability and regional export development. His work has been published in several prominent business journals and conferences.

Janice Jones is a Senior Lecturer in the Flinders Business School at Flinders University, Adelaide, Australia. Her research interests include human resource development and innovation, particularly in smaller enterprises, and the corporatisation of health care organisations.

Sanghyeon Kim is a PhD Candidate in Sociology at the University of Seoul, South Korea. His main research interests are big data analysis, social network analysis and economic sociology.

Yexin Liu is a Doctoral Student of Business Administration in the School of Management at the Harbin Institute of Technology, China.

Ingyu Oh is a Professor of Hallyu Studies in the Research Institute of Korean Studies at Korea University, Seoul, South Korea. His main research interests are economic sociology, cultural sociology and international business strategy.

Lloyd Oppelaar completed a BA of Business (Honours) Degree from the Flinders Business School at Flinders University, Adelaide, Australia. He is currently a Marketing Coordinator at Community Living Australia, an organisation that provides personalised services and support to people with disabilities.

Gordon Redding spent 24 years at the University of Hong Kong and was founding director of its business school. His main research has been on varieties of capitalism in Asia with a special interest in Chinese managerial ideology, published as *The Spirit of Chinese Capitalism*. He also directed the Euro-Asia Centre at INSEAD, and was founding director of The HEAD Foundation in Singapore. He recently co-edited *The Oxford Handbook of Asian Business Systems*.

Chris Rowley has affiliations with Kellogg College at the University of Oxford, UK; Cass Business School at the City University of London, UK; Griffith University, Nathan, Australia; and the Institute of Asia and Pacific Studies at Nottingham University, UK.

Pi-Shen Seet is a Professor of Entrepreneurship and Innovation in the Management discipline at Edith Cowan University's School of Business and Law, Joondalup, Australia, where he is also the Deputy Director of the Centre for Work and Organizational Performance. He conducts research and supervises research students in entrepreneurship, innovation, family business, international business and human resource management.

Yuliani Suseno is with the School of Business and Law at Edith Cowan University, Joondalup, Australia. Her research interests are in the areas of social capital, international HRM, knowledge management and innovation.

Aaron Tham is a Lecturer and Researcher in the School of Business, Faculty of Arts, Business and Law, with a focus in Tourism and Hospitality, at the University of the Sunshine Coast, Australia. Aaron has published in top-tier tourism journals and serves as an editor on various journals including *Tourism Management Perspectives*. He is also the Vice President of the Travel and Tourism Research Association Asia Pacific Chapter.

Weiwei Wu is a Professor of Business Administration in the School of Management at the Harbin Institute of Technology, China.

Graciela Corral de Zubielqui is a Senior Lecturer of the postgraduate Project Management and Innovation area in the Entrepreneurship, Commercialization and Innovation Centre at the University of Adelaide, Australia. Her research interests include innovation; knowledge transfer; collaboration activities among government, industry and university; and SMEs' performance and impact on regional economic development.

Preface

Ever since Putnam's remarkable revelation of the differences in societal structure between northern and southern Italy, and their implications for civil society, for economic structures and for the contrasting nature of ideals of cooperativeness that shape much social action, awareness of this powerful, intangible influence has been at the leading edge of much social science. It has been constantly reinforced by 30 years of the World Values Surveys. Studies of the exploding growth of East Asia in recent decades have confirmed two important social facts: across the region there is strong dependence on specific interpersonal relationships beyond family in making economies work; and the way this happens itself varies within the region. Asia cannot be treated as one category of social structure. Having said that there is still a fundamental cross-cultural difference globally between one large block of societies that are essentially collectivist and hierarchical, and another that are individualist and egalitarian. It may well be that, fortuitously for social science, Putnam had unwittingly discovered part of the global boundary between them running across the Italian peninsula.

Business people coming into the Asian region for the first time are usually told 'it is all about relationships'. They are not always told why, because people at the interface may know the fact, but not its origins, or even how its workings rest on a particular social psychology. Nor that the psychology varies between cultures, and why it does so.

This collection opens up such issues to view, as a contribution to understanding a powerful force in international business. Such an influence needs to be acknowledged by those responsible for work that blends the logics of such matters as market demand and cost effectiveness, with the less visible logics of special kinds of trust. The Western world tends to rely on trust in institutions and laws, plus some assistance from interpersonal reciprocities. In Asian cultures, for perfectly understandable reasons, it is the other way round, and the reciprocities come first. This is especially relevant in industries such as services where the personal aspect of transactions, such as qualifications, experience, contacts and reliability, are key to many success stories.

This collection of studies has the virtues of being grounded in reality, and also being varied enough to demonstrate that Asia Pacific is an area that repays attention to local traditions and ideals in the context of globalization.

Gordon Redding

Introduction: reflections on research on social capital and the services industry

Yuliani Suseno and Chris Rowley

ABSTRACT

Notwithstanding the substantial literature on social capital produced in recent years, there have been fewer attempts to examine social capital within the services industry. Our contribution highlights existing research on social capital particularly on the application and outcomes of social capital in the context of service-oriented firms in the Asia Pacific region. We structure our analysis of existing research around the different approaches of social capital studies – either ego-centric or sociocentric approach and the focus on the creation and outcomes of social capital. The analysis on the different perspectives of social capital research contributes to our further understanding in the areas of social capital and services industry in the Asia Pacific. The implications for theory and management practice are noted.

Introduction

For more than four decades since Loury's (1977) work, research on social capital has played an important role in advancing our knowledge and understanding of the impact of social relationships, networks and resources. Social capital is broadly conceptualized by scholars as consisting of resources and network ties embedded in the social structures and relationships that facilitate beneficial outcomes for the actors within those structures (Coleman 1988; Suseno and Pinnington 2018). Converging evidence from scholarly research highlights the effect of social capital at the individual (e.g. Bozionelos 2014; Hauser et al. 2016), organizational (e.g. Andrews 2010; Carmona-Lavado, Cuevas-Rodríguez, and Cabello-Medina 2010) and societal levels (e.g. Aldrich and Meyer 2015; Kwon and Arenius 2010; Lin, Fu, and Chen 2014).

However, notwithstanding the substantial literature on social capital over the years, there have been fewer attempts to examine social capital in the context of service-oriented firms. Yet, the service industry plays an important role in global services and trade activities. Services continue to account for significant levels of total foreign direct investment (FDI) in greenfield projects and merger and acquisition deals in the world (UNCTAD 2014). The trend towards personalization also drives manufacturing firms to be more customer- and service-focused (Gebauer and Kowalkowski 2012). Given the increasing demand for firms to be more service-oriented, it is important to understand and explore the dynamics of relationships and resources embedded in social networks of service-oriented firms. The set of contributions in this collection responds to calls for more insight into exploring social capital in the context of service-oriented firms.

We sought contributions from scholars on studies that examine the application and outcomes of social capital in the context of service-oriented firms in the Asia Pacific region. The Asia Pacific region has long been regarded as an interesting research context for management research (Rowley and Redding 2012). Many of the Asian economies can also be considered as economic powerhouses. For example, the 10 member states of the Association of South-east Asian Nations (ASEAN), currently the seventh largest economy in the world, is projected to be ranked as the fourth largest economy by 2050 (Vinayak, Thompson, and Tonby 2016). According to the World Bank's 2017 Global Economic Prospect, growth in developing East Asia and Pacific continued to be robust in 2018, at the growth rate of 6% in comparison to 1.9% growth in the advanced economies (The World Bank 2017). Furthermore, the population in many of the Asia Pacific countries is huge and they are also becoming less dependent on advanced industrial economies (Das 2012). The collection of research of social capital in the service context in the Asia Pacific region is, thus, a worthwhile avenue of inquiry.

Here, we highlight some aspects of existing research on social capital. We discuss two important issues: the different approaches of social capital studies and the creation and outcomes of social capital in existing research. We then illustrate how these aspects relate to the contributions that are part of this collection.

Reflections of existing research on social capital

Egocentric and sociocentric approaches of social capital

Research on social capital is varied in their approaches or perspectives of analysis. Many studies view social capital as an individual or private good in terms of 'how individuals access and use resources embedded in social networks to gain returns in instrumental actions (e.g. finding better jobs)' (Lin 2001, 21). The argument for the private good of social capital is primarily focused on the viewpoint that social capital benefits individuals who are linked to powerful others (Gubbins and Garavan 2015; Hadani et al. 2012). This view of the private good of social capital is generally referred to as the egocentric approach (Burt 2015; Kostova and Roth 2003; Lin 2001), which is related to the direct and indirect relationships with others whom one can reach through one's networks. Other scholars, such as Barroso-Castro, Villegas-Periñan, and Casillas-Bueno (2016) refer to this egocentric approach as the external view because it views social capital as a resource that ties a focal actor to the other actors in the social network.

Yet, other studies of social capital have viewed social capital as a public good. For instance, Woolcock (2001) argues that social capital is a classic public good because of its non-exclusive nature of benefits to members of the community. The public good perspective is often referred to as the sociocentric approach of social capital. The focus on the social collectivity is comparable to Fukuyama's (1995a) and Putnam's (2000) notion of social capital as the trust and cooperative norms within communities and society, or the social cohesion which is 'more than the simple sum of individuals' social capital due to the existence of externalities in the production of social capital' (Klein 2013, 896). Social capital can, thus, be considered as a societal-level attribute (Dakhli and De Clercq 2004; Fukuyama 1995b). It is a public good to enable the reduction of transaction and search costs and facilitate economic success (Kawachi and Berkman 2014; Putnam 2002).

Using the case of Italian regions, Putnam's (1993) highly influential work described the highly differentiated performance of the north-central regions of Italy and the south regions of Italy. The north-central regions of Italy were found to be linked by cooperative actions involving horizontal and open structures of government and society. On the other hand, regions in the south of Italy were marked by hierarchical and authoritative form of governance. Putnam (1993) found that the northern parts of Italy were in fact richer and more successful than the Southern regions because community members tend to be more involved in civic engagement to promote governmental efficiency. This civic engagement enhances collective norms and behaviours, which helps to build trust and connections among people. This sort of milieu underpins industrial districts and ideas of flexible specialization (see Rowley 1992, 1994, 1996). Fukuyama (1995b) also highlighted that trust within a given country (or even areas within a country) influences the functioning of the country's economy and hence its prosperity. In high-trust societies such as Japan, Germany and the United States, Fukuyama (1995b) indicated that organizations can expand in scope and efficiency to reach optimum economies of scale. In contrast, in low-trust societies, e.g. China, Italy, France and Korea, individuals are only able to organize within their own extended family to build commercial, social and political networks. Social capital, thus, becomes a necessary ingredient for the functioning of democracy and institutions.

Other studies that adopt the socioentric approach consider social capital as social trust that is important for health, and therefore, it is considered as the indicator of a region's well-being (Kawachi and Berkman 2014; Pickett and Wilkinson 2015). Social capital has also been shown to exhibit a positive relationship with innovation at the country level. Doh and Acs (2010) study, for instance, shows that the overall level of social capital (trust, passive and active membership and norms of civic behaviour) is an important driver of entrepreneurship and has a positive influence on the overall innovation of a country. Similarly, Kwon and Arenius (2010) argue for the case of national social capital as an important contributor to the nation's entrepreneurial activities. Other studies indicate the antecedents of social capital in the society. For example, for Portes and Vickstrom (2011) it is ethno-racial diversity from immigration that may reduce the level of public trust and cohesion as social capital.

Existing studies are illustrated in the literature with different underpinnings of social capital as a private good or a public good. In other words, extant studies differ in terms of the network approaches they adopt – either the egocentric or the sociocentric approach of social capital. The collection of studies here also highlights the different approaches of social capital.

Creation and outcomes of social capital

Existing research on social capital unfortunately has not comprehensively examined the creation of social capital (Bolino, Turnley, and Bloodgood 2002; Johnson et al. 2011), with the majority of existing social capital literature focusing on the outcomes of social capital. Extant research is predominantly based on a prevalent assumption that social capital leads to beneficial outcomes (Kwon and Adler 2014; Nahapiet and Ghoshal 1998). A cognate body of work has demonstrated that at the individual level of analysis, social capital enhances the efficiency of the actors' actions within the social structure (Bian, Huang, and Zhang 2015; Burt 1992; Hauser et al. 2016). An individual's social capital is positively related to favourable outcomes, such as finding jobs, attaining higher income or compensation and promoting occupational and status attainment (Bian, Huang, and Zhang 2015; Fernandez, Castilla, and Moore 2000; Hadani et al. 2012; Mouw 2003). Social capital has also been found to improve one's career success (Gubbins and Garavan 2015; Seibert, Kraimer, and Liden 2001).

At the organizational level, research suggests that social capital within organizations is an important resource for improving organizational performance (Ahearne, Lam, and Kraus 2014; Andrews 2010; Hollenbeck and Jamieson 2015). It reduces organizational dissolution and ensures higher survival chances (Fischer and Pollock 2004; Payne et al. 2011; Pennings, Lee, and Van Witteloostuijn 1998). It also leads to stronger organizational commitment and lower turnover rates (Dess and Shaw 2001; Ellinger et al. 2013; Watson and Papamarcos 2002). Organizational social capital, including managerial social capital, thus, improves a firm's economic performance and business operations, which in turn facilitates firm growth (Lins, Servaes, and Tamayo 2017; Maurer and Ebers 2006; Wu 2008). It further facilitates inter-unit resource exchange and product innovation (Camps and Marques 2014; Carmona-Lavado, Cuevas-Rodríguez, and Cabello-Medina 2010; Pérez-Luño et al. 2011; Tsai and Ghoshal 1998).

Moreover, social capital promotes cooperation and learning (Camps and Marques 2014; Hauser et al. 2016) and facilitates the development of knowledge networks in organizations (Dhanaraj et al. 2004; Phelps, Heidl, and Wadhwa 2012; Yu et al. 2013). It enables the creation of intellectual capital (Madhavaram and Hunt 2017; Subramaniam and Youndt 2005) and influences the development of human capital (Ellinger et al. 2013; Rowley and Redding 2012; Suseno and Pinnington 2018). In addition, social capital encourages entrepreneurship (Burt and Burzynska 2017; Gedajlovic et al. 2013; Kwon and Arenius 2010; Stam, Arzlanian, and Elfring 2014) as well as facilitates information flow and reduces transaction costs (Liu et al. 2016).

On the inter-firm level, social capital has been found to create industry networks of start-up companies (Kohtamäki et al. 2012; Manolova, Manev, and Gyoshev 2010), promote industry creation and resource acquisition (Bhagavatula et al. 2010), enable inter-organizational collaborations and innovation (Carnovale and Yeniyurt 2015; Demirkan and Demirkan 2012) and establish relationships between firms and financial institutions (Kreiser, Patel, and Fiet 2013). Indeed, scholars have indicated that maintenance and utilization of social capital can produce a number of positive outcomes for organizations and employees.

There are also increasingly studies that look at the multi-level perspectives of these approaches of social capital. For instance, Acquaah (2007) highlighted the effect of managerial social capital – the managers' social networking relationships and ties with community leaders – on organizational performance and that this relationship is contingent on the strategic orientation of the organization. Yu et al. (2013) indicated multi-level effects of social capital and knowledge sharing in teams. Similarly, Ahearne, Lam, and Kraus (2014) used an individual's ego-network to measure the centrality of the management network as a whole and found that there are curvilinear effects of middle managers' social capital on business unit performance. However, as noted by Payne et al. (2011), researchers have yet fully explored multi-level research in social capital to understand management and organizational issues.

On yet a higher level of analysis, social capital has been found to reduce crime rates in society (Beyerlein and Hipp 2005; Buonanno, Montolio, and Vanin 2009; Putnam 2000), enhance economic and community development (Aldrich and Meyer 2015; Woolcock 2010; Redding and Rowley 2017) and improve the performance of nations (Doh and Acs 2010; Doh and McNeely 2012; Fukuyama 1995a). Laursen, Masciarelli, and Prencipe's (2012) work, for instance, indicated that regional social capital – the localized norms and networks – enables the region to have a higher propensity to innovate. Kwon, Heflin, and Ruef (2013) similarly suggested that the benefits of social trust and organizational memberships accrue not just to the individual, but also to the whole community. This is sometimes referred to as civil social capital or governmental social capital (e.g. Knack 2002), outlining the role of social capital in creating positive outcomes of a country.

However, like any investment, social capital can produce negative outcomes, or what Gargiulo and Benassi (1999) refer to as the 'dark side'. Portes and Sensenbrenner's (1993) study, for instance, describe the suffocating issues faced by ethnic entrepreneurs in coping with particularistic demands and restrictions to freedom brought by the same strong ties supposedly accountable for enabling their initial access to the network. Gargiulo and Benassi (1999) highlight the negative effects of strong ties to cohesive contacts in limiting managers' adaptability to changing environments. Similarly, social capital in the form of strong bonding within a group leads to parochialism and inertia (Chenhall, Hall, and Smith 2010; Portes 2000). According to Kwon and Arenius (2010), strong social capital in the form of excessive in-group cohesion contributes to groupthink and further discourages the creativity of individual members and decreases the possibility for entrepreneurial activity. When examining the potential beneficial outcomes and disadvantages of social capital, Chenhall, Hall, and Smith (2010, 741) noted that 'the disadvantages of social capital, however, may outweigh these benefits'. As Putnam (2000) observed, positive benefits of social capital may come at a cost to individuals outside the collectivity (i.e. outside the group). For instance, a group of 'troubled' teenagers may have developed strong bonds within the group (i.e. has a high social capital) but the 'benefits' of this high social capital do not overflow to society at large.

Indeed, the often positive outcomes of social capital cited in the literature have been criticized as one-sided and as Portes and Landolt (1996, 21) stated that this is as 'an unmixed blessing' and that 'the one-sided picture of social capital produces a series of tautologies, truisms, and stereotypes'. They further pointed out that there are indeed several distinctly negative aspects of social capital, including conspiracies against the public, restrictions on individual freedom and business initiative and downward levelling pressures. Furthermore, Bian (2017) emphasized that obligational ties, an important element of Chinese *guanxi* networks (Wang and Rowley 2016), are deeply rooted in business circles and political spheres, and therefore, may contribute to illicit dealings and official corruption. These essentially are 'the ugly face of *guanxi*' and the dark side of social capital (Bian 2017, 266).

The evidence from the literature suggests the variety of outcomes of social capital. It is, therefore, important to view social capital in context in terms of its positive and negative outcomes in order to develop a much more thorough analysis of the concept. The collection of contributions in this volume is also varied in terms of studies examining the outcomes of social capital and also those that examine the creation of social capital. We now provide an overview of these to show the breadth and depth of our content.

Contributions

Table 1 provides a quick schematic overview of content within this collection. They are similar in that they are focused on social capital of service-oriented firms. The contributions are also distinct in terms of the context and methods employed, and consequently their findings. The contributions are wide-ranging in terms of approaches to social capital in terms of adopting either an egocentric or a sociocentric approach and social capital creation and outcomes.

The contributions address the different approaches to studying social capital and the implications for service-oriented firms in the Asia Pacific. They show that the creation and outcomes of social capital are dependent on the different contexts, while allowing for ties to develop across actors and societal members. Furthermore, the contributions are drawn from cases based in Thailand, Indonesia, South Korea, China and Australia and so emphasize the need to recognize cultural, social and economic contexts of these countries when examining social capital in the Asia Pacific region.

Implications

Social capital has been an important area of research particularly in recent years. Much has been known about the impact of social capital at different levels of analysis, from the individual, organizational and societal levels. Extant studies have provided a baseline of understanding social capital in terms of resources and network ties embedded in the social structures and relationships that facilitate beneficial outcomes. Our intention here is to draw attention to the different approaches to social capital as well as the creation and outcomes of social capital in studies examining service-oriented firms. The work here provides several important implications for theory and business and management practice.

First, the focus on the service industry is important as this industry plays a critical role in global services and trade activities and yet fewer attempts have been done to investigate social capital in the service context particularly in the Asia Pacific region. Academic research on this topic is instrumental in aspects such as relationship management including maximization and retention of client base and value assessment. Social capital is also important for business and management practice for service firms in order to improve their service quality and expansion of business networks particularly across emerging markets in the Asia Pacific region.

Second, Asia Pacific countries' historical perspectives with the political and institutional systems can influence the creation and outcomes of social capital. It cannot, therefore, be assumed that the application of social capital in the service context in Western countries is going to be even broadly similar to that of the Asia Pacific region. It is important to dedicate our research and understanding to each country's cultural, institutional, social and political nuances as being influential to establishing and examining social capital. The context of Asia Pacific in our case is a starting point to further building our knowledge in this area.

Third, the overview we provided is intended as a guide when analysing social capital and the many interactions between actors. The common way is to investigate either the egocentric or the sociocentric approach of social capital and the outcomes of social capital, either positive or negative. We found that little attention has, however, been paid to examining the creation of social capital. Social capital is important because research has

Table 1. Overview: context, method, approach, creation and outcomes of social capital, findings.

Author(s)	Context	Method	Social capital approach	Social capital creation and outcomes	Findings
Tham et al.	Thailand and Australia	Case study	Sociocentric, focusing on organizations and industry	Creation of social capital and positive outcomes	• Thai case – norms in Thai society produce social capital • Australian case – social capital enables creation of a strong organizational identity for economic and social outcomes as well as better service experience
Suseno	Indonesia	Case study	Sociocentric, focusing on organization and society	Creation of social capital and positive outcomes	• Innovative service offerings of an organization can enable creation of social capital in the forms of social connectedness, trust and mutual understanding in communities • Social capital is depicted in the context of urban communities in an emerging economy
Oh et al.	South Korea	Big data	Sociocentric, focusing on the society	Positive and negative outcomes	• Social networking service providers in cyber space enable downward social mobility and thus, create a negative effect of social capital that enforces divisions among citizens • Service providers enable trust in cyber space to be quickly developed to foster offline collective actions in order to restore social order in the country
Wu et al.	China	Survey	Egocentric, focusing on organization	Positive outcomes	• Social capital plays a role in relationship between a firm's technology management capability and its new product development performance
Seet et al.	Australia	Interviews	Egocentric, focusing on individual	Positive outcomes	• Social capital in the form of 'know-who' is essential in providing entrepreneurs with means to access 'know-what' as well as 'know-how' • Social capital enables entrepreneurs to enhance their entrepreneurial self-efficacy

indicated that actors possessing limited social capital do not gain as much benefits as those who have a high extent of social capital. Social capital facilitates the utilization of resources and enables trust and civic engagement. With economic, political and sociocultural changes, society therefore needs to adapt to building social ties and shared norms for creating social capital to improve societal well-being and economic prosperity. This is particularly important in the context of Asia Pacific where progress is needed to overcome various service challenges such as health, poverty reduction, social inequality and even good governance.

Conclusion

In the present study, we take stock of social capital research by examining its application in service-oriented firms in the Asia Pacific region. We have shown that research on social capital is varied in terms of its approaches and implications. We have also indicated the importance of recognizing cultural, social, economic, institutional and political contexts of countries in the Asia Pacific region to better understand the application of social capital. We hope that the present analysis will serve as the basis for further development on this topic.

Disclosure statement

No potential conflict of interest was reported by the authors.

References

Acquaah, M. 2007. "Managerial Social Capital, Strategic Orientation, and Organizational Performance in an Emerging Economy." *Strategic Management Journal* 28 (12): 1235–1255.

Ahearne, M., S. K. Lam, and F. Kraus. 2014. "Performance Impact of Middle Managers' Adaptive Strategy Implementation: The Role of Social Capital." *Strategic Management Journal* 35 (1): 68–87.

Aldrich, D. P., and M. A. Meyer. 2015. "Social Capital and Community Resilience." *American Behavioral Scientist* 59 (2): 254–269.

Andrews, R. 2010. "Organizational Social Capital, Structure and Performance." *Human Relations* 63 (5): 583–608.

Barroso-Castro, C., M. M. Villegas-Periñan, and J. C. Casillas-Bueno. 2016. "How Boards' Internal and External Social Capital Interact to Affect Firm Performance." *Strategic Organization* 14 (1): 6–31.

Beyerlein, K., and J. R. Hipp. 2005. "Social Capital, Too Much of a Good Thing? American Religious Traditions and Community Crime." *Social Forces* 84 (2): 995–1013.

Bhagavatula, S., T. Elfring, A. van Tilburg, and G. T. van de Bunt. 2010. "How Social and Human Capital Influence Opportunity Recognition and Resource Mobilization in India's Handloom Industry." *Journal of Business Venturing* 25 (3): 245–260.

Bian, Y. 2017. "The Comparative Significance of Guanxi." *Management and Organization Review* 13 (2): 261–267.

Bian, Y., X. Huang, and L. Zhang. 2015. "Information and Favoritism: The Network Effect on Wage Income in China." *Social Networks* 40 (3): 129–138.

Bolino, M. C., W. H. Turnley, and J. M. Bloodgood. 2002. "Citizenship Behavior and the Creation of Social Capital in Organizations." *Academy of Management Review* 27 (4): 505–522.

Bozionelos, N. 2014. "Careers Patterns in Greek Academia: Social Capital and Intelligent Careers, but for Whom?" *Career Development International* 19 (3): 264–294.

Buonanno, P., D. Montolio, and P. Vanin. 2009. "Does Social Capital Reduce Crime?" *The Journal of Law and Economics* 52 (1): 145–170.

Burt, R. S. 1992. *Structural Holes*. Cambridge, MA: Harvard University Press.

Burt, R. S. 2015. "Reinforced Structural Holes." *Social Networks* 43: 149–161.

Burt, R. S., and K. Burzynska. 2017. "Chinese Entrepreneurs, Social Networks, and Guanxi." *Management and Organization Review* 13 (2): 221–260.

Camps, S., and P. Marques. 2014. "Exploring How Social Capital Facilitates Innovation: The Role of Innovation Enablers." *Technological Forecasting & Social Change* 88 (1): 325–348.

Carmona-Lavado, A., G. Cuevas-Rodríguez, and C. Cabello-Medina. 2010. "Social and Organizational Capital: Building the Context for Innovation." *Industrial Marketing Management* 39 (4): 681–690.

Carnovale, S., and S. Yeniyurt. 2015. "The Role of Ego Network Structure in Facilitating Ego Network Innovations." *Journal of Supply Chain Management* 51 (2): 22–46.

Chenhall, R. H., M. Hall, and D. Smith. 2010. "Social Capital and Management Control Systems: A Study of a Non-Government Organization." *Accounting, Organizations and Society* 35 (8): 737–756.

Coleman, James S. 1988. "Social Capital in the Creation of Human Capital." *American Journal of Sociology* 94 (Supplement: Organizations and Institutions: Sociological and Economic Approaches to the Analysis of Social Structure): S95–S120.

Dakhli, M., and D. De Clercq. 2004. "Human Capital, Social Capital, and Innovation: A Multi-Country Study." *Entrepreneurship and Regional Development* 16 (2): 107–128.

Das, D. K. 2012. "The Asian Economy: Current State of Play and Future Prospects." *Asia Pacific Business Review* 18 (3): 441–447.

Demirkan, I., and S. Demirkan. 2012. "Network Characteristics and Patenting in Biotechnology, 1990-2006." *Journal of Management* 38 (6): 1892–1927.

Dess, G. G., and J. D. Shaw. 2001. "Voluntary Turnover, Social Capital, and Organizational Performance." *Academy of Management Review* 26 (3): 446–456.

Dhanaraj, C., M. A. Lyles, H. K. Steensma, and L. Tihanyi. 2004. "Managing Tacit and Explicit Knowledge Transfer in IJVs: The Role of Relational Embeddedness and the Impact on Performance." *Journal of International Business Studies* 35 (5): 428–442.

Doh, S., and Z. J. Acs. 2010. "Innovation and Social Capital: A Cross-Country Investigation." *Industry and Innovation* 17 (3): 241–262.

Doh, S., and C. McNeely. 2012. "A Multi-Dimensional Perspective on Social Capital and Economic Development: An Exploratory Analysis." *The Annals of Regional Science* 49 (3): 821–843.

Ellinger, A. E., C. F. Musgrove, A. D. Ellinger, D. G. Bachrach, A. B. E. Baş, and Y.-L. Wang. 2013. "Influences of Organizational Investments in Social Capital on Service Employee Commitment and Performance." *Journal of Business Research* 66 (8): 1124–1133.

Fernandez, R. M., E. J. Castilla, and P. Moore. 2000. "Social Capital at Work: Networks and Employment at a Phone Center." *American Journal of Sociology* 105 (5): 1288–1356.

Fischer, H. M., and T. G. Pollock. 2004. "Effects of Social Capital and Power on Surviving Transformational Change: The Case of Initial Public Offerings." *Academy of Management Journal* 47 (4): 463–481.

Fukuyama, F. 1995a. "Social Capital and the Global Economy." *Foreign Affairs* 74 (5): 89–103.

Fukuyama, F. 1995b. *Trust: The Social Virtues and the Creation of Prosperity*. New York: Free Press.

Gargiulo, M., and M. Benassi. 1999. "The Dark Side of Social Capital." In *Corporate Social Capital and Liability*, edited by R. T. A. J. Leenders and S. M. Gabbay, 298–322. Boston, MA: Kluwer.

Gebauer, H., and C. Kowalkowski. 2012. "Customer-Focused and Service-Focused Orientation in Organizational Structures." *Journal of Business & Industrial Marketing* 27 (7): 527–537.

Gedajlovic, E., B. Honig, C. B. Moore, G. T. Payne, and M. Wright. 2013. "Social Capital and Entrepreneurship: A Schema and Research Agenda." *Entrepreneurship Theory and Practice* 37 (3): 455–478.

Gubbins, C., and T. Garavan. 2015. "Social Capital Effects on the Career and Development Outcomes of HR Professionals." *Human Resource Management* 55 (2): 241–260.

Hadani, M., S. Coombes, D. Das, and D. Jalajas. 2012. "Finding a Good Job: Academic Network Centrality and Early Occupational Outcomes in Management Academia." *Journal of Organizational Behavior* 33 (5): 723–739.

Hauser, C., U. Perkmann, S. Puntscher, J. Walde, and G. Tappeiner. 2016. "Trust Works! Sources and Effects of Social Capital in the Workplace." *Social Indicators Research* 128 (2): 589–608.

Hollenbeck, J. R., and B. B. Jamieson. 2015. "Human Capital, Social Capital, and Social Network Analysis: Implications for Strategic Human Resource Management." *Academy of Management Perspectives* 29 (3): 370–385.

Johnson, S., K. Schnatterly, J. F. Bolton, and C. Tuggle. 2011. "Antecedents of New Director Social Capital." *Journal of Management Studies* 48 (8): 1782–1803.

Kawachi, I., and L. F. Berkman. 2014. "Social Cohesion, Social Capital and Health." In *Social Epidemiology*. 2nd ed, edited by L. Berkman, I. Kawachi and M. Glymour, 290–319. New York: Oxford University Press.

Klein, C. 2013. "Social Capital or Social Cohesion: What Matters for Subjective Well-Being?" *Social Indicators Research* 110 (3): 891–911.

Knack, S. 2002. "Social Capital, Growth and Poverty: A Survey of Cross-Country Evidence." In *The Role of Social Capital in Development: An Empirical Assessment*, edited by C. Grootaert and T. van Bastelaer, 42–84. Cambridge: Cambridge University Press.

Kohtamäki, M., J. Vesalainen, S. Henneberg, P. Naudé, and M. J. Ventresca. 2012. "Enabling Relationship Structures and Relationship Performance Improvement: The Moderating Role of Relational Capital." *Industrial Marketing Management* 41 (8): 1298–1309.

Kostova, T., and K. Roth. 2003. "Social Capital in Multinational Corporations and a Micro-Macro Model of Its Formation." *Academy of Management* 28 (2): 297–317.

Kreiser, P. M., P. C. Patel, and J. O. Fiet. 2013. "The Influence of Changes in Social Capital on Firm-Founding Activities." *Entrepreneurship Theory and Practice* 37 (3): 539–568.

Kwon, S.-W., and P. A. Adler. 2014. "Social Capital: Maturation of a Field of Research." *Academy of Management Review* 39 (4): 412–422.

Kwon, S.-W., and P. Arenius. 2010. "Nations of Entrepreneurs: A Social Capital Perspective." *Journal of Business Venturing* 25 (3): 315–330.

Kwon, S.-W., C. Heflin, and M. Ruef. 2013. "Community Social Capital and Entrepreneurship." *American Sociological Review* 78 (6): 980–1008.

Laursen, K., F. Masciarelli, and A. Prencipe. 2012. "Regions Matter: How Localized Social Capital Affects Innovation and External Knowledge Acquisition." *Organization Science* 23 (1): 177–193.

Lin, N. 2001. *Social Capital : A Theory of Social Structure and Action*. Cambridge: Cambridge University Press.

Lin, N., Y. C. Fu, and C. J. Chen. 2014. *Social Capital and Its Institutional Contingency: A Study of the United States, China and Taiwan*. New York: Routledge.

Lins, K. V., H. Servaes, and A. Tamayo. 2017. "Social Capital, Trust, and Firm Performance: The Value of Corporate Social Responsibility during the Financial Crisis." *The Journal of Finance* 72 (4): 1785–1824.

Liu, H., W. Ke, K. K. Wei, and Y. K. Lu. 2016. "The Effects of Social Capital on Firm Substantive and Symbolic Performance: In the Context of E-Business." *Journal of Global Information Management* 24 (1): 61–85.

Loury, G. C. 1977. "A Dynamic Theory of Racial Income Differences." In *Women, Minorities, and Employment Discrimination*, edited by P. A. Wallace and A. M. L. Mond, 153–186. Lexington, MA: Lexington Books.

Madhavaram, S., and S. D. Hunt. 2017. "Customizing Business-to-Business (B2B) Professional Services: The Role of Intellectual Capital and Internal Social Capital." *Journal of Business Research* 74 (1): 38–46.

Manolova, T. S., I. M. Manev, and B. S. Gyoshev. 2010. "In Good Company: The Role of Personal and Inter-Firm Networks for New-Venture Internationalization in a Transition Economy." *Journal of World Business* 45 (3): 257–265.

Maurer, I., and M. Ebers. 2006. "Dynamics of Social Capital and Their Performance Implications: Lessons from Biotechnology Start-Ups." *Administrative Science Quarterly* 51 (2): 262–292.

Mouw, T. 2003. "Social Capital and Finding a Job: Do Contacts Matter?" *American Sociological Review* 68 (6): 868–898.

Nahapiet, J., and S. Ghoshal. 1998. "Social Capital, Intellectual Capital, and the Organizational Advantage." *Academy of Management Review* 23 (2): 242–266.

Payne, G. T., C. B. Moore, S. E. Griffis, and C. W. Autry. 2011. "Multilevel Challenges and Opportunities in Social Capital Research." *Journal of Management* 37 (2): 491–520.

Pennings, J. M., K. Lee, and A. Van Witteloostuijn. 1998. "Human Capital, Social Capital, and Firm Dissolution." *Academy of Management Journal* 41 (4): 425–440.

Pérez-Luño, A., C. C. Medina, A. C. Lavado, and G. C. Rodríguez. 2011. "How Social Capital and Knowledge Affect Innovation." *Journal of Business Research* 64 (12): 1369–1376.

Phelps, C., R. Heidl, and A. Wadhwa. 2012. "Knowledge, Networks, and Knowledge Networks: A Review and Research Agenda." *Journal of Management* 38 (4): 1115–1166.

Pickett, K. E., and R. G. Wilkinson. 2015. "Income Inequality and Health: A Causal Review." *Social Science and Medicine* 128 (2): 316–326.

Portes, A. 2000. "Social Capital: Its Origins and Applications in Modern Sociology." In *Knowledge and Social Capital: Foundations and Applications*, edited by E. L. Lesser, 43–67. Boston, MA: Butterworth Heinemann.

Portes, A., and P. Landolt. 1996. "The Downside of Social Capital." *The American Prospect* 26: 18–21.

Portes, A., and J. Sensenbrenner. 1993. "Embeddedness and Immigration: Notes on the Social Determinants of Economic Action." *American Journal of Sociology* 98 (6): 1320–1350.

Portes, A., and E. Vickstrom. 2011. "Diversity, Social Capital, and Cohesion." *Annual Review of Sociology* 37 (1): 461–479.

Putnam, R. D. 1993. *Making Democracy Work: Civic Traditions in Modern Italy*. Princeton: Princeton University Press.

Putnam, R. D. 2000. *Bowling Alone: The Collapse and Revival of American Community*. New York: Simon and Schuster.

Putnam, R. D. 2002. *Democracies in Flux: The Evolution of Social Capital in Contemporary Society*. Oxford: Oxford University Press.

Redding, G., and C. Rowley. 2017. "Conclusion: The Central Role of Human and Social Capital." *Asia Pacific Business Review* 23 (2): 299–305.

Rowley, C. 1992. "The British Pottery Industry." *Environment & Planning a* 24: 1645–1650.

Rowley, C. 1994. "The Illusion of Flexible Specialisation: The Domesticware Sector of the Ceramics Industry." *New Technology Work & Employment* 9 (2): 127–139.

Rowley, C. 1996. "Flexible Specialisation: Comparative Dimensions and Evidence from the Tile Industry." *New Technology Work & Employment* 11 (2): 125–136.

Rowley, C., and G. Redding. 2012. "Building Human and Social Capital in Pacific Asia." *Asia Pacific Business Review* 18 (3): 295–301.

Seibert, S. E., M. L. Kraimer, and R. C. Liden. 2001. "A Social Capital Theory of Career Success." *Academy of Management Journal* 44 (2): 219–237.

Stam, W., S. Arzlanian, and T. Elfring. 2014. "Social Capital of Entrepreneurs and Small Firm Performance: A Meta-Analysis of Contextual and Methodological Moderators." *Journal of Business Venturing* 29 (1): 152–173.

Subramaniam, M., and M. A. Youndt. 2005. "The Influence of Intellectual Capital on The Types of Innovative Capabilities." *Academy of Management Journal* 48 (3): 450–463.

Suseno, Y., and A. H. Pinnington. 2018. "The Significance of Human Capital and Social Capital: Professional–Client Relationships in the Asia Pacific." *Asia Pacific Business Review* 24 (1): 72–89.

The World Bank. 2017. "Global Economic Prospects: East Asia and the Pacific." Accessed December 12, 2017. http://www.worldbank.org/en/region/eap/brief/global-economic-prospects-east-asia-pacific

Tsai, W., and S. Ghoshal. 1998. "Social Capital and Value Creation: The Role of Intrafirm Networks." *Academy of Management Journal* 41 (4): 464–476.

UNCTAD. 2014. *World Investment Report 2014: Investing in the SDGs: An Action Plan.* New York: United Nations Conference on Trade and Development.

Vinayak, H. V., F. Thompson, and O. Tonby 2016. "Understanding ASEAN: Seven Things You Need to Know." *McKinsey.* Accessed December 12, 2017. http://www.mckinsey.com/industries/public-sector/ourinsights/understanding-asean-seven-things-you-need-to-know

Wang, B., and C. Rowley. 2016. "Invisible Hand." In *Business Networks in East Asian Capitalisms*, edited by J. Nolan, C. Rowley and M. Warner, 93–118. Kidlington: Elsevier.

Watson, G. W., and S. D. Papamarcos. 2002. "Social Capital and Organizational Commitment." *Journal of Business and Psychology* 16 (4): 537–552.

Woolcock, M. 2001. "The Place of Social Capital in Understanding Social and Economic Outcomes." *ISUMA Canadian Journal of Policy Research* 2 (1): 11–17.

Woolcock, M. 2010. "The Rise and Routinization of Social Capital, 1988–2008." *Annual Review of Political Science* 13: 469–487.

Wu, W.-P. 2008. "Dimensions of Social Capital and Firm Competitiveness Improvement: The Mediating Role of Information Sharing." *Journal of Management Studies* 45 (1): 122–146.

Yu, Y., J.-X. Hao, X.-Y. Dong, and M. Khalifa. 2013. "A Multilevel Model for Effects of Social Capital and Knowledge Sharing in Knowledge-Intensive Work Teams." *International Journal of Information Management* 33 (5): 780–790.

Spilling the social capital beans: a comparative case study of coffee service enterprises within Asia-Pacific

Aaron Tham, David Fleischman and Peter Jenner

ABSTRACT
Despite the importance of social capital to organizational performance, there is scant insight within service contexts. Accordingly, this research explores social capital in two Asia-Pacific service enterprise cases – a Thai coffee franchise and a Coffee Roasters Guild in Australia. In the Thai case, social capital in the service experience emerged from norms common in Thai society and manifested via social enterprise initiatives. Findings from Australia indicate social capital helps form a strong organizational identity leading to better economic and social outcomes and an enhanced service experience, benefiting numerous stakeholders. The study demonstrates varying patterns of social capital in Asia-Pacific service enterprises, contributing to theory and practice.

Introduction

Social capital theory (SCT) emerged from the work of sociologists and political scientists (Bourdieu 1986; Coleman 1988; Putnam 1993). With its focus upon social relationships, SCT has evolved into 'a whole field of research' and increasingly found application in business (Kwon and Adler 2014, p. 412). Hence, the understanding of social capital as an 'organisational advantage has received considerable theoretical attention over recent years' (Lee 2009, p. 248). As a valuable asset inhered in social relations and their associated networks (Nahapiet and Ghoshal 1998; Lin 1999), social capital helps organizations access important resources, influence and support, representing a potential source of competitive advantage (Adler and Kwon 2002). Research has identified social capital as advantageous to organizations in a variety of contexts (Li, Barner-Rasmussen, and Bjorkman 2007; Lee 2009). For example, research demonstrates benefits in organizational areas such as entrepreneurial opportunity (Martinez and Aldrich 2011; McKeever, Anderson, and Jack 2014), information sharing and knowledge transfer (Levin and Cross 2004; Maurer, Bartsch, and Ebers 2011), innovation and the development of new practices (Gilsing and Nooteboom 2005; Huggins and Johnston 2010), resource exchange and lower transaction costs (Tsai and Ghoshal 1998; Uzzi 1999), collaboration (Brunetto and Farr-Wharton 2007), the performance of SMEs (BarNir and Smith 2002), social businesses (Jenner and Oprescu 2016) and the internationalization of firms

(Pinho and Prange 2016). However, Petrou and Daskalopoulou (2013) note the knowledge and application of social capital within service contexts remains under-researched.

In Asia-Pacific, one area of limited social capital scope is the coffee service context. Over the last thirty years, the coffee industry has undergone significant change. The rise of democratically controlled cooperatives have provided small farmers and communities with better organizational capital, economies of scale and more control over their livelihoods (Simpson and Rapone 2000). Likewise, Pine and Gilmore (1999) argue the consumption of coffee has transformed an agrarian commodity to one that is a manifestation of an experience economy. The experience economy has emerged for various reasons, including consumer literacy and a quest to know how food has been produced (Xie, Bagozzi, and Troye 2008; Antonio 2015). Consequently, consumers want and require a consumption experience, and are often thought of as 'prosumers' actively involved in service experiences (Humphries and Grayson 2008; Ritzer and Jurgenson 2010). The coffee service experience is illustrative of that desired experience.

Given the trends reflecting the sophistication of coffee cultures and consumers in the experience economy, recent literature has focused on coffee production and consumption as a tool for achieving economic and social development goals – often under guises like 'fair trade' (Simpson and Rapone 2000; Utting 2009; Ruben and Fort 2012). In fact, social capital plays an important role in the development of organizations with combined social and economic objectives (Meyskens, Carsrud, and Cardozo 2010). Thus, social capital is likely fundamental in the evolution and operation of the coffee service experience, but how it is developed and appropriated by such enterprises remains under-researched (Elder, Zerriffi, and Le Billon 2012; Ruben and Heras 2012).

To address this gap, a comparative case study approach is utilized to examine how two Asia-Pacific coffee service enterprises adopt social capital to enhance their coffee service experience. Resultantly, the study makes two main contributions. First, the study contributes to theory by building on existing social capital frameworks. In particular, the cross-comparative cases in the study offer insight to additional components that may be adapted in existing social capital frameworks, providing better theoretical understanding of social capital in varying service enterprise types and differing Asia-Pacific regions. Second, the study reveals how social capital manifests within the coffee service experience. This contributes practical insight for various types of service enterprises operating within Asia-Pacific to foster and apply social capital for the benefit of all stakeholders.

The study progresses as follows. The SCT literature is overviewed before the coffee service experience in the Asia-Pacific region is considered. Next, the method is detailed, followed by the findings of two coffee service enterprises, highlighting the development and application of social capital in each case. A discussion of the cases follows, resulting in adaptations to existing social capital frameworks. Contributions, future research directions and limitations conclude the study.

Background literature

Social capital

Social capital is an asset emanating from the interactions, networks, norms and trust of social relations (Coleman 1988; Bourdieu 1986; Putnam 1993). Representing 'the goodwill that is engendered by the fabric of social relations', social capital delivers beneficial access to 'information, influence and solidarity' (Adler and Kwon 2002, pp. 17–18). Such benefits may accrue at individual (Lin 1999), organizational, (Nahapiet and Ghoshal 1998) or communal network levels (Kwon and Adler 2014).

For an organization, social networks deliver a range of benefits. These include: collaboration (Brunetto and Farr-Wharton 2007), access and exchange of resources (Burt 1992, 1997; Tsai and Ghoshal 1998), access to information (Adler and Kwon 2002), knowledge transfer (Levin and Cross 2004; Maurer, Bartsch, and Ebers 2011), new business practices and innovation (Gilsing and Nooteboom 2005; Huggins and Johnston 2010), reduced transaction costs (Coleman 1988; Uzzi 1999), development of entrepreneurial opportunities (McKeever, Anderson, and Jack 2014) and the internationalization of firms (Pinho and Prange 2016). Accordingly, Kwon and Adler (2014, p. 412) state, 'there is no longer much need to refine and demonstrate the value of the overarching concept, but research can usefully continue to expand on specific aspects and mechanisms of social capital as they are relevant to specific disciplines and topics'. So, while organizational benefits of social capital are widely understood at the macro-level, there remains an absence of research examining how social capital is developed and appropriated in service contexts, such as the coffee service experience, hence the point of this study.

The development of social capital

Networks are pivotal in the mobilization of social capital. They provide access to the value inherent within relationships (Granovetter 1973; Bourdieu 1986; Adler and Kwon 2002). The intrinsic value of any network is therefore dependent on the relative strength and quality of its connections (Granovetter 1983). This has led to two important conceptualizations. First, closed or 'bonding' networks can eventuate from strong connections and bind members of a group or community (Coleman 1988; Putnam 1993; Woolcock 1998). Such networks typically display a high degree of homogeneity resulting from shared values, beliefs and norms leading to a prominent degree of trust and reciprocity (Coleman 1988; Portes 2000). Thus, strong closed networks provide opportunity for information sharing, support and cooperation (Woolcock 1998; Adler and Kwon 2002; Kwon and Adler 2014), and are advantageous for community development (Putnam 1993). They also fortify cooperation amongst a group due to group obligations of trust, and the potential of sanctions for un-cooperative members (Coleman 1988). Weaker network connections are also important and can lead to more open or 'bridging' networks (Burt 1992, 1997; Putnam 1993). These networks are comprised of heterogonous relationships and offer greater access to diverse information and influence (Burt 1992, 1997; Adler and Kwon 2002).

Both bonding and bridging networks offer advantages and disadvantages (Lin 1999; Gilsing and Nooteboom 2005), which vary depending on strength of connection and context (Granovetter 1983; Levin and Cross 2004). For example, strong homogenous (bonding) networks may suffer from a lack of new information and innovation, stifling economic activity (Uzzi 1999). Whereas weaker heterogeneous (bridging) networks provide avenues for new information, but may lack strong collective values (Granovetter 1983; Burt 1992, 1997). The most effective networks typically possess and balance strong (bonding) and weak (bridging) connections (Hoang and Antoncic 2003).

Moving beyond a predominant focus on the relational aspects of networks (i.e. bridging and bonding), Adler and Kwon (2002) developed a conceptual framework (Figure 1) of social capital addressing the reality of organizational networks. They argue other contingent factors, also impact the value of the social capital for organizations. They posit contingent factors as: (1) the opportunity provided by the network structure for interaction and transaction; (2) the inherent norms and values within the network, of which trust is a key element, providing the motivational force within network interactions; and (3) individual stakeholders' ability to access and utilize capabilities and resources within networks (Adler and Kwon 2002; Kwon and Adler 2014).

The framework illustrates the importance of the contingent factors of opportunity, motivation via trust, and stakeholder ability, along with external hierarchical and market forces that influence and moderate social capital development in organizations. For this study, the framework offers a foundation to consider the development and application of social capital in different industries, such as services.

Extant literature demonstrates support for these contingent factors and others. For example, an individual's personality characteristics and skills, such as the ability to network with relevant stakeholders, are vital in the creation and maintenance of relationships (Adler and Kwon 2002; De Koning 2003), making social skills important (Baron and Markman 2000). Moreover, the ability to utilize network connections to access beneficial resources also influences the effectiveness of a network (Adler and Kwon 2002; De Koning 2003). Thus, the strategic ability of an organizational leader is also salient, given enterprises make a range of decisions in attaining goals through the strategic utilization of their relationships (Burt 1997; Adler and Kwon 2002; Jenner and Oprescu 2016). Lack of expertise in leveraging existing network relationships may dilute social capital benefits, despite an individual's motivation (Adler and Kwon 2002).

Motivation is another important antecedent to social capital development (Lin 1999; Adler and Kwon 2002). The source of motivation emanates from shared values, norms and

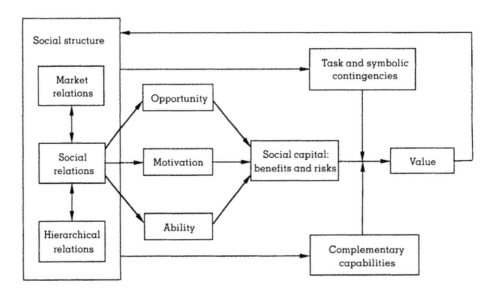

Figure 1. A conceptual model of social capital. Source: Adler and Kwon (2002).

trust of a group (Coleman 1988; Putnam 1993; Leana and Van Buren 1999). When present, such motivation is akin to notions of collective social capital (Portes 2000), and may lead to beneficial sharing of resources and support to other network members (Adler and Kwon 2002). In the context of an enterprise with economic and social goals, such as a coffee guild or socially driven coffee franchise, motivation is likely influenced by collective values, goals and associated trust in relation to the community (Jenner and Oprescu 2016).

Trust is a central tenet to the development and value social capital represents to an organization. Trust emanates from a willingness to be vulnerable and rely on others (Nahapiet and Ghoshal 1998; Brunetto and Farr-Wharton 2007). It underpins the collaboration, support and reciprocity associated with strong networks (Putnam 1993; Woolcock 1998). Trust also influences the complexity and level of exchanges within relationships (Gilsing and Nooteboom 2005). When trust is established, it enhances stakeholder benefits in networks (Adler and Kwon 2002; Nahapiet and Ghoshal 1998). Stakeholders are more likely to collaborate and undertake mutual exchange of resources (e.g. knowledge, skills) when trust is strong, which are critical for developing and supporting social capital (Nahapiet, Gratton, and Rocha 2005).

Overall, SCT is mature area of study with the critical elements well established in several areas of organizational research (Kwon and Adler 2014). For example, research has investigated broad organizational operations (Burt 1997; Nahapiet and Ghoshal 1998; Andrews 2010; Maurer, Bartsch, and Ebers 2011), entrepreneurial activity (Martinez and Aldrich 2011; McKeever, Anderson, and Jack 2014), SMEs (Brunetto and Farr-Wharton 2007; Pinho and Prange 2016), not-for-profit organizations (Jenner and Oprescu 2016), economic and regional development (Woolcock 1998; Hayami 2009) and multi-national environments (Tsai and Ghoshal 1998; Levin and Cross 2004). Consequently, future research is encouraged to become more topic specific (Kwon and Adler 2014). Thus, studies unpacking the nature of social capital in service contexts are germane. Gaps exist in understanding how social capital is developed and applied to support services focused on providing experiential value, such as the coffee experience, and particularly in an Asia-Pacific context. Our study addresses these gaps.

Coffee as a burgeoning service experience in Asia-Pacific

Within Asia-Pacific, coffee consumption has become commonplace, being synonymous with 'everyday' life and a popular social activity (Chen and Hu 2010; Yang 2010). This is a result of the experience economy, where coffee is undergoing growth beyond a commodity to a consumption experience (ICO 2016a, 2016b). Cafes and restaurants offering coffee as an alternative to tea products, reflects coffee's transition from a commodity to a service experience in Asia-Pacific (Grigg 2002; Collins 2008). Thus, the coffee industry provides a fitting context to explore how organizations have evolved to create service experiences with consumers (Pine and Gilmore 1999), and how social capital may potentially influence this experience.

Since the mid-1990s, many organizations, including those in Asia-Pacific, have transitioned from a sole focus on transactional economic exchange, towards designing service experiences with consumers. The focus on service experience creation is reflective of an overarching global trend commonly referred to as the *experience economy* (Pine and Gilmore 1999; Mathwick, Malhotra, and Rigdon 2001; Mehmetoglu and Engen 2011). The experience economy emerged because of consumer desire beyond transactional exchange centred on functional product value, to services that embed interactions and experiences with organizations, yielding additional value (Pine and Gilmore 1999; Poulsson and Kale 2004).

Drawn from the services marketing literature, the *experiential marketing* paradigm and notion of *experiential value*, provide insight for understanding how the experience economy has helped reshape commodity-focused industries, such as coffee, to service experiences. Both centre on the value consumers receive via experiences from their interactions with organizations and other stakeholders (Schmitt 1999; Yuan and Wu 2008; Brodie et al. 2011). Consumers are often seen as 'prosumers' invited to participate and interact in experiences where value is *co-created* with organizations and other stakeholders (Schembri 2006; Ritzer and Jurgenson 2010). Interaction yields value creation via mutual exchange of operant resources (e.g. knowledge, skills and relationships) amongst stakeholders, along with economic exchange (Grönroos and Ravald 2011; Vargo and Lusch 2016). At the onset of the experience economy, Starbucks pioneered the experiential marketing of coffee beyond a commodity, to a service experience where consumers can interact with the organization in value creation (Markides 1997; Pine and Gilmore 1999). Numerous Asia-Pacific franchises and local coffee shops have since followed Starbuck's approach of creating a 'coffee experience' with consumers. Consequently, research interest has piqued regarding experiential consumption in the coffee service context.

The extant research reveals two main trends associated with the burgeoning profile of coffee consumption: (1) consumer-orientated coffee service experiences; and (2) fair trade practices. For example, service research focusing on experiential value in the places and destinations where coffee is consumed, has demonstrated coffee shops as a 'third place' or social hub offering a comfortable and familiar place for consumers away from home and work (e.g. Markides 1997; Rosenbaum et al. 2007). Tourism research has focused on how coffee experiences offer novel opportunities to enhance tourism for consumers (Kleidas and Jolliffe 2010). In the Asia-Pacific context, for example, Yang (2010) discusses experiential marketing in the context of a coffee festival event in Taiwan; while other coffee research focuses on fair trade and scientific production practices (e.g. Simpson and Rapone 2000; Utting 2009; Ruben and Fort 2012).

To date, research sheds some light on the coffee service experience from the consumer perspective and fair trade practice within Asia-Pacific. Yet, understanding the coffee service experience from the organizational perspective in terms of how and what resources, skills and knowledge are needed for to develop a service experience, remains underdeveloped. For example, there is little understanding of how service enterprise stakeholders develop and apply social capital resources in the coffee service experience. An exception is Tan (2000), who found from the organizational viewpoint; coffee production is a highly networked process, with local identities and beliefs driving how coffee is then (re)presented to the consumer. Tan's work provides initial evidence that the coffee service experience and social capital are underpinned by similar elements (e.g. trust, relationships, networks and the exchange of mutually beneficial resources). Accordingly, from the organization perspective, there is scope for further development. Insight towards the contemporary development and application of social capital in service organizations may emerge as a result.

Method

Given this study's exploratory nature, a qualitative methodology was selected as it is suited to research exploring social and cultural phenomena (Creswell 2009; Yin 2011). A comparative case study approach was employed for this study. In brief, case studies are a qualitative technique used to explore a particular topic occurring within an individual, group or organization (Stake 1978). Case studies allow the researcher to examine differing perceptions and interpretations of reality, in 'real world' settings using a variety of data sources (Denzin and Lincoln 1994; Patton 2009). This allows theory development from empirical evidence, yielding greater conceptual understanding (Eisenhardt 1989; Yin 2011). A case study approach is not primarily seeking to test hypotheses or validate claims, but rather looking to uncover lesser known topics or trends (Flyvbjerg 2006), as in this research. Case studies are also well suited to understand the dynamics operating within small to medium enterprises, such as those in this study (Perren and Ram 2004), and been widely adopted across various industries, including health, business and social sciences (Yin 1994). A cross-comparative approach was used to enhance the rigour of this research (Eisenhardt 1989; Ogawa and Malen 1991; Yin 2011), as it enabled a deeper understanding of the similarities and differences in varying service enterprise types and Asia-Pacific regions.

From the literature, the research question developed to frame this study was:

How is social capital developed and applied in the Asia-Pacific coffee service experience?

To guide the exploration of the research question, case study interviews sought to address the following research objectives:

(1) Ascertain the participants' understanding and perceptions of social capital (Question 3 of Appendix 1);
(2) Identify prominent relationships/networks that influenced the evolution and development of the enterprise (Questions 5 and 7 of Appendix 1);
(3) Establish enabling/limiting factors in the application of social capital (Question 4 of Appendix 1); and
(4) Identify the advantages of social capital to the enterprise (Question 6 of Appendix 1).

To explore the research question and objectives, two cases were purposefully chosen, whereby the researcher identifies participants that possess the best experience associated with the topic under investigation (Creswell et al. 2007). This approach allowed the selection of accessible participants with permission to act as representatives of their respective service enterprises and address the research objectives in more depth (Teddlie and Tashakkori 2012). To determine participants' appropriateness for the research, they had to meet the following criteria: (1) be at least of a supervisory or managerial position, (2) granted permission and recognized by the enterprise as credible representatives, and (3) willing to voluntarily participate in the study.

Two participants from the Doi Chaang coffee franchise, and three from the Coffee Roasters Guild in regional Australia, were purposely identified and received permission to act as representatives of their enterprise's viewpoints. These individuals fulfilled the criteria as being someone holding a key role within their enterprise, either at a managerial or supervisory function and voluntarily became involved in the research. Each participant confirmed permission to speak on the enterprises' behalf. While there have been philosophical debates on sample sizes in qualitative studies, a central tenet of exploratory research is to gain insights from an emic perspective as to the nature of the phenomenon under study (Cho and Trent 2006; Rolfe 2006; Whittemore, Chase, and Mandle 2001). As such, rather than critiquing the paucity of samples, Boddy (2016) argued that the value of the research data should instead be judged on its merit of extending knowledge about a topic. To assess the ability of the research to further unpack social capital within the coffee service enterprises, theoretical saturation was applied to the data collection method. Theoretical saturation is the process of collecting data until it appears that no new themes further emerge (Bowen 2008; Guest, Bunce, and Johnson 2006; O'Reilly and Parker 2013).

Semi-structured interviews were used to obtain primary data from the participants regarding the research question and objectives. Such interviews allow for an open-ended, informal and interactive approach generating depth and richness of data for generating insights and thematic development (Eisenhardt 1989; Yin 2011). The interviews occurred over a period of approximately one hour. The interviews were conducted separately based on participants' availability. The conversations were digitally recorded and notes were made to capture the nuances of voice and gesture, along with the impressions of the researcher (Saldana 2010). Pseudonyms were used to maintain participant anonymity. A copy of the sample interview questions is provided in Appendix 1.

The data were manually coded and analysis undertaken to identify recurrent themes (Saldana 2010). The coding process incorporated several stages. First, descriptive coding was applied to categorize the data and prepare it for the second stage of analysis (Saldana 2010). Next, pattern coding, also known as analytical coding, further re-organized, reanalysed, and synthesized the initial coding. This allowed for the creation of more coherent themes by clustering the initial codes to attribute better meaning to the grouped data (Spiggle 1994; Baxter and Jack 2008; Saldana 2010).

To alleviate researcher bias and optimize the analysis, the transcripts were individually reviewed and coded by multiple researchers, using the per cent agreement technique, before being triangulated with secondary data via cross-examination to ensure consistency and validity of findings (Lincoln and Guba 1990; Patton 2009; Yin 2011). Per cent agreement is an often adopted process of enhancing inter-coder reliability. In brief, inter-coder reliability involves researchers independently coding the data-set before coming to agreement as to a consistent set of labels adopted for thematic analysis (Beam 2003; Hayes and Krippendorff 2007). The use of per cent agreement has often been the technique employed within qualitative exploratory studies examining small sample sizes (DeCuir-Gunby, Marshall, and McCulloch 2011; Lombard, Snyder-Duch, and Bracken 2002). As the data-set consisted of two case studies, per cent agreement was justified as acceptable for the scope of this research. According to Lombard, Snyder-Duch, and Bracken (2002), above 70 per cent agreement for exploratory research is acceptable, with 80 per cent or above adequate, and 90 per cent or above high quality of acceptance. Using Lombard, Snyder-Duch, and Bracken's (2002) suggested thresholds, themes with an agreement of 80 per cent or above amongst the researchers were grouped according to their commonalities with the research objectives (Attride-Stirling 2001; Braun and Clarke 2006) and the extant literature (Yin 2011). This enabled themes to be clustered together to attribute meaning to the data and facilitate analysis (Saldana 2010).

The coding sought to address four key elements: credibility, transferability, dependability and confirmability of the research (Creswell and Miller 2000). Credibility was achieved by employing a variety of strategies to corroborate findings. This included respondent validation and triangulation. Follow up calls with the participants confirmed validity by further clarifying findings. Triangulation occurred via the iterative process of thematic analysis whereby the transcripts were firstly reviewed and analysed by the three researchers individually, using the per cent agreement technique, before cross-examining of the findings and interpretations to ensure consistency. Secondary data from online news reports, social media content and websites were also used to triangulate information as suggested by numerous scholars (e.g. Cowton 1998; Harris 2001; Houston 2004; Jack and Raturi 2006; Yin 2011). Transferability was attained by producing depth and richness in the detailing of the activities via descriptive extracts illustrating key themes (Yin 2011). Dependability, which Lincoln and Guba (1990) liken to reliability in quantitative work, was achieved through consistency of practice and procedures in the research, particularly in transcription and analysis (Morse et al. 2002; Yin 2011). Finally, confirmability was achieved by outlining the steps taken in the analysis to minimize researcher bias (Patton 2009; Yin 2011).

Findings

Case Study 1 – Doi Chaang

Doi Chaang Coffee was established over a decade ago in Thailand. After 20 years of successfully cultivating and processing coffee, the coffee community was frustrated with the minimal prices paid by international coffee merchants (Ragavan 2013). The community of 8,000 inhabitants united to create its own single-estate Arabica coffee company – Doi Chaang. Doi Chaang quickly established itself as an independent coffee producer by successfully exporting its brand within the Asia-Pacific region and internationally, in collaboration with some Canadian coffee enthusiasts (Ragavan 2013). The company has developed into an award-winning and well-respected global coffee business, with its Thailand base now establishing branches in Malaysia, Singapore and Australia (Stakal 2011). The following discusses the findings of the Doi Chaang case.

Understanding and perceptions of social capital

Social capital, in the form of trust and reciprocity manifests itself in several aspects of the development and operations of Doi Chaang. At its onset, the company developed important relationships with a group of Canadian coffee enthusiasts to help brand the company and ensure its image is consistent across its entities (Ragavan 2013). Despite potential risks, company leadership convinced the local community that the Canadian partnership (a bridging network), built on trust based upon shared values and goals, was critical for Doi Chaang to have a successful future. The trusting relationships developed with its Canadian counterparts has helped Doi Chaang secure numerous awards for coffee, and carve its niche as a service experience built on organic and fair-trade coffee production (Stakal 2011).

Similarly, evidence of trust and reciprocity was uncovered in Doi Chaang's retail operations. Tess, a branch manager, stated, *'Some people from Doi Chaang Thailand sometimes pay a mystery visit to the store and catches us by surprise … This is not a spot check* per se, *but to come and encourage us and trust that we are doing business* [providing a service experience] *aligned with the company's ethos.'* Reciprocity also extends to consumers. For Tess, the Doi Chaang outlet (located within a residential area) brings in consumers who desire an experience where they can take their time to have their drink and chat with the employees. The resultant relationships that have developed over the months provides clear illustration of trust and reciprocity. Tess explained:

> Sometimes the customers forget to take their wallet or purse as their home is nearby … I will allow them to pay the next time they come in … Some of the customers are kind to me in return. For instance, one lady bought me lunch as she saw that I was quite busy the whole day and had hardly eaten.

The acts of kindness bestowed by Tess are emblematic of how Doi Chaang conducts its operations. The company prides itself as a fair-trade and organic coffee producer not because of the economic incentives, but as Bitti (2014) puts it, as a conduit to inculcate the social values of its story that reinforces the service experience provided to potential and existing consumers.

Prominent relationships/networks that influenced the evolution and development of the enterprise

The participants repeatedly highlighted the role of trust, and the shared beliefs and values underpinning the transformational leadership existing within Doi Chaang. There appeared to be a deference to, and implicit trust in, the company's founder, who was an inspiration in taking the brand and service experience to its current heights (Davids 2014). Tess commented on the trust and motivation she drew from the founder, '*Wicha* [the founder] *was the force behind why I wanted to be part of the vision for the company – to take coffee to a market that values and treasures the meanings behind how it is produced …*'

Rural communities, such as the northern Thailand hill tribes, are heavily reliant on two main exports – agriculture and tourism – as key paths to both development (Lacher and Nepal 2010) and to alleviating poverty and social ills (McKinnon 2008). Unlike tourism, agricultural exports in Northern Thailand are highly controlled by the government. Thailand practices a '*One Tambon, One Product*' (OTOP) programme, where each community village is prescribed what it can grow in terms of agriculture with its aim of alleviating poverty (Natsuda et al. 2012). However, this programme has resulted in some inherent challenges, as inclement weather and/or diseases can wipe out an entire harvest for communities with little contingency plans (Pruetipibultham 2010). Given the importance of and apparent inflexible nature of agricultural choices, these communities have much to gain from the strategic collaboration that can help create service experiences (e.g. coffee tourism). The trust and collaboration detailed in the Doi Chaang case bears witness to this.

Identification of enabling/limiting factors in the application of social capital

The Doi Chaang case exemplified collaboration across different facets of its operations. At the retail end, Tess mentioned she often spoke with others in the network located across different countries to discuss strategies moving forward. One of these individuals was Ignatius, a regional manager based in Malaysia. Ignatius revealed, '*I believe in open communication … that if Tess or anyone in the group encounter problems we can talk and help problem solve collectively.*' Additionally, Tess echoed she felt indebted to many others who contributed as she oversaw the new Doi Chaang outlet opening in Singapore. Tess added, '*Without the help of Ignatius and others in the network, this new store would not have progressed this far.*'

While the previous paragraph indicated collaboration at the end of the supply chain, there was also collaboration evidenced by backward integration. This was demonstrated by the willingness of the Doi Chaang outlets to not only source Arabica beans from Thai communities, but also other complementary items (e.g. brown sugar) to further build these important relationships. Tess highlighted the brown sugar obtained from the northern Thailand regions cost more than those readily available in Singapore and Malaysia. Yet, these outlets were adamant the brown sugar tasted better than other alternatives justifying the higher costs. Further validating her decision, she emphasized purchasing from local sources enhanced the welfare of the village communities. Ignatius expressed similar regards:

> Last year, the harvest of brown sugar decreased significantly due to terrible droughts … we had severe shortage in the supplies … while we raised prices of coffee for a short period of time explaining why this was the case to our customers, we gave more back to the communities from our sales revenue … This was our way of showing support for the villages who have repeatedly given us so much …

For coffee service enterprises, collaboration occurs in terms of forward and backward integration. Some other studies alluded to the roles of coffee service enterprises in leveraging on the synergies between, and within different groups in the network to build sustainable operations (e.g. Mawejje and Holden 2013; Mujawamariya, D'Haese, and Speelman 2013; Tobias, Mair, and Barbosa-Leiker 2013). However, what appears to drive collaboration in this instance is the shared vision of collective well-being as a choice, rather than a condition of collaboration. Tess articulated:

> Doi Chaang runs a coffee academy that some of us have participated in prior to becoming a franchiser. This experience was such an eye opener for me to witness how each member of the community chose to be part of this movement, and their participation had no strings attached … This is so anti-Singaporean [*laughs*] as there is no such thing as a free lunch here!

From her comments, Tess emphasized the communities were not coerced into collaboration, but developed from trust in the inspirational leadership and relationship building of the founder, who assembled an entourage of followers keen to seek a better quality of life. This finding also demonstrates social capital via developing relationships with all stakeholders, as important for creating a unique service experience.

It is also worth positioning the research within a cultural context, as a contingent factor. Thailand embodies a collective society, with Buddhism underpinning much of the nation's social and economic fabric (Maisrikrod 1999; Niffenegger, Kulviwat, and Engchanil 2006). These characteristics emphasize harmony, societal well-being and conflict avoidance (Onishi and Bliss 2006; McCann, Honeycutt, and Keaton 2010). For this reason, any attempt at agricultural entrepreneurship in Thailand would have necessitated a key individual, or group, to envision the benefits of collaboration with the entire community, an area in which the inspirational leadership of Doi Chaang's founder excelled (Sapsuwan 2014). In turn, the culture in community leadership and collaboration developed from social capital are contingent factors that help embed a shared vision into a unique coffee service experience for the franchise.

Advantages of social capital to the enterprise

Overall, the Doi Chaang narrative has illuminated the benefits of adopting a social capital approach. Compared with the Adler and Kwon (2002) framework (Figure 1), the characteristics of Doi Chaang are similar in that social structures are antecedents to the conceptualization of social capital. These took the form of strong trusting relations that enabled the company to grow. These relationships are further operationalized by the contingent moderating factors of opportunity, motivation and abilities to derive positive gains from social capital. For example, founders of Doi Chaang approached a Canadian entrepreneur with similar values and goals relating to coffee, and via this relationship extended networks important for funding and drawing on business expertise to help Doi Chaang expand globally (Stakal 2011). This collaboration helped leverage the existing network relationships based on the strategic leadership of Wicha and the shared similar vision of select external parties needed for global expansion. The discussion also demonstrates the role of external factors, namely political, economic, legal, socio-cultural and environmental considerations in directing how and why social capital should be appropriated within the network (Woolcock 1998; Adler and Kwon 2002; Hayami 2009). These contexts are country, culture and sector specific, but nonetheless contribute valuable insights to theory and practice, especially in an environment where service enterprises such as coffee are experiencing steady growth.

Case Study 2 – A Coffee Roasters Guild in regional Australia

The second case is a regional Australian Coffee Roasters Guild. The Guild is a group of eight coffee roasters formed in 2015. The Guild's main purpose is to make the local region the 'ultimate coffee destination' in Australia (Bowling 2015). The Guild aims to achieve its purpose by maintaining their financial autonomy as individual roasters, while pooling effort, energy and time to create collaborative experiences around coffee. This takes the form of events, workshops, training, and education incorporating numerous stakeholders (e.g. consumers, suppliers, retailers, local tourism bodies) interacting and building relationships to generate mutual benefit for regional stakeholders. An understanding of the development and application of social capital is therefore germane to this organization.

Understanding and perception of social capital

Members of the Guild suggested social capital centres on the value they derived from working in networks where mutually beneficial relationships are established. Thoughts that came to mind when members were asked to give their understanding of social capital were, 'connections rather than isolation', 'local networks', 'power in numbers', 'sharing skills and learning', 'mutual advantage and viability'. One member, Don, a head roaster, stated a more specific understanding of social capital as, 'A starting point [for social capital] is the sharing of information via networks for the benefit of each other [other Guild members].' While another member, Jen, a business owner, posited, 'It [social capital] is about learning with each other, instead of feeling isolated as a business. It makes what you do more enriching if you have allies … it also opens connections outside of business, for example friendships.' These findings corroborate with social capital attributes such as influence and solidarity (Adler and Kwon 2002), reflecting central tenets of social capital such as networks, and social interactions that drive collaboration and mutual benefit (Coleman 1988; Putnam 1993).

Prominent relationships/networks that influenced the evolution and development of the enterprise

The Guild participants identified several key networks developed from and supported by the group's inherent social capital. For example, playing a central role in the continued development of the Guild are the relationships among the coffee roasters themselves. In this sense, social capital is what brought the roasters together. Jen noted:

> A single roaster pitched the idea that we [*the roasters*] should not be working as individual competitors within all levels of our businesses, but rather working together to ensure that retailers in the region are all using product from one of us as a local roaster, as opposed to a large commercial supplier. There was likeminded vision of what being part of a guild could potentially provide us all.

As the Guild continues to develop, the social capital between them has become more robust as motivation and trust builds. For example, Don suggested, *'Before we were a part of the Guild, roasters would never share information on roasting techniques, but now I know I can openly call other members to bounce ideas off of them'.* This type of horizontal network sharing is symbolic of a bonding network, where strong group memberships form based on common values and beliefs supported by trust and reciprocity (Coleman 1988; Putnam 1993; Portes 2000).

Supply chain networks are also viewed as important for the Guild. In particular, another member, Katrina, the founding Guild chair member, posited, *'Relationships with suppliers and producers helps us ensure the quality and integrity of our product and make us all more viable as individual businesses financially, and can also reduce difficulties associated with processes like logistics.'*

This finding offers insight into the service component of the coffee experience and how the relationships formed within the supply chain help convey the story of coffee to consumers. From a service experience perspective, interactions with consumers mark a key opportunity to develop relationships. As Don explained, *'Customers desire ethically sourced, speciality and fresh coffee, so traceability is key. It's about starting the conversation on what is good coffee and educating people about the supplier's process.'* Katrina added, *'... the Guild's brand can serve as symbol of assurance and help create relationships with customers. It allows us to educate customers on the product ... the customers then ask more ... building the relationship.'*

Hence, educational experiences offer a platform for the Guild to develop reciprocal relationships with consumers. This finding suggests the Guild's relationships with consumers are enhanced via the strength of relationships the Guild has within its producer and supplier network. That is, the stronger the social capital developed within the Guild's supplier and producer networks, the better education and service experience the Guild can build into consumer relationships and networks.

Findings also showed relationships with external organizations as an important factor in the Guild's development. Specifically, the Guild was interested in leveraging connections with other regionally based organizations and groups that share similar vision and values. As Katrina suggested:

> The development of external relationships is important; especially connecting to other local groups/organisations that share the same focus and ideas ... working with local organisations like regional tourism bodies is good for both parties. They have expertise in areas such as promotion of the local region, while we provide them with knowledge to how we may be represented within their campaigns.

This highlights the benefit bridging between networks can provide in the form of access to diverse information, influence and resources not available within the Guild's internal networks (Burt 1997; Adler and Kwon 2002).

Identification of enabling/limiting factors in the application of social capital

The findings revealed three main factors that influence the application of social capital by the Guild. The most common factor discussed was trust, a salient element of social capital (Putnam 1993; Woolcock 1998; Portes 2000). Don stated, *'Trust is key. It drives the transparency and communication needed to sustain this* [the Guild]. Jen expressed to achieve trust in building social capital, *"It* [trust] *takes time to build … when its established value can emerge … having a focus helps build trust for us … working on a few small projects that have some tangible outcomes so members can experience getting a win together.'* Establishing trust amongst Guild members was an important antecedent towards developing social capital amongst themselves, and the lynchpin for developing trust and social capital in other external networks such as suppliers, consumers, and local tourism and event organizations. Jen noted, *'After trust is established within the Guild, then we can look to establish external relationships.'*

Relevant skill sets are another factor found influencing the development and application of social capital for the Guild. Katrina stated, *'Smaller organisations … like our members … don't have all the skills … it's important to find others that have skills and to share them … skills could be marketing, management, barista, network and relationship building skills.'* This finding suggests sharing skills supports social capital in the form of mutually beneficial resource exchange (Tsai and Ghoshal 1998), via the ability to network and build relationships (Brunetto and Farr-Wharton 2007). Jen suggested, *'Learning how to share skills is a skill in itself and is difficult. Once people learned this, they saw the value in the skills they could share and contribute … this enhanced trust and mutual benefit for us and others* [consumers, suppliers] *we work with or service.'* This finding reflects how relationships deliver beneficial collaboration for organizations (Nahapiet and Ghoshal 1998) and implies collaboration may lead to a better overall service experience for consumers.

Motivation was another factor important to the development of social capital within the Guild and external network organizations. Katrina expressed, *'You have to be motivated to contribute to the group in the interest of outcomes for all … the members that decided to participate in the Guild were simply keen to try something different … of course it helped that there were likeminded values that everyone was driven by.'* This finding aligns with intrinsic contingent factors such as motivation, often based on shared values and goals, which influence the development of social capital (Adler and Kwon 2002). Echoing Adler and Kwon (2002), the findings suggest trust and skill sets are important in developing and applying social capital; and motivation built on common value systems, influences the degree to which social capital is leveraged to generate a better service experience.

Advantages of social capital to the enterprise

Advantages of utilizing social capital surfaced in the form of two themes, internal and external benefits. Don stated:

Building, using and communicating about our social capital networks … for example, Guild roasters, roasters and local tourism bodies, roasters and consumers, roasters and supply chain members, roasters and community … generates better benefit financially to everyone … and ensures the best product and service to customers.

Concerning internal benefits, Jen posited, *'Working within a group gives you more influence and power.'* Katrina conveyed, *'… it* [social capital] *keeps orgs from cannibalising customers by using a cooperative-competitor approach … not just transferring customers from one to another, but working collectively though our relationships to consider how to improve the financial viability of all.'* In service experience terms, Don added, *'Customers are amazed when you recommend a business other than your own … customers think, these businesses* [members] *in the Guild really care about what I want as a customer … when I go get a coffee from a Guild member, they will take care of me.'*

One benefit of working in external networks was the potential relationships created with suppliers. Don noted, *'By coming together we can influence suppliers … and work with them to create relationships and take us more seriously in this region.'* Benefits with the local community also emerged. Katrina suggested, *'Being in a regional location is a good fit … we feel that the local community is part of our identity … we benefit by connecting with it and want them to benefit by connecting with us … it's more viable for all of us.'* Both themes centred on common advantages of social capital like access to resources, and cooperation and influence derived from the strength of group affiliations (Nahapiet and Ghoshal 1998; Adler and Kwon 2002; Kwon and Adler 2014). It further illustrates how the presence of trust is beneficial throughout the service experience, including the critical connection with the end-consumer.

Discussion

The application of social capital has allowed both service enterprise cases to develop and leverage relationships that have underpinned their growth. In addition, it appears social capital has helped each service enterprise develop and support the coffee service experience, beyond a commodity. The findings coalesce an understanding as to how different service enterprises create a better coffee experience for all stakeholders as a result of social capital. Importantly, this includes the consumer relationships that are enhanced through the high quality coffee experiences many consumers seek. However, both cases demonstrate differences in terms of their appropriation of social capital.

In the case of Doi Chaang, the findings demonstrate the influence of national culture as a contingent factor and indicative antecedent to conceptualizing how social capital manifests within an Asian service enterprise experience. The existing national cultures within Thailand have shaped communal behaviours reflecting social capital as a process of re-engineering the agricultural environment, which is echoed in Doi Chaang's operations as a service enterprise. Individuals, such as Doi Chaang's founder, provided the strategic ability to facilitate collaboration within coffee production and other supporting crops (e.g. sugar and tea) to effect what Parnwell (2007) terms 'renascent social capital'. Renascent social capital is a neo-local perspective that embraces local identities and values drawn from a charismatic leader that activates desired communal outcomes across numerous sectors (Parnwell 2007). Woolcock (1998) also argued such a bottom-up approach is effective in negotiating resistance and apprehensiveness to the notion of social capital by embedding local practices and cultural affinity. Such conditions enhance community buy-in for trust and reciprocity to be realized, for the manifestation of social capital in a service experience.

The finding also resonates and extends Adler and Kwon's (2002) observation where the value derived from social capital is contingent. The case identifies how culture represents a contingent factor, along with how Doi Chaang's social capital is impacted by established contingent factors such as motivation, ability and opportunity, in the form of strategic and transformational leadership guided by shared vision and goals. Further aligning with Adler and Kwon (2002), Doi Chaang's social capital relationships are also influenced by contingent external forces (e.g. government regulations), along with socio-cultural and natural environment factors. In the case of Doi Chaang, the development and application of social capital has charted a valuable trajectory for creating a unique coffee service experience for consumers and other associated stakeholders (e.g. local community villages). From the findings and drawn from the Adler and Kwon (2002) and Parnwell (2007) frameworks, Figure 2 depicts a framework of Doi Chaang's social capital.

In contrast to Doi Chaang, the precipitating factors for the regional Coffee Roasters Guild in Australia focused on the benefits of social capital to build a stronger coffee narrative. In turn, this provides a better consumer service experience and economic viability for each member. Presumably, each operator could function as an independent entity without necessarily being part of the Guild. However, the relationships formed within the Guild help pool together its collective knowledge, skills and relational ties to create a stronger value proposition for all members in the region to deliver an enhanced coffee service experience. This supports Adler and Kwon's (2002) view that while the value of social capital is inherently relational, other contingent factors have a mediating influence.

The activities of the Guild reflect the value of social capital as contingent on the capabilities (i.e. knowledge, skills) of the actors in a network. This value is the aggregated benefits available within the organization's internal network and its associated weaker connections

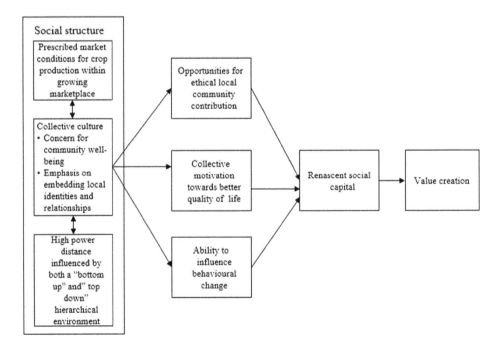

Figure 2. Doi Chaang social capital framework. Adapted from Adler and Kwon (2002) and Parnwell (2007).

with other extended networks (Adler and Kwon 2002). The Guild case identifies members are not only strategically accessing value from its strong bonding network, but are further realizing the value associated with utilising weaker ties to bridge between external networks (e.g. local tourism bodies) (Burt 1997). Thus, the Guild appear to be benefiting from strategically leveraging strong and weak network connections (Hoang and Antoncic 2003) as an optimal approach to developing social capital in their service experience.

The work of Tsai and Ghoshal (1998) is also reflected in the Guild's application of social capital. Specifically, where the structural (social interaction) and cognitive (shared vision) dimensions of social capital develop beneficial trust and resource exchange to create value for an organization (Tsai and Ghoshal 1998). This conceptualization is prompted by a common set of motivational beliefs and goals about enhancing the local region's coffee service experience. As a result, Guild members build resilience in their individual business models and develop the capacity to strategically align and leverage internal and external relationship networks. Drawn from Tsai and Ghoshal (1998) and Adler and Kwon (2002), Figure 3 conceptualizes the social capital for the regional Coffee Roasters Guild in Australia.

Apart from some of the differences illustrated in the adapted frameworks, the variation in social capital between the two cases may also be connected to the service enterprise type. With franchises, the goal is to create a consistent service experience that maintains the culture and values of an organization anywhere it is established. Whereas, the Guild's objectives encourage each member to maintain their individual unique service experience, but work together to educate, support and establish mutual benefit for stakeholders that share and wish to enhance the regional identity.

Overall, the findings lend further structure and extend current frameworks concerning social capital by mapping the emic perspectives from a comparative case study approach. In doing so, the role of culture was highlighted as a contingent influence on social capital

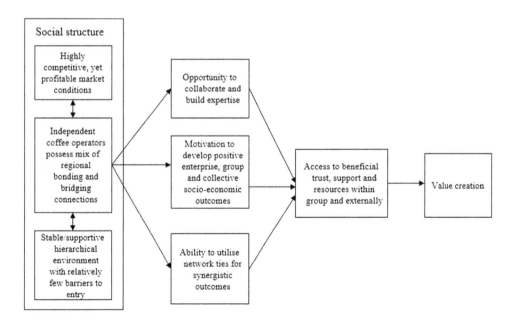

Figure 3. Regional coffee roasters guild social capital framework. Adapted from Tsai and Ghoshal (1998) and Adler and Kwon (2002).

development and appropriation, which we acknowledge large body of literature that exists concerning culture in a social capital context (e.g. Chui, Lloyd, and Kwok 2002; Ji et al. 2010). However, national culture, in and of itself, is insufficient to explain how social capital is developed and applied in organizations and the legitimacy it holds for different stakeholders varies (Jackman and Miller 1998; Beugelsdijk and Van Schaik 2005; Kwon and Arenius 2010). As such, this research sought to make explicit links to overlay the findings onto the broad conceptualizations of social capital from the organizational perspective. This answered the call from Kwon and Adler (2014) to coalesce more nuanced associations of social capital with contingent factors such as opportunity, motivation, ability, in addition to national culture, in the scope of service enterprises, within the under-researched space of the coffee industry service experience. In doing so, a micro-level understanding of how social capital is developed and applied in service experiences starts to emerge.

Conclusion, limitations and future research

This study sought to explore how social capital is developed and applied from an organizational perspective, within a service experience context in two Asia-Pacific regions. The study demonstrated the nuance of contingent factors, including culture, along with business types (i.e. franchises, guilds), are important considerations to the development and appropriation of social capital in service enterprise experiences. Resultantly, the study reveals there is not likely a singular way for social capital to be developed and applied across the coffee service experience in Asia-Pacific. Rather, how social capital is appropriated, is contextually bound to the specific nomenclature and processes identified in each service enterprise case.

Theoretically, existing SCT frameworks within the organizational literature provide a general framework for understanding the potential value of social capital, but they lack a nuanced understanding of aspects and mechanisms required in specific industries and disciplines (Adler and Kwon 2002). The study therefore contributes adapted theoretical frameworks that include specific aspects and mechanisms reflecting how social capital is contextualized in each service enterprise case to influence the service experience. For service enterprises in Asian cultures, collective cultural values stemming from charismatic and trusted leaders, known as renascent social capital, are reflected in how the service organization seeks to enhance the service experience, support existing theory. Adding to this theory, our study demonstrates that Asian service enterprises tend to embed and leverage this type of social capital in such mechanisms as supporting community causes, and operating in and encouraging more sustainable business behaviour to enhance the value of the service experience. In the case of Western-based service enterprises, common views of social capital, such as creating relational networks to help drive the financial viability of individual stakeholders, appear dominant and are consistent with existing theory. Following suggestions from Adler and Kwon (2002) and Kwon and Adler (2014), our study expands on this theory via uncovering more nuanced aspects of developing social capital. Aspects like opportunities for collaboration, desire for collective outcomes and the ability to share network resources surfaced in our study and contribute to enhancing the service experience.

From a practical standpoint, the study contributes initial insight towards how social capital is actually developed and applied in the coffee service experience within different Asia-Pacific regions. For example, in both case examples, although mechanized with varying initiatives, creating relationships with community stakeholders via social capital, help improve the service experience. The study also offers insight to service organizations seeking to enhance their service experience by understanding how social capital manifests within varying business models and in different Asia-Pacific regions.

This study is not without limitations. Given the exploratory nature of the study, it was restricted to two Asia-Pacific locations and cases. Employing a similar study to other Asia-Pacific regions and service enterprise types would add robustness to future work. Future studies could also incorporate expert opinions in the form of the Delphi technique to enhance and validate the findings. Contributing to a known gap, the findings were based on interviews from the service enterprise (organizational) perspective and only focused on the benefits of social capital. While social capital presents benefits, potential risks in the form of exclusion, freeloading and group think can emerge (Nahapiet and Ghoshal 1998; Portes 2000). Accordingly, future studies seeking insight from other stakeholders (e.g. consumers, suppliers, external community organizations) could provide additional rigour and insights into the interpretation, development, application and potential disadvantages of social capital in service experiences. We also note that our focus on the service organization perspective resulted in theoretical and practical contributions based on preliminary findings of how social capital may be developed and applied in the service experience. As a result, theoretical findings related to cultural differences in the two cases are preliminary, but offer a platform for future theoretical work on the relationship between social capital, culture and the service experience.

Quantitative methods would also contribute further rigour. They could explore large service organizations operating on a global scale, examining similarities and differences across social capital nomenclature, and application within different Asia-Pacific regions and cultures. A future longitudinal study would provide a more nuanced perspective of how social capital evolves and may be used to enhance service enterprises over time.

Disclosure statement

No potential conflict of interest was reported by the authors.

References

Adler, P. S., and S. W. Kwon. 2002. "Social Capital: Prospects for a New Concept." *Academy of Management Review* 27 (1): 17–40.

Andrews, R. 2010. "Organizational Social Capital, Structure and Performance." *Human Relations* 63 (5): 583–608.

Antonio, R. J. 2015. "Is Prosumer Capitalism on the Rise?" *The Sociological Quarterly* 56 (3): 472–483.

Attride-Stirling, J. 2001. "Thematic Networks: An Analytic Tool for Qualitative Research." *Qualitative Research* 1 (3): 385–405.

Baron, R. A., and G. D. Markman. 2000. "Beyond Social Capital: How Social Skills Can Enhance Entrepreneurs' Success." *Academy of Management Executive* 14 (1): 106–117.

BarNir, A., and K. Smith. 2002. "Inter-Firm Alliances in the Small Business: The Role of Social Networks." *Journal of Small Business Management* 40 (3): 219–232.

Baxter, P., and S. Jack. 2008. "Qualitative Case Study Methodology: Study Design and Implementation for Novice Researchers." *The Qualitative Report* 13 (4): 544–559.

Beam, R. A. 2003. "Content Differences between Daily Newspapers with Strong and Weak Market Orientations." *Journalism & Mass Communication Quarterly* 80 (2): 368–390.

Beugelsdijk, S., and T. Van Schaik. 2005. "Differences in Social Capital between 54 Western European Regions." *Regional Studies* 39 (8): 1053–1064.

Bitti, M. T. 2014. *For Coffee Purveyors, Fair Trade is No Longer a Differentiator*. Accessed February 29, 2016. http://business.financialpost.com/entrepreneur/for-coffee-purveyors-fair-trade-is-no-longer-a-differentiator

Boddy, C. R. 2016. "Sample Size for Qualitative Research." *Qualitative Market Research: An International Journal* 19 (4): 426–432.

Bourdieu, P. 1986. "The Forms of Capital." In *Handbook of Theory and Research for the Sociology of Education*, edited by J. G. Richardson, 241–258. New York: Greenwood.

Bowen, G. A. 2008. "Naturalistic Inquiry and the Saturation Concept: A Research Note." *Qualitative Research* 8 (1): 137–152.

Bowling, D. 2015. *Coffee Roasters Guild Established in Sunshine Coast*. Accessed February 29, 2016. http://www.hospitalitymagazine.com.au/beverage/coffee-roasters-guild-established-in-sunshine-coas

Braun, V., and V. Clarke. 2006. "Using Thematic Analysis in Psychology." *Qualitative Research in Psychology* 3 (2): 77–101.

Brodie, R. J., L. D. Hollebeek, B. Juric, and A. Ilic. 2011. "Customer Engagement - Conceptual Domain, Fundamental Propositions, and Implications for Research." *Journal of Service Research* 14 (3): 252–271.

Brunetto, Y., and R. Farr-Wharton. 2007. "The Moderating Role of Trust in SME Owner/Managers' Decision-Making about Collaboration." *Journal of Small Business Management* 45 (3): 362–387.

Burt, R. 1992. *Structural Holes: The Social Structure of Competition*. Cambridge, MA: Harvard University Press.

Burt, R. S. 1997. "The Contingent Value of Social Capital." *Administrative Science Quarterly* 42 (2): 339–365.

Chen, P., and H. Hu. 2010. "The Effect of Relational Benefits on Perceived Value in Relation to Customer Loyalty: An Empirical Study in the Australian Coffee Outlets Industry." *International Journal of Hospitality Management* 29 (3): 405–412.

Cho, J., and A. Trent. 2006. "Validity in Qualitative Research Revisited." *Qualitative Research* 6 (3): 319–340.

Chui, A. C. W., A. E. Lloyd, and C. C. Y. Kwok. 2002. "The Determination of Capital Structure: Is National Culture a Missing Piece to the Puzzle." *Journal of International Business Studies* 33 (1): 99–127.

Coleman, J. S. 1988. "Social Capital in the Creation of Human Capital." *American Journal of Sociology* 94 (Supplement): S95–S120.

Collins, F. L. 2008. "Of Kimchi and Coffee: Globalisation, Transnationalism and Familiarity in Culinary Consumption." *Social & Cultural Geography* 9 (2): 151–169.

Cowton, C. J. 1998. "The Use of Secondary Data in Business Ethics Research." *Journal of Business Ethics* 17 (4): 423–434.

Creswell, J. W. 2009. "Editorial: Mapping the Field of Mixed Methods Research." *Journal of Mixed Methods Research* 3 (2): 95–108.

Creswell, J. W., W. E. Hanson, V. L. C. Plano, and A. Morales. 2007. "Qualitative Research Designs – Selection and Implementation." *The Counselling Journalist* 35 (2): 236–264.

Creswell, J. W., and D. L. Miller. 2000. "Determining Validity in Qualitative Inquiry." *Theory into Practice* 39 (3): 124–130.

Davids, K. 2014. *A Tribute to the Life of Wicha Promyong, Doi Chaang Coffee*. Accessed February 29, 2016. http://www.coffeereview.com/a-tribute-to-the-life-of-wicha-promyong-doi-chaang-coffee/

De Koning, A. 2003. "Opportunity Development: A Socio-Cognitive Perspective." In *Advances in Entrepreneurship Firm Emergence and Growth*, Vol. 6, edited by J. Katz and I. Shepard, 265–314. Bingley: Emerald Group Publishing.

DeCuir-Gunby, J. T., P. L. Marshall, and A. W. McCulloch. 2011. "Developing and Using a Codebook for the Analysis of Interview Data: An Example from a Professional Development Project." *Field Methods* 23 (2): 136–155.

Denzin, H., and Y. Lincoln. 1994. *Handbook of Qualitative Research*. Thousand Oaks: Sage.

Elder, S. D., H. Zerriffi, and P. Le Billon. 2012. "Effects of Fair Trade Certification on Social Capital: The Case of Rwandan Coffee Producers." *World Development* 40 (11): 2355–2367.

Eisenhardt, E. 1989. "Building Theories from Case Study Research." *Academy of Management Review* 14 (4): 532–550.

Flyvbjerg, B. 2006. "Five Misunderstandings about Case-Study Research." *Qualitative Inquiry* 12 (2): 219–245.

Gilsing, V., and B. Nooteboom. 2005. "Density and Strength of Ties in Innovation Networks: An Analysis of Multimedia and Biotechnology." *European Management Review* 2 (3): 179–197.

Granovetter, M. S. 1973. "The Strength of Weak Ties." *American Journal of Sociology* 78 (6): 1360–1380.

Granovetter, M. 1983. "The Strength of Weak Ties: A Network Theory Revisited." *Sociological Theory* 1: 210–233.

Grigg, D. 2002. "The Worlds of Tea and Coffee Consumption." *GeoJournal* 57 (4): 283–294.

Grönroos, C., and A. Ravald. 2011. "Service as Business Logic: Implications for Value Creation and Marketing." *Journal of Service Management* 22 (1): 5–22.

Guest, G., A. Bunce, and L. Johnson. 2006. "How Many Interviews Are Enough? An Experiment with Data Saturation and Variability." *Field Methods* 18 (1): 59–82.

Harris, H. 2001. "Content Analysis of Secondary Data: A Study of Courage in Managerial Decision-Making." *Journal of Business Ethics* 34 (3): 191–208.

Hayami, Y. 2009. "Social Capital, Human Capital and the Community Mechanism: Toward a Conceptual Framework for Economics." *Journal of Development Studies* 45 (1): 96–123.

Hayes, A. F., and K. Krippendorff. 2007. "Answering the Call for a Standard Reliability Measure for Coding Data." *Communication Methods and Measures* 1 (1): 77–89.

Hoang, H., and B. Antoncic. 2003. "Network-Based Research in Entrepreneurship: A Critical Review." *Journal of Business Venturing* 18 (2): 165–187.

Houston, M. B. 2004. "Assessing the Validity of Secondary Data Proxies for Marketing Constructs." *Journal of Business Research* 57 (2): 154–161.

Huggins, R., and A. Johnston. 2010. "Knowledge Flow and Inter-Firm Networks: The Influence of Resources, Spatial Proximity and Firm Size." *Entrepreneurship & Regional Development* 22 (5): 457–484.

Humphries, A., and K. Grayson. 2008. "The Intersecting Roles of Consumer and Producer: A Critical Perspective of Co-Production, Co-Creation and Presumption." *Sociology Compass* 2 (3): 963–980.

International Coffee Organization (ICO). 2016a. *Total Production by All Exporting Countries*. Accessed February 29, 2016. http://www.ico.org/prices/po-production.pdf

International Coffee Organization (ICO). 2016b. *World Coffee Consumption in Thousand 60 Kg Bags*. Accessed February 29, 2016. http://www.ico.org/prices/new-consumption-table.pdf

Jack, E. P., and A. S. Raturi. 2006. "Lessons Learned from Methodological Triangulation in Management Research." *Management Research News* 29 (6): 345–357.

Jackman, R. W., and R. A. Miller. 1998. "Social Capital and Politics." *Annual Review of Political Science* 1 (1): 47–73.

Jenner, P., and F. Oprescu. 2016. "The Sectorial Trust of Social Enterprise: Friend or Foe?" *Journal of Social Entrepreneurship* 7 (2): 236–261.

Ji, Y. G., H. Hwangbo, J. S. Yi, P. Rau, X. Fang, and C. Ling. 2010. "The Influence of Cultural Differences on the Use of Social Network Services and the Formation of Social Capital." *International Journal of Human-Computer Interaction* 26 (11–12): 1100–1121.

Kleidas, M., and L. Jolliffe. 2010. "Coffee Attraction Experiences: A Narrative Study." *Turizam* 58 (1): 61–73.

Kwon, S., and P. Adler. 2014. "Social Capital: Maturation of a Field of Research." *Academy of Management Review* 39 (4): 412–422.

Kwon, S., and P. Arenius. 2010. "Nations of Entrepreneurs: A Social Capital Perspective." *Journal of Business Venturing* 25 (3): 315–330.

Lacher, R. G., and S. K. Nepal. 2010. "Dependency and Development in Northern Thailand." *Annals of Tourism Research* 37 (4): 947–968.

Leana, C., and H. Van Buren. 1999. "Organisational Social Capital and Employment Practices." *Academy of Management* 24 (3): 538–555.

Lee, R. 2009. "Social Capital and Business and Management: Setting a Research Agenda." *International Journal of Management Reviews* 11 (3): 247–273.

Levin, D. Z., and R. Cross. 2004. "The Strength of Weak Ties You Can Trust: The Mediating Role of Trust in Effective Knowledge Transfer." *Management Science* 50 (11): 1477–1490.

Li, L., W. Barner-Rasmussen, and I. Bjorkman. 2007. "What Difference Does the Location Make?: a Social Capital Perspective on Transfer of Knowledge from Multinational Corporation Subsidiaries Located in China and Finland." *Asia Pacific Business Review* 13 (2): 233–249.

Lin, N. 1999. "Building a Network Theory of Social Capital." *Connections* 22 (1): 28–51.

Lincoln, Y. S., and E. G. Guba. 1990. "Judging the Quality of Case Study Reports." *International Journal of Qualitative Studies in Education* 3 (1): 53–59.

Lombard, M., J. Snyder-Duch, and C. C. Bracken. 2002. "Content Analysis in Mass Communication: Assessment and Reporting of Intercoder Reliability." *Human Communication Research* 28 (4): 587–604.

Maisrikrod, S. 1999. "Joining the Values Debate: The Peculiar Case of Thailand." *Journal of Social Issues in Southeast Asia* 14 (2): 402–413.

Markides, C. 1997. "Strategic Innovation." *Sloan Management Review* 38 (3): 9–23.

Martinez, M., and H. Aldrich. 2011. "Networking Strategies for Entrepreneurs: Balancing Cohesion and Diversity." *International Journal of Entrepreneurial Behavior & Research* 17 (1): 7–38.

Mathwick, C., N. Malhotra, and E. Rigdon. 2001. "Experiential Value: Conceptualization, Measurement and Application in the Catalog and Internet Shopping Environment." *Journal of Retailing* 77 (1): 39–56.

Maurer, I., V. Bartsch, and M. Ebers. 2011. "The Value of Intra-Organisational Social Capital: How It Fosters Knowledge Transfer, Innovation, Performance and Growth." *Organization Studies* 32 (2): 157–185.

Mawejje, J., and S. T. Holden. 2013. "Does Social Network Capital Buy Higher Agricultural Prices? A Case of Coffee in Masaka District." *Uganda. International Journal of Social Economics* 41 (7): 573–585.

McCann, R. M., J. M. Honeycutt, and S. A. Keaton. 2010. "Toward Greater Specificity in Cultural Value Analyses: The Interplay of Intrapersonal Communication Affect and Cultural Values in Japan, Thailand, and the United States." *Journal of Intercultural Communication Research* 39 (3): 157–172.

McKeever, E., A. Anderson, and S. Jack. 2014. "Entrepreneurship and Mutuality: Social Capital in Processes and Practices." *Entrepreneurship & Regional Development* 26 (5–6): 453–477.

McKinnon, K. 2008. "Taking Post-Development Theory to the Field: Issues in Development Research." *Northern Thailand. Asia Pacific Viewpoint* 49 (3): 281–293.

Mehmetoglu, M., and M. Engen. 2011. "Pine and Gilmore's Concept of Experience Economy and Its Dimensions: An Empirical Examination in Tourism." *Journal of Quality Assurance in Hospitality and Tourism* 12 (4): 237–255.

Meyskens, M., A. Carsrud, and R. Cardozo. 2010. "The Symbiosis of Entities in the Social Engagement Network: The Role of Social Ventures." *Entrepreneurship and Regional Development* 22 (5): 425–455.

Morse, J. M., M. Barrett, M. Mayan, K. Olson, and J. Spiers. 2002. "Verification Strategies for Establishing Reliability and Validity in Qualitative Research." *International Journal of Qualitative Methods* 1 (2): 13–22.

Mujawamariya, G., M. D'Haese, and S. Speelman. 2013. "Exploring Double Side-Selling in Cooperatives, Case Study of Four Coffee Cooperatives in Rwanda." *Food Policy* 39 (Apr): 72–83.

Nahapiet, J., and S. Ghoshal. 1998. "Social Capital, Intellectual Capital, and the Organizational Advantage." *Academy of Management Review* 23 (2): 242–266.

Nahapiet, J., L. Gratton, and H. Rocha. 2005. "Knowledge and Relationships: When Cooperation is the Norm." *European Management Review* 2 (1): 3–14.

Natsuda, K., K. Igusa, A. Wiboonpongse, and J. Thoburn. 2012. "One Village One Product – Rural Development Strategy in Asia: The Case of OTOP in Thailand." *Canadian Journal of Development Studies* 33 (3): 369–385.

Niffenegger, P., S. Kulviwat, and N. Engchanil. 2006. "Conflicting Cultural Imperatives in Modern Thailand: Global Perspectives." *Asia Pacific Business Review* 12 (4): 403–420.

Ogawa, R. T., and B. Malen. 1991. "Towards Rigor in Reviews of Multivocal Literatures: Applying the Exploratory Case Study Method." *Review of Educational Research* 61 (3): 265–286.

Onishi, J., and R. E. Bliss. 2006. "In Search of Asian Ways of Managing Conflict: A Comparative Study of Japan, Hong Kong, Thailand and Vietnam." *International Journal of Conflict Management* 17 (3): 203–225.

O'Reilly, M., and N. Parker. 2013. "'Unsatisfactory Saturation': A Critical Exploration of the Notion of Saturated Sample Sizes in Qualitative Research." *Qualitative Research* 13 (2): 190–197.

Parnwell, M. J. G. 2007. "Neolocalism and Renascent Social Capital in Northeast Thailand." *Environment and Planning D: Society and Space* 25 (6): 990–1014.

Patton, M. 2009. *Qualitative Research & Evaluation Methods*. Thousand Oaks: Sage.

Perren, L., and M. Ram. 2004. "Case-Study Method in Small Business and Entrepreneurial Research." *International Small Business Journal* 22 (1): 83–101.

Petrou, A., and I. Daskalopoulou. 2013. "Social Capital and Innovation in the Services Sector." *European Journal of Innovation Management* 16 (1): 50–69.

Pine, B. J., and J. H. Gilmore. 1999. *The Experience Economy: Work is Theatre & Every Business a Stage*. Boston, MA: Harvard Business Press.

Pinho, J. C., and C. Prange. 2016. "The Effect of Social Networks and Dynamic Internationalisation Capabilities on International Performance." *Journal of World Business* 51 (3): 391–403.

Portes, A. 2000. "The Two Meanings of Social Capital." *Sociological Forum* 15 (1): 1–12.

Poulsson, S. H. G., and S. H. Kale. 2004. "The Experience Economy and Commercial Experiences." *The Marketing Review* 4 (3): 267–277.

Pruetipibultham, O. 2010. "The Sufficiency Economy Philosophy and Strategic HRD: A Sustainable Development for Thailand." *Human Resource Development International* 13 (1): 99–110.

Putnam, R. 1993. *Making Democracy Work: Civic Traditions in Modern Italy*. Princeton: Princeton University Press.

Ragavan, J. F. 2013. *The Buzz about Doi Chaang Coffee*. Accessed February 29, 2016. http://www.thestar.com.my/lifestyle/food/features/2013/11/18/the-buzz-about-doi-chaang-coffee/

Ritzer, G., and N. Jurgenson. 2010. "Production, Consumption, Prosumption: The Nature of Capitalism in the Age of the Digital 'Prosumer'." *Journal of Consumer Culture* 10 (1): 13–36.

Rolfe, G. 2006. "Validity, Trustworthiness and Rigour: Quality and the Idea of Qualitative Research." *Journal of Advanced Nursing* 53 (3): 304–310.

Rosenbaum, M. S., J. Ward, B. A. Walker, and A. L. Ostrom. 2007. "A Cup of Coffee with a Dash of Love – An Investigation of Commercial Social Support and Third-Place Attachment." *Journal of Service Research* 10 (1): 43–59.

Ruben, R., and R. Fort. 2012. "The Impact of Fair Trade Certification for Coffee Farmers in Peru." *World Development* 40 (3): 570–582.

Ruben, R., and J. Heras. 2012. "Social Capital, Governance and Performance of Ethiopian Coffee Cooperatives." *Annals of Public and Cooperative Economics* 83 (4): 463–484.

Saldana, J. 2010. *The Coding Manual for Qualitative Researchers*. London: Sage.

Sapsuwan, P. 2014. *Beyond Fair: Doi Chaang Coffee Beans and Development*. Accessed February 29, 2016. http://borgenproject.org/beyond-fair-doi-chaang-coffee-beans-and-development/

Schembri, S. 2006. "Rationalizing Service Logic, or Understanding Services as Experience?" *Marketing Theory* 6 (3): 381–392.

Schmitt, B. 1999. "Experiential Marketing." *Journal of Marketing Management* 15 (1-3): 53–67.

Simpson, C. R., and A. Rapone. 2000. "Community Development from the Ground up: Social-Justice Coffee." *Human Ecology Review* 7 (1): 46–57.

Spiggle, S. 1994. "Analysis and Interpretation of Qualitative Data in Consumer Research." *Journal of Consumer Research* 21 (3): 491–503.

Stakal, K. 2011. *Doi Chaang Coffee: Beyond Exceptional, beyond Fair Trade*. Accessed February 29, 2016. http://www.organicauthority.com/foodie-buzz/doi-chaang-coffee-beyond-exceptional-beyond-fair-trade.html

Stake, R. E. 1978. "The Case Study Method in Social Inquiry." *Educational Researcher* 7 (2): 5–8.

Tan, S. B. 2000. "Coffee Frontiers in the Central Highlands of Vietnam: Networks of Connectivity." *Asia Pacific Viewpoint* 41 (1): 51–67.

Teddlie, C., and A. Tashakkori. 2012. "Common "Core" Characteristics of Mixed Methods Research – A Review of Critical Issues and Call for Greater Convergence." *American Behavioral Scientist* 56 (6): 774–788.

Tobias, J. T., J. Mair, and C. Barbosa-Leiker. 2013. "Toward a Transformative Entrepreneuring: Poverty Reduction and Conflict Resolution in Rwanda's Entrepreneurial Coffee Sector." *Journal of Business Venturing* 28 (6): 728–742.

Tsai, W., and S. Ghoshal. 1998. "Social Capital and Value Creation: The Role of Intrafirm Networks." *Academy of Management Journal* 41 (4): 464–476.

Utting, K. 2009. "Assessing the Impact of Fair Trade Coffee: Towards an Integrative Framework." *Journal of Business Ethics* 86 (S1): 127–149.

Uzzi, B. 1999. "Embeddedness in the Making of Financial Capital: How Social Relations and Networks Benefit Firms Seeking Financing." *American Sociological Review* 64 (4): 481–505.

Vargo, S. L., and R. F. Lusch. 2016. "Institutions and Axioms: An Extension and Update of Service-Dominant Logic." *Journal of the Academy of Marketing Science* 44 (1): 5–23.

Whittemore, R., S. K. Chase, and C. L. Mandle. 2001. "Validity in Qualitative Research." *Qualitative Health Research* 11 (4): 522–537.

Woolcock, M. 1998. "Social Capital and Economic Development: Toward a Theoretical Synthesis and Policy Framework." *Theory and Society* 27 (2): 151–208.

Xie, C., R. P. Bagozzi, and S. V. Troye. 2008. "Trying to Prosume: Toward a Theory of Consumers as Co-Creators of Value." *Journal of the Academy of Marketing Science* 36 (1): 109–122.

Yang, W. 2010. "The Study of Consumer Behavior in Event Tourism - a Case of the Taiwan Coffee Festival." *The Journal of Human Resource and Adult Learning* 6 (2): 119–126.

Yin, R. K. 1994. "Discovering the Future of the Case Study Method in Evaluation Research." *Evaluation Practice* 15 (3): 283–290.

Yin, R. K. 2011. *Qualitative Research from Start to Finish*. New York: Guilford Press.

Yuan, Y., and C. Wu. 2008. "Relationship among Experiential Marketing, Experiential Value, and Customer Satisfaction." *Journal of Hospitality and Tourism Research* 32 (3): 387–410.

Appendix 1. Semi-structured interview question guide.

(1) Can you share how and why you got involved and how the enterprise has evolved in the coffee service industry?

(2) What's the background of the enterprise (how did it start, what's its purpose and what role do you see it playing in the region)?

(3) What does the idea of social capital mean to you and the enterprise?

(4) What elements of social capital have you incorporated or would like to incorporate into the enterprise's practice?

(5) How do you believe social capital can benefit the coffee industry on whole, along with the enterprise itself?

(6) How do you believe social capital can benefit other stakeholder in the enterprise's network (e.g. local government organizations, suppliers, customers)?

(7) If social capital is potentially beneficial to the enterprise and its stakeholders, what unlocks the value of social capital (i.e. do stakeholders that are working with each other have to have trust, similar principles, aligned objectives, something of value to each other, etc.)?

(8) Is there anything else you would like to add?

Disruptive innovation and the creation of social capital in Indonesia's urban communities

Yuliani Suseno

ABSTRACT

Existing research on social capital has primarily focused on examining the outcomes of social capital, whether these are about individual, organizational or even societal outcomes. However, much research is still needed in terms of examining how social capital is created. We contribute to filling this gap by examining the ways in which social capital is created in urban communities in an emerging economy. Social capital, in this study, is viewed as being created as a consequence of an organization's disruptive innovation. We analyse the context of Go-Jek, a rather newly established service firm in Indonesia, and examine how the disruptive innovation of Go-Jek's service provision influences the creation of social capital in terms of social connectedness, trust, and shared understanding, in Indonesia's urban communities.

Introduction

The importance of social capital for understanding social relations within societies has been acknowledged in a growing body of literature (e.g. Woolcock 2010; Portes and Vickstrom 2011; Kwon and Adler 2014; Lin, Fu, and Chen 2014). Social capital, defined as the resources derived from social relationships (Payne et al. 2011), enables actors, be it individuals, groups or teams, or organizations, to coordinate action to gain benefits and achieve desired outcomes. The outcomes of social capital are profound, from enabling family support and education (Coleman 1988) to explaining firm growth and success (e.g. Andrews 2010) and community resilience (Aldrich and Meyer 2015).

While there is a plethora of research on social capital, extant research on social capital has primarily focused on examining the outcomes of social capital, whether individual outcomes (e.g. Gubbins and Garavan 2015), organizational outcomes (e.g. Tsai and Ghoshal 1998; Pérez-Luño et al. 2011), or even societal outcomes (e.g. Doh and Acs 2010; Aldrich and Meyer 2015). Although substantial progress has been made on understanding the concept of social capital, our comprehension on how social capital is created in the first place, is still limited. In fact, there is little knowledge on what needs to be done to cultivate and create social capital for the good of society. Much work is therefore needed to investigate the *creation* of social capital (Bolino, Turnley, and Bloodgood 2002; Glaeser, Laibson, and Sacerdote 2002; Johnson et al. 2011), particularly on the creation of social capital within the wider community in emerging countries (Li, Lin, and Arya 2008) that still remains poorly understood.

Drawing on social capital theory, this work examines social capital in an emerging economy – Indonesia. Indonesia, the largest economy in Southeast Asia and the fourth most populated country in the world with a population of nearly 255.5 million people (The World Bank 2016), contributes to approximately 40 per cent of the economic output of Southeast Asia (Vinayak, Thompson, and Tonby 2016). A McKinsey's report by Oberman et al. (2012) outlines that Indonesia is forecasted to be one of the largest economies in the world by 2030 with $1.8 trillion worth of economic opportunities in various sectors such as in agriculture and fisheries, consumer services, education and resources. The study is thus a worthwhile contribution to the literature of social capital as it attempts to advance our understanding of the creation of social capital in an emerging economy, in this case Indonesia.

In addition, the study is novel in addressing the multi-level relationship in social capital research. As noted by Payne et al. (2011, 492), 'researchers have largely limited their studies to a single level of analysis and have failed to fully recognize that social capital have alternative meanings, antecedents, and consequences at different levels'. Research on social capital often examines individual outcomes such as compensation or job opportunities (e.g. Hadani et al. 2012), team-level outcomes (e.g. Oh, Chung, and Labianca 2004), as well as organizational-level outcomes (e.g. Andrews 2010; Carmona-Lavado, Cuevas-Rodríguez, and Cabello-Medina 2010; Sanchez-Famoso, Maseda, and Iturralde 2014). Extant studies therefore have predominantly examined social capital as an antecedent predicting various outcomes (Payne et al. 2011).

In this study, we address this gap in the literature by examining the relationship between an organizational-level attribute and its impact on the creation of social capital at the societal level. In examining the organizational-level attribute, we focus on innovation as a crucial strategic resource that influences a firm's competitive advantage (Jiménez-Jiménez and Sanz-Valle 2011). Innovation can be defined as the successful introduction and implementation of novel ideas (Amabile et al. 1996). Organizations that are innovative are more likely to attain competitiveness and successful long-term outcomes (Tseng and Wu 2007; Berry 2014). More specifically, in this study, we contribute to filling the gap in the literature of innovation and social capital by examining the relationship between innovation as a firm-level attribute, and the creation of social capital in urban communities as societal-level outcomes. Our study is embedded in examining an innovative service concept in Indonesia, brought forward by Go-Jek, a social enterprise that creates an exciting new service provision for users/commuters and providers. Capitalizing on the demand for technology and innovation, Go-Jek offers Indonesian customers with the possibility to arrange transportation quickly, safely and easily using a smartphone application – a unique service provision to tackle the issue of traffic congestion in the heavily congested urban cities of Indonesia. The focus on societal-level outcomes is important as existing research on social entrepreneurship (SE) research 'has paid too little attention to the community as a centrally important locus of SE activity, and a distinguishing feature of the SE domain' (Lumpkin, Bacq, and Pidduck 2018, 38).

The service offering of Go-Jek is disruptive as it capitalizes on a unique mode of transportation, i.e. using *ojeks* (or motorcycle taxis) in Indonesia, and by being the linkage between *ojek* drivers and their customers. *Ojeks* are a popular mode of transportation, particularly in the bigger, notoriously congested cities like Jakarta and Surabaya. Its value proposition is simple: to increase customers' productivity while ensuring their safety and convenience when commuting using *ojek*s in many cities of Indonesia. In Jakarta alone, it is common for commuters to spend three to four hours a day in their cars on the roads with an average speed of travel of 8.3 km per hour (Owen 2015). Go-Jek however guarantees service delivery within 60 minutes to anywhere within the city, an idea that used to be seemingly impossible considering the massive congestion in the city. Based on archival news about Go-Jek in the media, we examine how the company's disruptive innovation influences the creation of social capital in Indonesia's urban communities.

The structure of the work is as follows. We first provide a literature review of social capital, including our focus on the three dimensions of social capital – structural, relational and cognitive dimensions, as outlined by Nahapiet and Ghoshal (1998). Second, we proceed with explaining the context of Indonesia and its urban communities. Third, we illustrate the case of Go-Jek, and clarify how the company's disruptive innovation creates social capital in the urban communities of Indonesia in the forms of social connectedness, trust and shared understanding. Finally, we discuss the study's implications for research and practice on disruptive innovation in service provision and the creation of social capital in urban communities, as well as its limitations and directions for future research.

Social capital

A multifaceted definition of social capital is nothing short of surprising as the concept has received overwhelming interest in wide range of areas of research and application. The main idea of social capital refers to actors' relationships or ties with others that provide resources or benefits that can create value and facilitate the achievement of instrumental outcomes. The study by Gu, Wang, and Wang (2013), for example, highlights that social capital facilitates innovation, while the study by Suseno and Pinnington (2018) describes the outcome of social capital in enabling the development of human capital in professional-client relationships.

Two different strands of approach illustrate how social capital is illustrated. Proponents of the first school of thought regard social capital in terms of the structure of one's network (e.g. Daskalaki 2010). For example, researchers such as Granovetter (1973) view social capital as one's ties in the network that provide benefits in terms of privileged access to vast and new opportunities. Similarly, Burt and Burzynska (2017) describe social capital as the opportunity or advantage that one gets because of one's position and relations in the social structure.

The second school of thought defines social capital not only in terms of social structures and resources but to also include the features or attributes of networks within which these arrays of relationships are embedded. Proponents from this side of the fence suggest that the nature or quality of 'value' derived from such networks is instrumental for attaining positive outcomes. Putnam (1993, 167), for instance, views social capital as the 'features of social organization such as trust, norms, and networks' that facilitates coordinated action, further enabling a society to be efficient. Suseno and Pinnnington (2017) also outlines that the interrelationships of the network ties of social capital and human capital are important for the internationalization of service firms.

In their seminal paper, Nahapiet and Ghoshal (1998) provide an invaluable starting point for theoretical conceptualization of social capital as a multidimensional construct, comprising of structural, relational and cognitive dimensions. The structural dimension of social capital refers to the fact that actors who are better connected are more likely to achieve instrumental outcomes as they are able to access their network contacts for resources (Burt, Kilduff, and Tasselli 2013; Kemper, Schilke, and Brettel 2013; Daspit and Long 2014). In other words, networks can provide opportunities or impose constraints on the focal actor to access resources. As Burt (2005, 4) indicates, social capital often explains 'how people do better because they are somehow better connected with other people', with better connected networks predicting business success (Burt and Burzynska 2017).

The second dimension of social capital – relational dimension, refers to the qualities of interpersonal relationships. Nahapiet and Ghoshal (1998) suggest that this dimension of social capital is essentially concerned with the ideas of trust, obligations, norms and identification that facilitate coordinative actions and lessen opportunism and malfeasance. Existing research has shown that the relational dimension of social capital is important for knowledge acquisition, in particular for tacit knowledge (Liu, Ghauri, and Sinkovics 2010; Levin et al. 2016). It also promotes entrepreneurship (Kwon and Arenius 2010; Kwon, Heflin, and Ruef 2013) and social cohesion (Portes and Vickstrom 2011; Schiefer and van der Noll 2017). Essentially, there is evidence that the relational dimension of social capital facilitates positive individual and organizational outcomes (Kohtamäki et al. 2012; Hauser et al. 2016).

The third dimension of social capital – cognitive dimension, is about language and narratives in communication that provide shared, or mutual, understanding in relationships (Nahapiet and Ghoshal 1998; Madhavaram and Hunt 2017). Shared understanding or values and common goals not only provide information to parties but also influence the perceptions in relationships (Youndt and Snell 2004). Similarly, Lang and Ramírez (2017) find that investment in building the cognitive dimension of social capital further facilitates the development of structural and relational dimensions of social capital.

Interestingly, while there is ample literature suggesting the link between social capital and beneficial outcomes such as innovation (e.g. Alguezaui and Filieri 2010; Pérez-Luño et al. 2011), the relationship between an organization's innovation and the creation of social capital in the community, has not been extensively explored. For example, The Bill and Melinda Gates Foundation's work on transformative technologies as well as innovative methods and approaches for better sanitation would potentially lead to the development of many rural communities. Such innovation consequently promotes a better way of life and creates social capital for a sustainable future for these communities. While it has been noted that regions with high levels of social capital are more likely to introduce product innovations (Laursen, Masciarelli, and Prencipe 2012), it is equally possible for a firm's innovation to have an impact on the creation of social capital in communities. It is this idea of the possible link between organizational innovation and social capital at the societal level that this study attempts to explore by focusing on Indonesia, a country with immense potential as an economic powerhouse.

Background: Indonesia

Indonesia is considered as one of the most promising emerging market economies of the world. With its huge population, Indonesia's economy is a significant contributor to the economic output of Southeast Asia (Woetzel et al. 2014; Vinayak, Thompson, and Tonby 2016). Based on the purchasing power parity (PPP), Indonesia is the eighth largest economy in the world (Lagarde 2015). Its GDP growth was around 5.3% in 2016 (Ismail 2015). In recent years, the country even outperformed its neighbouring countries, and together with China and India, is the only G20 country members that posted growth (Forbes 2015). In its annual assessment, the International Monetary Fund (IMF) has noted that Indonesia is one of the best performing emerging market economies with its strong economic growth among the highest in emerging market economies (Dieng 2016), even though the country has several structural policy challenges in terms of maritime infrastructure, social security and food security (OECD 2015a).

Indonesia reached a political milestone in 2014 with two key events. The first event is the country's fourth democratic elections since the country's independence from the Dutch and Japanese rules in 1945. The second event is the presidential race with the election of Mr Joko Widodo (popularly known as Jokowi) as the president of Indonesia and Mr Jusuf Kalla as the vice-president of the country. Mr Widodo made the famous Time Magazine's cover page titled 'A New Hope' in 2014, with the magazine highlighting the fact that the election of a new president suggests a progress in Indonesia's democratic movement (Beech 2014a, 2014b). Under Mr Widodo's leadership, the Indonesian government is committed on reducing/eliminating corruption, and investing for the development of infrastructure for the future of the country.

With these events, many structural and economic changes start happening in Indonesia, a country long known for its rich resources despite its troubled past. After the Asian economic crisis and the Global Financial Crisis, the Indonesian government introduced various fiscal and monetary policies to promote economic growth and maintain inflation at low rates. The majority of Indonesian population remains confident in the government which hopefully paves the way for the government to implement a more effective implementation of reforms. Indonesia is an emerging economy that certainly looks set to sustain its strong economic growth and development with the government's focus to strengthening the business environment, increasing investment in infrastructure, and removing regulatory constraints and complex legislations (Dieng 2016).

Go-Jek: a case of disruptive innovation

Go-Jek was started by Nadiem Makarim in 2010, and began operating in 2011. Go-Jek creates what Christensen (1997) named as disruptive innovation. Such disruptive innovation often uses new technologies and/or business models and replaces archaic ways of doing business, creating new demands, new competitors and new ways of doing business. Christensen, Raynor, and McDonald (2015) highlight that disruption is a process whereby newer, often smaller companies with fewer resources, can challenge established businesses. Go-Jek started off in Jakarta, a city notorious for its congestion. The city in fact is considered as one city with the worst traffic congestion in the world (Schonhardt 2015; Wardhani and Budiari 2015). Go-Jek targets niche 'overlooked' market segments, essentially using technology to disrupt the traditional method of transportation, with its motto of speed, innovation, and social impact.

Although the offering is similar to San Francisco-based Uber, Go-Jek differentiates itself by operating a motorcycle taxi service to provide door-to-door transportation. Go-Jek is essentially a motorcycle ride-hailing app which works with iOS and Android. Instead of getting an *ojek* off the street which can be unsafe because it is often unlicensed, and troublesome due to the often need to haggle the price, users can 'order' a Go-Jek motorcycle service through phone and mobile applications. The smartphones' Global Positioning System (GPS) capabilities allow drivers and passengers to know the pick-up and destination locations, making such services reliable while ensuring the safety of passengers. Not only can users easily track the location of their Go-Jek driver through the GPS, the improved Go-Jek system has become even more innovative since 2014. Users can also check pricing and use the 'Go-Jek Credit' or 'Go-Pay', a cashless in-app wallet when using Go-Jek's services. Go-Jek has undeniably become very popular in Indonesia as it is easy to access, cheap, safe, in addition to providing convenience. Their trademark of green jackets and green helmets has become part of the everyday sights in Indonesia's urban communities. Go-Jek is now available in 50 cities in Indonesia including Jakarta, Bandung, Denpasar, Surabaya, Makassar, Yogyakarta, Medan, Semarang, Palembang, and Balikpapan (www.go-jek.com), with a reported 900,000 providers (Balea 2017). Go-Jek is also planning to expand to other Southeast Asian countries including Malaysia, Vietnam and Thailand (Straits Times 2017), with the first international operation being in the Philippines in early 2018 (Reuters 2017).

The company has now diversified its service offerings, and by 2017, it has developed 12 services, from a courier service, food delivery, salon and beauty services to grocery and shopping delivery services. It also plans to expand its operations in four ASEAN countries (The Jakarta Post 2017) and has recently acquired three local fintech firms as the company expands its digital payments services (Balea 2017). With its innovative service offerings, Go-Jek won the Global Entrepreneurship Program Indonesia in 2011 (Kurniawati 2015a) and becomes Indonesia's first billion-dollar start-up (Lee 2017). It is an example of a successful social enterprise and it is recently ranked as number 17 of the world's innovative companies which are changing the world for good (Fortune 2017). Go-Jek is certainly revolutionizing the logistics and transportation industry, providing benefits for the users, providers and the communities of Indonesia. The focus on examining Go-Jek's disruptive innovation on the creation of social capital in Indonesia's urban communities addresses a fundamental research issue within the social entrepreneurship domain that is currently lacking, that of focusing on the community as the locus of social entrepreneurship activity (Lumpkin, Bacq, and Pidduck 2018).

Methodology

We used the case study analysis in examining the case of Go-Jek using publicly available media as a source of our data analysis. In our context, news media is especially useful 'as the primary site where discussion of scientific, legal, cultural, and economic issues coexists' (Andrews and Caren 2010, 842). The use of news media as a data source is common in political process research (e.g. Earl et al. 2004; Baumgarten and Grauel 2009) and is increasingly used in HRM research (Ramsay, Branch, and Ewart 2016).

Publicly available media enables us to understand the company, Go-Jek, and also provide up-to-date information on Indonesia. The archival materials of Go-Jek and Indonesia also provide us with a broader view of understanding of this organization and the impact its service provision on its users, providers and the communities. In addition, our case study approach that is based on media material further enables us to identify gaps for a more confirmatory study. Our secondary data collection involves an extensive literature search from the press, online reports and social media platforms while synthesizing all the relevant information pertaining to Go-Jek and Indonesia's urban communities.

We adopted the suggestions by Lincoln and Guba (1985) and Malhotra et al. (2006) for evaluating secondary data and qualitative approach. We ensured the dependability and accuracy of the data by gathering data from reputable publications such as those published by the World Bank and the International Monetary Fund, media reports such as from the ABC, BBC, Bloomberg, Reuters, CNN, Channel News Asia, and Metro TV, newspapers and articles from the Jakarta Post, The Straits Times and the Wall Street Journal, publications by a renowned consulting firm (McKinsey & Company), and various prominent websites such as Tech in Asia – an organization that runs media and events (conferences) and provides social platform for the tech communities within Asia. In this study, we also attempted to ensure the reliability and validity of the information through the use of a variety of sources where the journalists themselves also conduct their own primary research, for example by interviewing Go-Jek's drivers (e.g. Freischlad 2015a). The accuracy of the data is also maintained by gathering and analysing recent information, with the majority of reports in this study being published between 2015 and 2017.

Disruptive innovation and the creation of social capital in Indonesia's urban communities

Using the context of Go-Jek, we examine its entrepreneurial ideas and innovation and its impact on the creation of social capital in Indonesia's urban communities. The following section highlights the case of Go-Jek's disruptive innovation in creating the different dimensions of social capital in Indonesia's urban communities.

The case of Go-Jek and the creation of the structural dimension of social capital

Social capital enables the formation of structures of connections between actors. In the case of Go-Jek, their drivers can be easily connected with customers needing a ride, cutting the waiting time for both drivers and customers (Schonhardt 2015). The drivers are also potentially better connected to their customers with routes, information and recommendations saved in the app.

The company's disruptive innovation also enables the formation of a network of individuals offering services beyond simply providing personal transportation, but also in terms of shopping services, and food delivery services. Go-Jek's offerings include a multitude of services such as Go-Ride, Go-Car, Go-Food, Go-Send, Go-Mart, Go-Box, Go-Massage, Go-Clean, Go-Glam, Go-Tix, Go-Busway, and Go-Pay, and these services interestingly bring together individuals who are previously disconnected. The Go-Jek system allows users to input their friend contacts, indirectly promoting the Go-Jek services to others, thus creating connectivity within the networks. In addition, these businesses thrive on referral services. If users are satisfied with a service provided by Go-Jek, for example if they are satisfied with Go-Ride – the company's transportation services, there is a high likelihood that these customers will be using other services offered by the company such as Go-Box – the moving services using trucks or vans, or Go-Clean – the cleaning services of the rooms, homes, or offices. Indeed, Go-Jek's innovation not only facilitates repeat businesses from individual users, but also enables the formation of connections between actors – between users and users (referral services to use Go-Jek's services) and between users and business providers (from transportation services to food delivery services).

Go-Jek also builds social connections by partnering with many other organizations to essentially build social connections between service providers. The partnerships include one with Tokopedia, Indonesia's popular ecommerce marketplace, to offer delivery services (Freischlad 2015b). Go-Jek also partners with many banking institutions such as Permata Bank to allow customers to top-up their Go-Pay account using Internet banking, mobile banking, or SMS banking (Hermansyah 2017). Customers can then use their Go-Pay virtual wallet to make payment of any transactions within Go-Jek applications. Interestingly, Go-Jek has also partnered with Indonesia's biggest taxi operator, Blue Bird, in technology, payment and promotion, to empower passengers and at the same time, accelerate Indonesia's digital economy (Wijaya 2016a). With its drive to continuously innovate, Go-Jek is also partnering with Indonesia's largest telecommunication provider, Telkomsel, to allow Go-Jek's drivers to make free calls to each other, to pay less when calling to the call centre, and to give them more competitive rates when making calls to customers (Pribadi 2016). The partnership between Go-Jek and Telkomsel also helps to launch Go-Pulsa with Go-Jek's drivers becoming agents to sell Telkomsel's products (Setyanti 2016). Indeed, Go-Jek is reported to partner with more than 125,000 partner merchants (Balea 2017). The innovative service provisions of Go-Jek and its partnerships thus create social connections amongst various organizations.

Go-Jek also offers services such as Go-Mart where customers can purchase from a range of more than 50,000 products across different stores such as from grocery stores, convenience stores, health and pharmacy stores, optical and eyewear stores, electronic and gadget stores, books and stationeries shops, pet shops, hair and beauty shops or bakeries. These products can then be delivered quickly within 60 minutes and with a relatively competitive fare of Rp 10.000 (Aus$1 or £0.59) per trip. Through this offering, the disruptive innovation of the company's service provision once again creates connections between partners. Indeed, with Go-Jek rapidly expanding across Indonesia, it has so much opportunities with partners and other service providers across Indonesia, potentially linking networks of service providers and users, and creating more social capital. Such structural connections of social capital inspire individuals to be entrepreneurs. Many of them inspire to own their own small business, and they can then sell their products and services via Go-Jek's services of Go-Mart. It also helps local shops to flourish with Go-Jek's ability to reach a bigger network of customers across urban communities in Indonesia.

Go-Jek has also expanded into providing a variety of other options for their users. In October 2015, Go-Jek came up with another app with new features called Go-Life in which users can order a house cleaner (Go-Clean), a massage therapist (Go-Massage), or even a manicurist (Go-Glam) to the client's doorstep (Freischlad 2015c). In this way, users are once again provided with a network of service providers who can be called almost instantaneously when their services are required. More recently, Go-Jek also expanded its services by cooperating with PT TransJakarta, the dedicated bus services provided by the municipal government of Jakarta, to create a project called Go-Busway. This is a new innovative initiative to enable user passengers to know, at the touch of a button on their phone/tablet, when their scheduled buses will arrive at a particular bus shelter. The buses will be equipped with GPS and with Go-Jek's technology, passengers can be seamlessly updated of the buses' arrival times so that they are able to arrange their schedules and get to their destinations more effectively. Such innovative system is useful in Indonesia's urban communities where endless congestion could entirely disrupt one's travel and appointment plans. Once again, Go-Jek's innovation is disrupting the transportation industry in Indonesia. Users can also use a multitude of Go-Jek's service offerings in a day – from 'ordering' the services of Go-Ride to go the bus stations to using Go-Busway service and be in time for the arrival of their buses. Go-Jek's service provisions not only improve the efficiency and safety of commuting in Indonesia's urban communities but also enhance the standard of living of their partners, providers and users.

The company's use of social media has also promoted the creation of social connections. Go-Jek has blogs on its website to increase the exposure of its services to their customers and to do any promotional or publicity efforts. Go-Jek has active Twitter, Facebook and Instagram accounts, and its YouTube channel. The fact that Jakarta is the number one Twitter city and Facebook's fourth most active country in the world (Aly 2013) shows that Indonesians not only use social media to socialize with each other but they also use these media to access and share information more frequently, and more than ever before. Indeed, Indonesia's population, particularly the youthful demographic, is keen to be innovative through capitalizing on the power of technologies and social media.

Go-Jek's social media activities empower users to find out about what and how the company is doing, thereby creating connections amongst users. In addition, the company is very proactive in its attempt to connect users more extensively by giving them opportunities to acknowledge Go-Jek's service providers that are good and exceptional, and also 'condemning' the unsatisfactory service providers, using various social media platforms. For instance, several reviews on Tripadvisor noted the 5* service of Go-Jek, for example, with some users commenting on the good service provided by the company when ordering from a particular restaurant in Bali. Such positive comments consequently encourage others to use the services of Go-Jek and/or the particular restaurant more frequently. Other bloggers do the same, for example Villa-Bali.com – a blog designed for expatriates living in Bali, highlights the joy of relying on Go-Jek's services in Bali rather than being stuck in the Bali traffic jam (Cezanne 2015). At the same time, customers could also lodge complaints about the company. For example, there are various websites where customers can write about their negative experiences when using Go-Jek's services. This can serve as an invaluable feedback for the company to improve its services. In essence, Go-Jek's presence in the virtual world and its innovative services enable Indonesians to not only build new social connections but to also allow them to maintain existing ones. The company's innovation further helps to develop support networks that otherwise would not be possible. These connections are increasingly instrumental in urban communities – amidst the busy lifestyle and often isolated by distance, individuals could still feel emotionally connected in the digital world through the use of various social media platforms because of Go-Jek's innovation and service offerings.

The case of Go-Jek and the creation of the relational dimension of social capital

Putnam's (1993, 167) definition of social capital as the 'features of social organization, such as trust, norms and networks, that can improve the efficiency of society by facilitating coordinated actions', suggests that trust is the lubricant to social life. Trust underpins social capital through norms of reciprocity, which then creates a society that is more efficient and cooperative. Trust, in Putnam's (1993) view, is what social capital is essentially all about.

Trust has been noted as an important factor in enabling market acceptance of new products and services or new organizational innovation (Camps and Marques 2014; Shazi, Gillespie, and Steen 2015). Go-Jek's disruptive innovation is unique in that it also essentially creates trust in the minds of customers and providers. As a relatively new service provider, the company may not possess brand equity that is based on trust and prestige that is commonly associated with global brands. However, the company has been able to identify a niche market gap in Indonesia and in the process of providing this unique service provision, the company does well in creating brand awareness and trust amongst Indonesians. Go-Jek has also won several funding, including more than $550 million in the second half of 2016 (Lee 2016) and a US$1.2 billion deal led by China's Tencent, raising the company's worth to be around US$3 billion (Freischlad 2017). Indeed, Go-Jek has created massive brand awareness through television, media invites, various social media news and its own website (www.go-jek.com), by empowering both the providers and customers to share their experiences and providing value-added service provisions in the country (there are several driver stories and customer testimonials on their website). Its innovative business approach consequently becomes 'trusted innovation', with the company continuously emphasizing on its desire to improve people's lives and strengthening trust in the communities.

There are additional ways in which Go-Jek's innovative service provision helps to foster trust in the community. For Go-Jek's drivers, they feel increasingly confident that they are taken care of by the company. Firstly, these drivers are provided with training which is previously unheard of in the transportation industry in Indonesia. Secondly, the drivers are provided with benefits such as medical and accident insurance, thus providing certainty to their livelihood. Go-Jek's website notes that the company has partnered with Allianz Insurance (PT Asuransi Allianz Life Indonesia) to provide health insurance not only for Go-Jek's drivers but also the family of the drivers. The life insurance provides benefits such as hospital cover, doctor's consultation, surgery, diagnostic tests and even immunizations, with the convenient use of cashless payment using Go-Pay in certain hospitals. Go-Jek also recently partners with Bank Tabungan Negara (BTN), Bank Negara Indonesia (BNI) Syariah and Permata Bank Syariah to provide the drivers with micro financing such as subsidized mortgages (Hermansyah 2017). Thirdly, Go-Jek's drivers are equipped with technology which helps them to be safe as their movements are tracked. Fourthly, they also represent a company where the price offering of their service provision is fixed. In this way, they do not have to haggle for a price with customers which can often result in unhappiness and/or potential physical and verbal abuse.

In much the same way, the service offerings of Go-Jek creates trust in the minds of the users. The pricing is transparent in that customers know the price they will have to pay at the time of booking since the company fixes the rate per kilometre basis. Its promotional prices are also known and advertised on the website. For example, there is a promotional fixed tariff during non-peak period of Rp. 15,000 fare (roughly US$1) for a maximum distance of 25 kilometres (Budiari 2016) or a discount of 50% (maximum Rp. 10,000) when customers pay for the services rendered using Go-Pay (www.go-jek.com). Such fixed pricing and the convenience of paying creates a sense of trust in the service delivery and provision. In addition, because Go-Jek's drivers are equipped with technology, Go-Jek's users know the driver's name at the time of booking. Users can call and speak to their driver, and vice versa. Users are also kept informed of the status of the service provision delivery or offering. If, for example, Go-Mart shopping services are used, users will receive a notification of the delivery of their shopping. Ultimately, the transactions become more personal and efficient.

Go-Jek's disruptive innovation changes the method of conventional motorcycle taxis, or *ojek*, by providing safer alternatives for both drivers and customers. Customers trust the transparent pricing; they trust the exceptional service; and they trust that they are safe when using Go-Jek's services. Go-Jek's drivers go through vetting process and are registered. The customers are informed of the driver's name and details at the time of transaction. Their loved ones are also able to track where they are, providing a peace of mind. In an emerging economy such as Indonesia, safety is still a major issue particularly when using conventional and/or 'unlicensed' transportation services. Most people are wary of using conventional *ojek*s in the big cities such as Jakarta because price must be haggled and it is not fixed, and drivers have no identifications whatsoever, making it problematic to trust them. Anyone in fact could be an *ojek* driver if they have a motorcycle. However, with Go-Jek's vetting process, the green attire, the smartphone and the GPS system, as well as the consequences if drivers are not delivering a certain level of service that is expected, the safety of both providers and customers is assured. The risk of crime and fraud is also lessened. Go-Jek thus not only solves traffic problems in Indonesia's cities but the company is also successful in its attempt to minimize fraud and safety crimes. At the same time, its service offerings enable members of the society to be more trusting of one another, essentially creating social capital in the society.

Go-Jek's services also create public confidence and trust of the government and institutions. The Indonesian government is pushing to create a digital economy with virtual banking and cashless payments. Many banks are already offering digital banking services but the penetration of such new innovation still faces obstacles in many parts of Indonesia. However, since Go-Jek's offering of Go-Pay (a cashless payment service), customers are becoming more confident in the government's push for the digital economy. Users see the convenience of using cashless payment – they do not need to bring a large amount of cash with them at all times. At the same time, providers also do not need to have small change or cash. The use of cashless payment using Go-Pay thus not only makes the transactions more practical and safe, but also creates a sense of trust and confidence in the new digital initiatives by the Indonesian government.

The case of Go-Jek and the creation of the cognitive dimension of social capital

The provision of Go-Jek's disruptive innovation provides various benefits that are mutually shared by the users and providers. For Go-Jek's service providers (e.g. drivers and partners), they come to understand and appreciate the importance of excellent service provision and their reputation. Go-Jek's innovative service offering also opens up new opportunities for people to earn money and improve their standard of living. Individual drivers can be employed by Go-Jek after passing through rigorous checks. They are able to work anytime and anywhere. They could also potentially maximize their daily incomes as they do not have to waste time looking for passengers which can be a tricky situation given the heavy traffic congestion in many Indonesian cities. The company has essentially been described as a social enterprise as its service provision solves underemployment issue in many of the urban communities of Indonesia. Reports have indicated that several have even quit their jobs to become Go-Jek drivers (Cosseboom 2015). Indeed, many of the drivers of the company proudly wear Go-Jek's green helmet and green jacket and claim that their livelihoods have been made better with Go-Jek (Aziz 2016).

There is also a shared understanding of repeat and new business. Drivers are trained to be polite to their customers. Drivers know that customers want to be treated with respect and professionalism. Customers also understand that drivers rely on good service and recommendations to have continuity in their source of income from being Go-Jek's providers. Indeed, if good service is delivered, providers are more likely to have repeat business from their customers, not only in the transportation business but also in courier, food delivery services, personal shopping or other services offered by the company. This is an important phenomenon that was unheard of in Indonesia until now – in fact, until recently, customers were not likely to 'return' to use the services of the same *ojek* drivers because there was no way of contacting them or knowing where they were. Mr Makarim as the CEO of the company, noted that many of the customers are indeed repeat customers (Kevin 2012). This repeat business is a powerful narrative to motivate the service providers to deliver an exceptional level of service at all times. In addition, the customers' ratings of drivers and service providers provide powerful incentives to keep service level at high standard, as these give opportunities for new business from other potential customers. Thus, both sides of the parties mutually understand the importance of professional service delivery.

Users of Go-Jek's services also have mutual understanding towards the providers and the company. First, they are provided with a service with a transparent price. For example, when Go-Jek launched its service in Surabaya, Indonesia's second largest city, on 8 June 2015, it launched a promotional tariff of Rp 10.000 (£0.58 or AUD$1.00) until the end of the holy month of Ramadan. With such promotional tariff, a large number of customers are able to try out Go-Jek's services from transport, instant courier, shopping to Go-Food. Second, customers are provided with peace of mind when using Go-Jek's services – there is a driver in uniform who is committed to fulfil the customer's demands and who is held accountable. Third, customers also understand that they are offered the benefit of practicality to access various services without the need to leave their house or office. Fourth, many customers understand the good intention of the company, with Go-Jek offering passengers with helmets and facemasks that are guaranteed to be cleaned. This type of service is again rather unheard of in Indonesia where passengers' health and safety is often not a priority.

Fifth, users are also empowered to share their experiences with others. After using the services, users can provide a rating of the service provision quality that they have received. Such an opportunity and a 'voice' that allow customers to express and share their views with others create mutual understanding of what the company stands for. Customers are able to acknowledge those who have provided a superb service in the hope that more users will be getting a similar level of outstanding service quality. At the same time, customers are also able to 'punish' those who fall short of service expectations through the community rating of drivers. Users recognize that their feedback is heard and taken seriously by the company. Such word-of-mouth marketing is a powerful means for a company to engage with the customers and improve its customer service satisfaction.

Go-Jek's innovation also promotes a shared understanding of what the business is all about by sharing the vision and mission of the company. When being asked on the success of the company, Mr Makarim commented that Go-Jek provides convenience in our increasingly busy world. '[Not only] is Go-Jek the fastest door-to-door transport and delivery booking service in Indonesia, but it also has an incredible social impact by empowering our drivers to take orders wherever they are and whenever they want, democratising the ability to make money for anyone who wants to work harder' (Cezanne 2015). With many *ojeks* under the company's banner, the company is indeed driven to improve the welfare of their drivers (Nugrahanto 2015) and ensure the safety of their passengers.

The company is also keen to promote its mission and values using the digital platforms of social media. This once again fosters a shared understanding between the company and the customers. The use of social media such as Twitter empowers customers to make better use of their time. One of the tweets by Go-Jek, for example, 'Some people like wasting time in traffic. For everyone else, there's the Go-Jek app', creates shared feelings among users and drivers that they could instead rely on Go-Jek's services to be more productive in their daily activities.

Finally, Go-Jek's innovation creates a sense of community belongingness. In the various cities where Go-Jek offers its services, there are many makeshift cafes for Go-Jek drivers to gather and share stories. For example, in *Go-Jek Warkop* in central Jakarta, drivers gather around to have a chat, recharge their phones, have a cigarette break and even help each other to solve technical issues (Freischlad 2015a). The news and tweets about a Go-Jek driver who helped a wounded bombing victim to evacuate from the bombing site in Sarinah in Jakarta, on the 14th January 2016, has worked really well for the company. The company has been praised for its quick response to the Jakarta bombing by offering free Go-Ride services in the Greater Jakarta area for their users to evacuate – a gesture that once again creates a sense of community togetherness. In addition, the company through its Go-Clean service provision recently cleaned up 100 mosques in Jakarta and the surrounding areas during the holy month of Ramadan. Community work, known as *gotong royong* in Indonesian, is practised by the company with employees regularly engaging themselves in civic participation in neighbourhood activities. Indeed, Go-Jek has inspired many Indonesians to support one another in building a stronger community while helping them to resolve their transportation needs and commuting demands.

Figure 1 illustrates the framework of how organizational innovation could facilitate the creation of social capital in communities. The framework also highlights the different ways in which social capital in terms of social connectedness, trust and shared understanding can be built within the communities.

Since Go-Jek was launched, the company has triggered disruptions and controversies with respect to social and culture issues (e.g. new ways for interaction and transaction), regulation issues (e.g. the service is battling legalization under the current transportation law), and competition (e.g. price war with other transportation rivals and competition with other logistic companies) (OECD 2015b). It is thus important to note that disruptive technology also introduces negative social capital. This is what Gargiulo and Benassi (1999) refer to as the 'dark side' of social capital. In the case of Go-Jek, there have been numerous media reports highlighting that Go-Jek drivers are increasingly fearful of threats, assaults and violent resistance from regular traditional *ojek* drivers who are often unregistered (Budiari 2015). Some reports have also highlighted that traditional *ojek* drivers have put up banners of 'Anti Go-Jek' (Budiari 2016) and 'Go-Jek drivers are not welcome here' (Freischlad 2015a; Kurniawati 2015b). The company headquarter was also attacked in the morning of November 2015, with its window being shattered. The motive of the attack seemed to be intimidation and fear (Florentin 2015). In recent times, the rivalry between Go-Jek's drivers and the traditional transportation drivers has escalated. A correspondent of ABC, Harvey

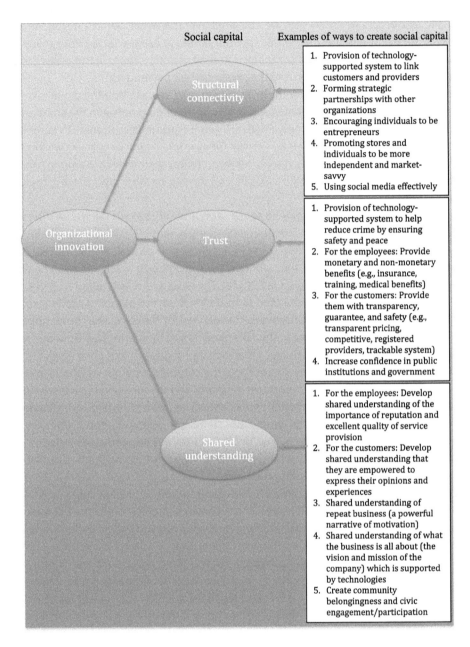

Figure 1. A framework of disruptive organizational innovation and the creation of social capital in communities.

(2016) noted the ugly protests against Go-Jek, with car and bus windows being smashed, resulting in injuries to Go-Jek drivers/riders. Similar reports have also been reported in various media where hundreds of taxi drivers and Go-Jek's drivers were engaged in a brawl with rocks being thrown, causing injuries to several individuals (Wijaya 2016b).

The dominant position of Go-Jek in their respective markets may also create rigidity and monopoly in terms of coping with demands and restrictions to freedom. For instance, there are various reports about the sudden suspension of drivers by Go-Jek, causing hundreds of drivers to gather and protest in the company's offices in Indonesia. Go-Jek claims that there have been suspicious bookings made by drivers, which made the company to systematically review the bookings and their drivers' activities. More than 7000 drivers have been suspended for alleged fraud, with some who are unsatisfied with such suspension staging protests in Jakarta, Surabaya, Bali and Bandung (Freischlad 2015a). Go-Jek also dictates the rules of the game; the company has recently lowered the fares in order to increase demand, angering many drivers across Indonesia's urban communities (Freischlad 2016). Drivers need to follow the company's rules and procedures even to the extent of paying exorbitant fees to reactivate their suspended accounts in order to continue being Go-Jek's drivers (Maulani 2015). Protests have been held in several cities with drivers claiming that the company's performance management policies are unfair, resulting in many not receiving their bonuses (Wijaya 2016c). However, despite the existence of negative social capital brought by the success of Go-Jek's innovation, Go-Jek is still deemed as the poster child of Indonesia's new, digital economy (Freischlad 2015a).

Discussion

In the ever increasingly competitive world, social capital plays an important role in the society particularly in urban communities across many countries. However, despite the fact that social capital is generally considered to have a positive impact in developing a more dynamic economy, there is a lack of understanding on how social capital is created in the first place (Bolino, Turnley, and Bloodgood 2002; Glaeser, Laibson, and Sacerdote 2002; Johnson et al. 2011), particularly how it is created within communities in emerging countries. In addition, in spite of more than forty years of research on social capital, the literature is still limited with regards to examining social capital at different levels of analysis. Thus, this study is novel in addressing several research gaps as outlined in the following.

Our study contributes to the social capital literature on exploring a perspective on the creation of social capital within an emerging country, Indonesia, and integrating different levels of analysis in the study of social capital. In our case, we examine an organizational-level output and its implications on societal-level outcomes, by providing an exploratory review of how a firm's innovation influences the creation of social capital in Indonesia's urban communities. The study thus paves the way for further exciting research on providing empirical support for the relevance of organizational innovation as an antecedent to the creation of social capital in communities.

We also contribute to the innovation literature by demonstrating that radical and disruptive innovation not only brings about positive outcomes for the organization but it can also create an impact at the societal level, as demonstrated in the case of Go-Jek.

The work examines the case of one of Indonesia's social enterprises and its effects on the community, which is presently lacking in existing research (Lumpkin, Bacq, and Pidduck 2018). While extant research findings largely document the fact that innovative companies will be more likely to achieve better outcomes and competitive advantage, no studies have yet examined the social impact of such innovation on a wider scale. Our study thus provides a wider picture of the importance of organizational innovation in enabling something good within the society.

The analysis of Go-Jek also provides a guideline to managers on how to fully benefit from their innovation. Go-Jek's innovative services provide social connectedness, trust, and shared understanding not only between the organization and the users, but also between users and users, as well as between individual providers and other organizations. A company could also benefit through the use of social media by encouraging dialogue and participative contributions from their customers as a way to publicize the innovative services and consequently enhance the customer service experience.

This study also has important practical implication for other emerging countries. An entrepreneurial company like Go-Jek has as much 'power' and responsibilities as the larger organizations in enabling the creation of social capital that is important in promoting the growth of the society. Innovative service provisions offered by companies such as Go-Jek may facilitate social connectedness, enable trust and create shared understanding in the society. However, efforts from the government, particularly those in emerging economies, are required to promote such entrepreneurial activities. The provision of network and infrastructure support as well as the access to capital may provide the much needed assistance to build these companies further. In Indonesia, the government has pushed for its social initiative to ensure that employees, either those who are formally or informally employed as in the case of Go-Jek's drivers, will be covered in terms of workplace injury and safety (including accidents). The government has also pushed for education programmes to change the mindset of drivers about the risks and opportunities associated with their job (Abrar 2016). It is also important for emerging countries like Indonesia to put in place a legislation to bring legal certainty for businesses in the creative sector (Aziz 2016). Such legislation will promote the creative industry to prosper further as a key to maintaining the country's growth, stimulating job creation, and tackling the problems of increasing inequality and youth unemployment (Aziz 2016). In addition, while disruptive innovation may create social capital, it is also important for organizations and societies to recognize the negative outcomes of social capital and formulate strategies and policies to minimize and counteract such potential negative outcomes.

The major limitation of the study is secondary information research methodology. While online media provide very recent information, it is challenging to sift through the vast amount of relevant information. Moreover, aspects such as the attitudinal or behavioural perspectives of Go-Jek's drivers or customers cannot be truly obtained from such secondary research. Cross-checking of information also has to be done consistently with cross-referencing of reputable various websites that are published in English and Indonesian.

While we acknowledge the limitations of the research, there are various ways in which future research could consider in examining the creation of social capital in communities, particularly in the context of an emerging country. One way is to quantitatively measure the extent of social capital in the communities. Putnam, as highlighted in his interview published by Li (2011), noted that the extent of social capital in the United States has been analysed through various indicators such as the frequency of volunteering to political participation (Putnam 2000, 2002). Similarly, such indicators could be developed to measure social capital in the urban community context in terms of, for example, their membership in social organizations such as sports or arts clubs, and their involvement in community or neighbourhood activities like being involved in community food fairs or other voluntary work. The extent of social capital in communities can even be measured using indicators of economic success, for example, by comparing the employment/unemployment rates, crime rates, poverty and cleanliness in different communities, which can be addressed in future research. Go-Jek as one of South-east Asia's largest on-demand transport company and its intention to expand to overseas markets also provides an interesting case in examining the creation of social capital in different countries, which can be explored in the future.

Conclusion

This study takes a fresh look at examining the creation of social capital in the context of an emerging country of Indonesia. The study proposes a framework that suggests how disruptive innovation can create social capital in urban communities. In exploring this interesting phenomenon, the study seeks to contribute to our understanding of the relationship between organizational-level disruptive innovation and societal-level social capital. The study also highlights the different means by which an organization and its innovative service offerings could promote social connectedness, trust and mutual understanding in the communities. Although this is an exploratory study outlining the case of Go-Jek and its disruptive innovation, it provides a starting context in examining organizational innovation and its changing impact on the creation of social capital in a country's urban communities.

Disclosure statement

No potential conflict of interest was reported by the author.

References

Abrar, A. 2016. "Ribuan pengemudi GoJek serbu kantor pusat BPJS Ketanagakerjaan." *Metro TV*, 17 April. http://news.metrotvnews.com/read/2016/04/17/514808/ribuan-pengemudi-gojek-serbu-kantor-pusat-bpjs-ketanaga.

Aldrich, D. P., and M. A. Meyer. 2015. "Social Capital and Community Resilience." *American Behavioral Scientist* 59 (2): 254–269.

Alguezaui, S., and R. Filieri. 2010. "Investigating the Role of Social Capital in Innovation: Sparse Versus Dense Network." *Journal of Knowledge Management* 14 (6): 891–909.

Aly, W. 2013. "Welcome to Jakarta, the World's Number One Twitter City." *ABC*, 29 May. http://www.abc.net.au/radionational/programs/drive/social-media-in-indonesia/4720678.

Amabile, T. M., R. Conti, H. Coon, J. Lazenby, and M. Herron. 1996. "Assessing the Work Environment for Creativity." *Academy of Management Journal* 39 (5): 1154–1184.

Andrews, K. T., and N. Caren. 2010. "Making the News: Movement Organizations, Media Attention, and the Public Agenda." *American Sociological Review* 75 (6): 841–866.

Andrews, R. 2010. "Organizational Social Capital, Structure and Performance." *Human Relations* 63 (5): 583–608.

Aziz, M. F. 2016. "Indonesia Needs Creative Economy Law to Spur Job Creation." *The Conversation*, 12 January. http://theconversation.com/indonesia-needs-creative-economy-law-to-spur-job-creation-52901.

Balea, J. 2017. "Go-Jek Buys 3 Fintech Firms to Conquer Indonesia Payments." *Tech in Asia*, 15 December. https://www.techinasia.com/go-jek-acquisition-kartuku-mapan-midtrans.

Baumgarten, B., and J. Grauel. 2009. "The Theoretical Potential of Website and Newspaper Data for Analysing Political Communication Processes." *Historical Social Research* 34 (1): 94–121.

Beech, H. 2014a. "A New Hope." *Time*, 27 October.

Beech, H. 2014b. "Joko Widodo Sworn in as Indonesia's President and Faces these 5 Challenges." *Time*, 19 October. http://time.com/3523168/indonesia-jokowi-inauguration-president/.

Berry, H. 2014. "Global Integration and Innovation: Multicountry Knowledge Generation Within MNCs." *Strategic Management Journal* 35 (6): 869–890.

Bolino, M. C., W. H. Turnley, and J. M. Bloodgood. 2002. "Citizenship Behavior and the Creation of Social Capital in Organizations." *Academy of Management Review* 27 (4): 505–522.

Budiari, I. 2015. "GoJek Drivers Fearing Violent Resistance from Traditional Ojek." *The Jakarta Post*, 11 June. http://www.thejakartapost.com/news/2015/06/11/GoJek-drivers-fearing-violent-resistance-traditional-ojek.html.

Budiari, I. 2016. "2015, Year of the Rise of App-Based Motorcycle Taxi." *The Jakarta Post*, 6 January. http://www.thejakartapost.com/news/2016/01/06/2015-year-rise-app-based-motorcycle-taxi.html.

Burt, R. S. 2005. *Brokerage and Closure: An Introduction to Social Capital*. New York: Oxford University Press.

Burt, R. S., and K. Burzynska. 2017. "Chinese Entrepreneurs, Social Networks, and Guanxi." *Management and Organization Review* 13 (2): 221–260.

Burt, R. S., M. Kilduff, and S. Tasselli. 2013. "Social Network Analysis: Foundations and Frontiers on Advantage." *Annual Review of Psychology* 64 (1): 527–547.

Camps, S., and P. Marques. 2014. "Exploring How Social Capital Facilitates Innovation: The Role of Innovation Enablers." *Technological Forecasting & Social Change* 88 (1): 325–348.

Carmona-Lavado, A., G. Cuevas-Rodríguez, and C. Cabello-Medina. 2010. "Social and Organizational Capital: Building the Context for Innovation." *Industrial Marketing Management* 39 (4): 681–690.

Cezanne. 2015. "Go-Jek, the Indonesian Transport App that'll Deliver Anything to Your Door." *Villa-Bali.com*, 1 April. http://blog.villa-bali.com/2015/04/go-jek-app-delivers-anything-to-your-door.

Christensen, C. M. 1997. *The Innovator's Dilemma*. Boston, MA: Harvard Business School Press.

Christensen, C. M., M. E. Raynor, and R. McDonald. 2015. "What is Disruptive Innovation?" *Harvard Business Review*. https://hbr.org/2015/12/what-is-disruptive-innovation.

Coleman, J. S. 1988. "Social Capital in the Creation of Human Capital." *American Journal of Sociology* 94 (Supplement: Organizations and Institutions: Sociological and Economic Approaches to the Analysis of Social Structure): S95–S120.

Cosseboom, L. 2015. "If You Work at GoJek, Nadidem Makarin is Your 'Coach, Sugar Daddy, and Friend.'" *Tech in Asia*, 15 November. https://www.techinasia.com/tech-in-asia-jakarta-2015-indonesia-GoJek.

Daskalaki, M. 2010. "Building 'Bonds' and 'Bridges': Linking Tie Evolution and Network Identity in the Creative Industries." *Organization Studies* 31 (12): 1649–1666.

Daspit, J. J., and R. G. Long. 2014. "Mitigating Moral Hazard in Entrepreneurial Networks: Examining Structural and Relational Social Capital in East Africa." *Entrepreneurship Theory and Practice* 38 (6): 1343–1350.

Doh, S., and Z. J. Acs. 2010. "Innovation and Social Capital: A Cross-Country Investigation." *Industry and Innovation* 17 (3): 241–262.

Dieng, I. 2016. "Indonesia Navigates Safely Through Uncertain Times." *International Monetary Fund Survey 2016*, 15 March. http://www.imf.org/external/pubs/ft/survey/so/2016/CAR031416A.htm.

Earl, J., A. Martin, J. D. McCarthy, and S. A. Soule. 2004. "The Use of Newspaper Data in the Study of Collective Action." *Annual Review of Sociology* 30: 65–80.

Florentin, V. 2015. "Gojek's Office Attacked by Gunmen." *Tempo*, 1 November. http://en.tempo.co/read/news/2015/11/01/057714927/Gojeks-Office-Attacked-by-Gunmen.

Forbes. 2015. "Forbes Lists: Best Countries for Business: Indonesia." *Forbes*, December 2015. http://www.forbes.com/places/indonesia/.

Freischlad, N. 2015a. "Is GoJek Evil? Drivers Share Thoughts on How it Could Improve." *Tech in Asia*, 4 December. https://www.techinasia.com/gojek-evil-drivers-share-thoughts-improve.

Freischlad, N. 2015b. "The Future of Tokopedia Could Lie in an Alliance with GoJek." *Tech in Asia*, 19 August. http://www.techinasia.com/tokopedia-announces-partnership-with-GoJek.

Freischlad, N. 2015c. "Here's GoJek's Massive Plan for an Everything-On-Demand Empire." *Tech in Asia*, 29 November. https://www.techinasia.com/GoJek-go-life-improve-informal-labor-indonesia.

Freischlad, N. 2016. "Go-Jek Lowers Prices to Spur Demand, Drivers Protest. Again." *Tech in Asia*, 15 August. https://www.techinasia.com/gojek-lowers-prices-spur-demand-drivers-protest.

Freischlad, N. 2017. "Brief: Go-Jek Reported to Have Raised $1.2b Round, Led by Tencent." *Tech in Asia*, 4 May. https://www.techinasia.com/gojek-signs-deal-tencent-worth-12-billion.

Fortune. 2017. *Change the World*. http://fortune.com/change-the-world/list.

Gargiulo, M., and M. Benassi. 1999. "The Dark Side of Social Capital." In *Corporate Social Capital and Liability*, edited by R. Th. A. J. Leenders and S. M. Gabbay, 298–322. Norwell, MA: Kluwer Academic Publishers.

Glaeser, E. L., D. Laibson, and B. Sacerdote. 2002. "An Economic Approach to Social Capital." *The Economic Journal* 112 (483): F437–F458.

Granovetter, M. 1973. "The Strength of Weak Ties." *American Journal of Sociology* 78 (6): 1360–1380.

Gu, Q., G. G. Wang, and L. Wang. 2013. "Social Capital and Innovation in R&D Teams: The Mediating Roles of Psychological Safety and Learning from Mistakes." *R&D Management* 43 (2): 89–102.

Gubbins, C., and T. Garavan. 2015. "Social Capital Effects on the Career and Development Outcomes of HR Professionals." *Human Resource Management* 55 (2): 241–260.

Hadani, M., S. Coombes, D. Das, and D. Jalajas. 2012. "Finding a Good Job: Academic Network Centrality and Early Occupational Outcomes in Management Academia." *Journal of Organizational Behavior* 33 (5): 723–739.

Harvey, A. 2016. "Jakarta's Taxi Industry Battles Against App-Based Motorcycle Service GoJek." *ABC*, 7 April. http://www.abc.net.au/news/2016-04-02/jakarta-embraces-app-based-transport/7291518.

Hauser, C., U. Perkmann, S. Puntscher, J. Walde, and G. Tappeiner. 2016. "Trust Works! Sources and Effects of Social Capital in the Workplace." *Social Indicators Research* 128 (2): 589–608.

Hermansyah, A. 2017. "Banks Offer Micro Finance to GoJek Drivers." *The Jakarta Post*, 10 May, http://www.thejakartapost.com/news/2017/05/10/banks-offer-micro-finance-to-gojek-drivers.html.

Ismail, S. 2015. "Indonesia's Economy Expected to Grow 4.7% in 2015: World Bank." *Channel News Asia*, 15 December. http://www.channelnewsasia.com/news/business/indonesia-s-economy/2348248.html.

Jiménez-Jiménez, D., and R. Sanz-Valle. 2011. "Innovation, Organizational Learning, and Performance." *Journal of Business Research* 64 (4): 408–417.

Johnson, S., K. Schnatterly, J. F. Bolton, and C. Tuggle. 2011. "Antecedents of New Director Social Capital." *Journal of Management Studies* 48 (8): 1782–1803.

Kemper, J., O. Schilke, and M. Brettel. 2013. "Social Capital as a Microlevel Origin of Organizational Capabilities." *Journal of Product Innovation Management* 30 (3): 589–603.

Kevin, J. 2012. "Go-Jek Solves Your Motorcycle Taxi Needs in Jakarta." *Tech in Asia*, 13 February. https://www.techinasia.com/go-jek-indonesia.

Kohtamäki, M., J. Vesalainen, S. Henneberg, P. Naudé, and M. J. Ventresca. 2012. "Enabling Relationship Structures and Relationship Performance Improvement: The Moderating Role of Relational Capital." *Industrial Marketing Management* 41 (8): 1298–1309.

Kurniawati, D. 2015a. "Digital Style Motorcycle Service "GoJek" Thrives Despite Resistance from Traditional Competitors." *The Parrot*, 23 October. http://theparrot.co/2015/10/23/digital-style-motorcycle-service-GoJek-thrives-despite-resistance-from-traditional-competitors/.

Kurniawati, D. 2015b. "GoJek, the Poor Man's Uber in Jakarta." *Asia Sentinel*, 22 October. http://www.asiasentinel.com/econ-business/GoJek-the-poor-mans-uber-in-jakarta/.

Kwon, S.-W., and P. A. Adler. 2014. "Social Capital: Maturation of a Field of Research." *Academy of Management Review* 39 (4): 412–422.

Kwon, S.-W., and P. Arenius. 2010. "Nations of Entrepreneurs: A Social Capital Perspective." *Journal of Business Venturing* 25 (3): 315–330.

Kwon, S.-W., C. Heflin, and M. Ruef. 2013. "Community Social Capital and Entrepreneurship." *American Sociological Review* 78 (6): 980–1008.

Lagarde, C. 2015. "Poised for Take-Off: Unleashing Indonesia's Economic Potential." *International Monetary Fund (IMF)*, University of Indonesia, Jakarta, 1 September. https://www.imf.org/external/np/speeches/2015/090115.htm.

Lang, T., and R. Ramírez. 2017. "Building New Social Capital with Scenario Planning." *Technological Forecasting and Social Change* 124 (Supplement C): 51–65.

Laursen, K., F. Masciarelli, and A. Prencipe. 2012. "Regions Matter: How Localized Social Capital Affects Innovation and External Knowledge Acquisition." *Organization Science* 23 (1): 177–193.

Lee, Y. 2016. "Go-Jek Raises Over $550 Million in KKR, Warburg-Led Round." *Bloomberg*, 4 August. https://www.bloomberg.com/news/articles/2016-08-04/go-jek-said-to-raise-over-550-million-in-kkr-warburg-led-round.

Lee, Y. 2017. "Indonesia's First Billion-Dollar Startup Looks to Expand Abroad." *Bloomberg*, 2 October. https://www.bloomberg.com/news/articles/2017-10-01/go-jek-to-expand-beyond-indonesia-on-track-to-clash-with-grab.

Levin, D. Z., J. Walter, M. M. Appleyard, and R. Cross. 2016. "Relational Enhancement: How the Relational Dimension of Social Capital Unlocks the Value of Network-Bridging Ties." *Group & Organization Management* 41 (4): 415–457.

Li, X. 2011. "Putnam: S'pore can't Afford to Stop Building Social Capital." *The Straits Times*, 31 March. http://lkyspp.nus.edu.sg/wpcontent/uploads/2013/06/20110331_SG_cant_afford_to_stop_building_social_capital.pdf.

Li, L., Z. Lin, and B. Arya. 2008. "The Turtle-Hare Race Story Revisited: Social Capital and Resource Accumulation for Firms from Emerging Economies." *Asia Pacific Journal of Management* 25 (2): 251–275.

Lin, N., Y. C. Fu, and C. J. Chen. 2014. *Social Capital and its Institutional Contingency: A Study of the United States, China and Taiwan*. New York: Routledge.

Lincoln, Y. S., and E. G. Guba. 1985. *Naturalistic Inquiry*. Beverly Hills, CA: Sage.

Liu, C.-L., P. N. Ghauri, and R. R. Sinkovics. 2010. "Understanding the Impact of Relational Capital and Organizational Learning on Alliance Outcomes." *Journal of World Business* 45 (3): 237–249.

Lumpkin, G. T., S. Bacq, and R. J. Pidduck. 2018. "Where Change Happens: Community-Level Phenomena in Social Entrepreneurship Research." *Journal of Small Business Management* 56 (1): 24–50.

Madhavaram, S., and S. D. Hunt. 2017. "Customizing Business-to-Business (B2B) Professional Services: The Role of Intellectual Capital and Internal Social Capital." *Journal of Business Research* 74 (1): 38–46.

Malhotra, N., J. Hall, M. Shaw, and P. Oppenheim. 2006. *Essentials of Marketing Research*. 2nd ed. Frenchs Forest, NSW: Pearson Education Australia.

Maulani, A. M. A. 2015. "Go-Jek Suspends and Fines 1400 Drivers; Protest Ensues." *e27 news*, 30 November. https://e27.co/go-jek-suspends-fines-1400-drivers-protest-ensues-20151130/.

Nahapiet, J., and S. Ghoshal. 1998. "Social Capital, Intellectual Capital, and the Organizational Advantage." *Academy of Management Review* 23 (2): 242–266.

Nugrahanto, P. 2015. "Go-Jek perluas layanan ke Surabaya." *Tech in Asia*, 8 June. https://id.techinasia.com/go-jek-hadir-di-surabaya.

Oberman, R., R. Dobbs, A. Budiman, F. Thompson, and M. Rossé 2012. "The Archipelago Economy: Unleashing Indonesia's Potential." *McKinsey Global Institute*, September 2012. http://www.mckinsey.com/global-themes/asia-pacific/the-archipelago-economy.

OECD. 2015a. "Economic Outlook for Southeast Asia, China and India 2016: Enhancing Regional Ties." *OECD iLibrary*. http://www.oecd.org/dev/asia-pacific/SAEO2016_Overview%20with%20cover%20light.pdf.

OECD. 2015b. "Enforcement Issues in Disruptive Technology – Indonesian Case Study from Go-Jek Apps." DAF/COMP/GF/WD(2015)40, OECD Competition Division, Global Forum on Competition: The Impact of Disruptive Innovations on Competition Law Enforcement: Contribution by Indonesia – Session III. http://www.oecd.org/officialdocuments/publicdisplaydocumentpdf/?cote=DAF/COMP/GF/WD(2015)40&docLanguage=En.

Oh, H., M.-H. Chung, and G. Labianca. 2004. "Group Social Capital and Group Effectiveness: The Role of Informal Socialising Ties." *Academy of Management Journal* 47 (6): 860–875.

Owen, N. 2015. "Jakarta's Ill-Famed Traffic Grief to Residents But Boon for Some." *Reuters*, 11 June. http://www.reuters.com/article/us-indonesia-traffic-idUSKBN0OR09Z2015061.

Payne, G. T., C. B. Moore, S. E. Griffis, and C. W. Autry. 2011. "Multilevel Challenges and Opportunities in Social Capital Research." *Journal of Management* 37 (2): 491–520.

Pérez-Luño, A., C. C. Cabello Medina, A. C. Carmona Lavado, and G. C. Cuevas Rodríguez. 2011. "How Social Capital and Knowledge Affect Innovation." *Journal of Business Research* 64 (12): 1369–1376.

Portes, A., and E. Vickstrom. 2011. "Diversity, Social Capital, and Cohesion." *Annual Review of Sociology* 37 (1): 461–479.

Pribadi, S. D. 2016. "Digandeng Telkomsel, sopir GoJek bersiap jadi agen pulsa." *CNN Indonesia*, 15 February. http://www.cnnindonesia.com/teknologi/20160215132233-213-110977/digandeng-telkomsel-sopir-gojek-bersiap-jadi-agen-pulsa/.

Putnam, R. D. 1993. *Making Democracy Work: Civic Traditions in Modern Italy*. Princeton, NJ: Princeton University Press.

Putnam, R. D. 2000. *Bowling Alone: The Collapse and Revival of American Community*. New York: Simon and Schuster.

Putnam, R. D. 2002. *Democracies in Flux*. New York: Oxford University Press.

Ramsay, S., S. Branch, and J. Ewart. 2016. "The Use of News Media as a Data Source in HRM Research: Exploring Society's Perceptions." In *Handbook of Qualitative Research Methods on Human Resource Management*, edited by K. Townsend, R. Loudoun and D. Lewin, 74–91. Massachusetts: Edward Elgar Publishing.

Reuters. 2017. "Indonesian Ride-Hailing Firm Go-Jek to Expand to Philippines in 2018." 7 December. https://www.reuters.com/article/gojek-southeast-asia/indonesian-ride-hailing-firm-go-jek-to-expand-to-philippines-in-2018-idUSL3N1O72FL.

Sanchez-Famoso, V., A. Maseda, and T. Iturralde. 2014. "The role of Internal Social Capital in Organisational Innovation. An Empirical Study of Family Firms." *European Management Journal* 32 (6): 950–962.

Schiefer, D., and J. van der Noll. 2017. "The Essentials of Social Cohesion: A Literature Review." *Social Indicators Research* 132 (2): 579–603.

Schonhardt, S. 2015. "Apps Give a Boost to Motorcycle Taxis." *The Wall Street Journal*, 12 June. http://blogs.wsj.com/indonesiarealtime/2015/06/12/apps-give-a-boost-to-motorcycle-taxis/.

Setyanti, E. P. 2016. "Repot beli pulsa? Telkomsel siap permudah lewat kerja sama dengan Go-Jek." *Tech in Asia*, 15 February. https://id.techinasia.com/telkomsel-gandeng-go-jek-mudahkan-pengguna-isi-ulang-pulsa.

Shazi, R., N. Gillespie, and J. Steen. 2015. "Trust as a Predictor of Innovation Network Ties in Project Teams." *International Journal of Project Management* 33 (1): 81–91.

Straits Times. 2017. "Indonesia's Go-Jek Aims to Expand Ride-Hailing Services to 3 or 4 South-East Asian Nations." 2 October. http://www.straitstimes.com/asia/se-asia/indonesias-go-jek-looks-to-take-fight-to-uber-grab-in-3-4-south-east-asian-countries.

Suseno, Y., and A. H. Pinnnington. 2017. "Building Social Capital and Human Capital for Internationalization: The Role of Network Ties and Knowledge Resources." *Asia Pacific Journal of Management*. https://link.springer.com/article/10.1007/s10490-017-9541-0.

Suseno, Y., and A. H. Pinnington. 2018. "The Significance of Human Capital and Social Capital: Professional–Client Relationships in the Asia Pacific." *Asia Pacific Business Review* 24 (1): 72–89.

The Jakarta Post. 2017. *Go-Jek to Expand Operations in Four ASEAN Countries*. http://www.thejakartapost.com/news/2017/10/02/go-jek-to-expand-operations-in-four-asean-countries.html.

The World Bank. 2016. *Overview – Indonesia*. http://www.worldbank.org/en/country/indonesia/overview.

Tsai, W., and S. Ghoshal. 1998. "Social Capital and Value Creation: The Role of Intrafirm Networks." *Academy of Management Journal* 41 (4): 464–476.

Tseng, C. Y., and L. Wu. 2007. "Innovation Quality in the Automobile Industry: Measurement Indicators and Performance Implications." *International Journal of Technology Management* 37 (1/2): 162–177.

Vinayak, H. V., F. Thompson, and O. Tonby. 2016. *Understanding ASEAN: Seven Things you Need to Know*. McKinsey & Company. http://www.mckinsey.com/industries/public-sector/our-insights/understanding-asean-seven-things-you-need-to-know.

Wardhani, D. A., and I. Budiari. 2015. "Jakarta has 'Worst Traffic in the World.'" *The Jakarta Post*, 5 February. http://www.thejakartapost.com/news/2015/02/05/jakarta-has-worst-traffic-world.html.

Wijaya, C. A. 2016a. "Blue Bird Teams up with GoJek." *The Jakarta Post*, 10 May. http://www.thejakartapost.com/news/2016/05/10/blue-bird-teams-up-with-gojek.html.

Wijaya, C. A. 2016b. "GoJek and Taxi Drivers Brawl Amid Jakarta Protest." *The Jakarta Post*, 22 March. http://www.thejakartapost.com/news/2016/03/22/go-jek-and-taxi-drivers-brawl-amid-jakarta-protest.html.

Wijaya, C. A. 2016c. "Hundreds of Go-Jek Drivers Protest 'Unfair Policy.'" *The Jakarta Post*, 3 October. https://www.thejakartapost.com/news/2016/10/03/hundreds-of-go-jek-drivers-protest-unfair-policy.html.

Woetzel, J., O. Tonby, T. Fraser, P. Burtt, and G. Lee. 2014. *Three Paths to Sustained Economic Growth in Southeast Asia – Southeast Asia at the Crossroads: Three Paths to Prosperity*. McKinsey & Company, McKinsey Global Institute. http://www.mckinsey.com/global-themes/asia-pacific/three-paths-to-sustained-economic-growth-in-southeast-asia.

Woolcock, M. 2010. "The Rise and Routinization of Social Capital, 1988–2008." *Annual Review of Political Science* 13: 469–487.

Youndt, M. A., and S. A. Snell. 2004. "Human Resource Configurations, Intellectual Capital, and Organizational Performance." *Journal of Managerial Issues* 16 (3): 337–360.

Selling trust in cyber space: social networking service (SNS) providers and social capital amongst netizens in South Korea

Ingyu Oh (ID), Wonho Jang and Sanghyeon Kim

ABSTRACT

Apart from excessive bonding amongst co-ethnics, social capital studies have sparsely discussed the negative effects of social capital, including excessive collective actions towards downward social mobility (e.g. imprisonment of social and political elites). As Bourdieu has noted, social capital can conflate problems of upward social mobility through various glass ceilings in the reproduction of elite power groups. However, it is also important to notice that less fortunate groups can debunk the dominant elite social network by participating excessively in social networking service (SNS) platforms, where they exchange distorted information about the elites to organize collective actions towards their downward social mobility. Gleaned from the recent cases of ferry sinking and candlelight vigilance in South Korea, SNS providers can sell trust in cyber space that can be easily transformed into social capital for collective character assassinations, political demonstrations, and economic sabotages at workplace. Based on the big data gathered from Naver, one of the leading SNS providers in South Korea, we find that Naver provides SNS users with a rare opportunity to encounter myriad opinion groups who will over time converge into one or two similar opinion groups that can be easily mobilized towards collective actions. Selling trust in cyber space on the internet and mobile devices is a unique commercial development in South Korea and its neighbouring countries, including Japan and Taiwan.

Introduction

South Korea has celebrated its economic and business success for decades due mainly to its closed and homogenous structures of chaebol (or conglomerate) organizations that had organized highly committed various social and state agents towards export-oriented economic development through conventional (i.e. Confucian) social capital – densely networked trust and hierarchy systems that were tightly conjoined based on regionalism, school ties and family ties (see *inter alia* Hattori 1984; Cho 2001; Chang 2003; Siegel 2003, 2007; Siegel, Pyun, and Cheon 2010). However, many economic pundits in the field have also pointed out the negative aspect of chaebol organizations that have relied heavily on the state for both legitimate and illegitimate social capital resources, ranging from simple state financing to the chaebol projects, to credible threats for contract execution amidst the absence of property rights protection and to outright rent-seeking and/or rent-sharing (Baik and Lee 1997; Wedeman 1997; Kang 2002; Morck and Yeung 2004; Oh and Varcin 2010; Oh and Jun 2016). What appears to be drastically different from the previous chaebol in the recent arrest of the Samsung's Vice Chairperson, Jae-young Yi, is the fact that the chaebol is now being mobilized by the state for state's soft power or national-branding projects that involve advertising Korea's national image to foreign nationals (for soft power, see Nye 2004). In the process, the prosecution office has confirmed with limited evidence that Yi's public donations to the state-sponsored cultural and sports foundations were bribes to the president herself, who sought personal gains in exchange of the government favours given to Samsung, which had sought government sanctions of Yi's succession to the ownership of Samsung without paying 50+% inheritance taxes (Kang 2016). Previously, public donations by the chaebol to government authorized not-for-profit foundations and public organizations had been considered legitimate, if such donations were transparently raised publicly and donated to organizations that were created to promote public and state interests in the advancement of Korean culture or sports (No 2016).

This drastically shifts the prosecutors' decisions over some of the transparent South Korean market activities, such as public donations, derives from the candlelight vigilance organized by South Korean netizens (i.e. citizens who conduct citizenship behaviour on cyber space). These protesters seem to have been heavily influenced by their own groupthink propagated by left-wing organizations that dominated some of the SNS platforms, including Naver, the largest South Korean portal and SNS service provider. These groups successfully exploited social capital in cyber space in the nation to topple the right-wing government, headed by Park Geun-hye, the daughter of the late President Park Chung-hee and the first democratically elected female president in the nation. She is also the first South Korean president that has ever been impeached by the Constitutional Court and imprisoned by the prosecutor's office for investigations during her term.

Unlike the previous candlelight demonstrations by the left-wing cyber groups during the Yi Myong-bak administration over the issue of the US mad cow disease, the current candlelight vigilance that finally impeached the former president has persisted on a weekly basis since 29 October 2016 with an estimated total of 16 million participants. On 15 April 2017, the 22nd weekly vigilance is scheduled to be held from 17:30 h to commemorate the Sewol ferry victims and to demand a thorough investigation of the ship to uncover missing corpses. These figures and facts are historic in the South Korean political scene, as these political rallies demonstrate a unique South Korean political and economic phenomenon, where social capital in cyber space in the country clearly works as a crucial instigator and organizer of massive political rallies amongst the underrepresented populace of the nation who want to purge and topple corrupt politicians and their incumbent governments. In fact, trust in cyber space sold by Naver, the biggest social networking service provider in the country, is appearing much more crucial than the conventional social networking based on regional and school ties in the formation of 'downward' social mobility. If South Korea's upward social mobility had been provided by the state and the chaebol that had actively nurtured regional and school ties, the twenty-first century South Korea has massively cherished trust in cyber space to endorse downward social mobility of some elite groups.

This study analyses

(1) The process of downward social mobility that social capital in cyber space is ratifying in South Korea;
(2) identifies SNS providers' role in selling trust as social capital in cyber space;
(3) analyses how South Korean users of SNS services change their attitudes over time as they interact with netizens to form one or two dominant opinion groups that are eventually mobilized to street demonstrations; and
(4) some of the policy implications for service firms that seek business opportunities in South Korea and its neighbouring countries, including Japan, China and Taiwan.

We first provide literature review, followed by a big data analysis of the comments made by anonymous netizens regarding newspaper reports on either the ferry sinking or the candle-light vigilance against the presidential corruption. We finally provide discussions of our findings and policy implications for business corporations operating in South Korea.

Social capital in cyber space in South Korea

This study uses the social capital model developed by Redding (2005) and slightly revised by Redding and Rowley (2017b, 301) to analyse the South Korean social capital in cyber space in its success in impeaching and imprisoning the former President Park, her political allies and presidential aides. According to this model, order is maintained by capital, human capital and social capital, where 'cooperativeness shows its effects' by the human being who 'is instinctively willing to make friends and to cooperate' if safeguards against opportunism exists (Redding and Rowley 2017a, 163). Furthermore, the 'ways in which financial, human and social capital come into play and are expressed in societal systems and structures, become highly complex and highly varied', even though 'the way they work reflects the society in which they have evolved' (Redding and Rowley 2017a, 163). Therefore, in East Asia, social capital derives from 'trust' with two types of institutional means that support action, namely, *guanxi* (Wang and Rowley 2012) and a reliable accounting system, or a codified and trusted legal system (Redding and Rowley 2017b, 300).

In sociology, however, order can also be construed as a form of suppression as evident in Bourdieu's concept of social capital (Bourdieu 1985, 1989, 1996, 2005). Social capital, interpreted as 'the sum of the resources, actual or virtual, that accrue to an individual or a group by virtue of possessing a durable network of more or less institutionalized relationships of mutual acquaintance and recognition' (Bourdieu and Wacquant 1992, 119), works as an obstructive force against any attempt to attain upward social mobility. Exclusive (closed) school ties that are strong and densely networked are another tool in the armoury of the elite who make sure that 'wrong' kind of people do not find their way into elite inner circles (Bourdieu 2011). Here, strong bondage amongst elite groups works as a force binding them together in the perpetuation of their social networks and social capital (Figure 1).

Whether *guanxi* and inner circles can work as either a promoter or prohibitor of upward social mobility requires social capital in the form of collective trust in each group. Trust works in two directions: the first towards upward social mobility through landing good jobs; the second towards downward social mobility through losing such jobs. Downward social mobility occurs when certain groups find no trust within their communities, such as immigrants. Another example would be individuals who lose trust due to economic downturns

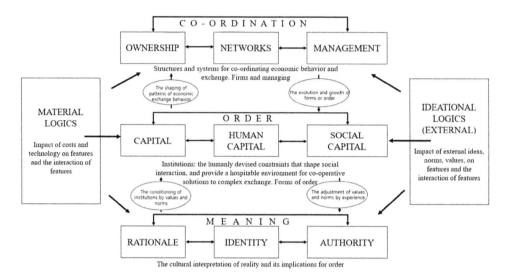

Figure 1. A model of capital, human capital and social capital. Source: Redding (2005) and Redding and Rowley (2017a, 2017b).

and social transformations, such as the middle-class people who get laid off from time to time due to economic cycles, or even white and Asian American people who lose jobs due to the affirmative actions (Newman 1988; Nicklett and Burgard 2009; Guo 2013). However, as our current South Korean case reveals, elites can also lose their social network privileges and experience a drastic downward social mobility due to excessive collective actions organized by the working-class people via cyber social networks. Therefore, our study presented here focuses on how digital social network can change institutions (order) by altering both meaning and co-ordination, which in turn changes ideational and material logics of social capital in one society that is undergoing rapid changes in the economic and digital realms of a country.

Using the South Korean case, Jang (2004, 2007) found that trust in cyber space is based on communicative rationality, whereas regional and school ties are prioritized by instrumental rationality (Table 1). Habermas (1984) has already pointed out the importance of the levelling effect amongst members of a community who exercise communicative rationality to maximize discursive and ethical cooperation (i.e. rationality achieved not by simple calculations but by in-depth and long-term discussions with affected parties who have fine-grained information from their daily living environments). The result of discursive and ethical cooperation is to liberate people from the yoke of authoritarian arbitration commonly found in regional and school-ties that are regulated by sanctions and instrumental rationality. In this sense, cyber communities can engender stronger community norms and trust-based social capital than conventional communities that operate on an off-line basis. However, as the cyber communities tend to disregard knowledge, status, age, gender and class distinctions amongst members, it can easily lead to the alienation of some members from the community majority. In South Korea, mature people would naturally distance themselves from young people, as the latter would not necessarily use honorifics and respectable language in addressing

Table 1. Conventional social capital vs. social capital in cyber space.

	Conventional social capital	Social capital in cyber space
Field	Regional, school-ties	Cyber community
Motivation	Instrumental rationality (Weberian rationality)	Communicative rationality (Habermasian rationality)
Conditions of trust	Sanctions	Discursive, ethical cooperation
Hierarchy	Vertical	Horizontal
Knowledge formation	Procedural	Innovative
Types of social capital	Bonding, cognitive	Bridging, relational

Source: Jang (2007, 188).

others in the cyber space. Furthermore, in the South Korean cyber communities, mature people can easily feel infuriated as they are not well trained in communicative rationality. Therefore, downward social mobility looms large in cyber communities, where mature, male, high status or upper-class people are treated equally (i.e. demoted) with the 'socially inferior' members in the same community.

The above discussions about the trust in cyber space opens a new horizon of social capital that can restore social order by ensuring elites' downward social mobility (i.e. impeachments of public officials, imprisonments of social elites) on a regular basis. Less powerful groups of societies form a cyber-community with an organizing principle of communicative rationality and discursive cooperation, which in turn creates a new social narrative of constructing political corruption committed by political elites and their inner circle members. The cyber construction of political corruption will then lead to excessive collective actions in the street demanding the imprisonment of the corrupt elites. The periodic social purge of elites would then restore social order by reinforcing ethical cooperation, innovative knowledge formation, and relational social capital amongst the majority of citizens. What is intriguing shall be the provision of the service of selling trust in cyber space by a leading service firm in South Korea, Naver, a company that provides a comprehensive portal and SNS service to South Korean netizens. Without Naver and its commercial service, no trust in cyber space would have formed in South Korea towards massive and excessive collective actions in the form of street demonstrations and candlelight vigilance (Cha and Jin 2012).

Based on the discussion so far, we propose the following three hypotheses to be tested against the big data we compiled for this study:

Hypothesis 1. When private portal servers provide free SNS, blog and news services to the public at large like in South Korea, trust in cyber space will be quickly developed between two opposite groups of those who support social capital among elites vs. those who try to demote such social capital among elites.

Hypothesis 2. Heated online confrontations between two opposition groups in a cyber community created by SNS firms in South Korea can lead to excessive offline collective actions (i.e. from online confrontations to offline collective actions).

Hypothesis 3. The social cleavages between elites and opposition groups will be resolved with the restoration of social order, when elites are demoted through downward social mobility (i.e. the restoration of social order after the downward social mobility of elites).

A big data method using R

The purpose of the big data analysis is to corroborate the three hypotheses proposed in the previous section. The process of the data analysis is as follows. First, from the Naver site (www.naver.com), we collected comments on any news that contained keywords, the 'Sewol Ferry', a keyword that has clearly divided the twenty-first century South Korean people into the progressive and the conservative camps. The Sewol incident indeed was ranked in the top five most momentous events in post-1945 South Korean history (Ji 2014). To measure the spread and evolution of the comments published on Naver, we collected those published from 29 October 2017 to 15 April 2017, a total of twenty-two weeks.

Second, we divided six types of news we collected from Naver into conservative and progressive. Conservative news had originally been published by the *Chosun Daily*, the *Joong-Ang Daily* and the *Dong-A Daily*, whereas progressive news had first appeared on the *Hankyeoreh*, the *Kyunghyang Daily* and the *Oh My News*. Conservative and progressive comments posted on each news article were then put on a graph based on their keywords to show which keywords affected the formation of trust in cyber space within conservative and progressive groups, respectively.

Third, Beautiful Soup, a library of the programming language Python 2.7, helped us to collect the news article comments published on Naver. We used the programming language R version 3.2.2 to analyze the keyword networks from the collected comments in newspaper articles. The R packages employed in this project were tm, KoNLP, igraph, arules, combinate, RColorBewer and ggplot2. Table 2 shows the summary of the newspaper articles and their attached comments we collected for this project. All these cases contain the keywords of the Sewol Ferry and/or candlelight vigilance.

Fourth, we illustrated the network maps for each keyword we identified from the collected sample discourses to analyse commentators' communication rationality from one period to another. The analysis of keyword networks involves extracting word roots of nouns and verbs after rearranging the collected texts into sentence units. To extract word roots, we used the dictionary published by the National Institute of Korean Language.

The network maps for each keyword represent the relationship between major keywords and their mutual relatedness in each period of investigation. If the size of the circle that encloses a keyword gets larger, it means commentators to news articles have mentioned the keyword more frequently than others. In a similar vein, the greener the colour gets, the more significant a keyword becomes (i.e. betweenness centrality increases). In other words, the significance of a keyword ostensibly surges, even as it increases the frequency of its relatedness with other words. For example, in the following two sentences (S1, S2), the keyword 'accident' is mentioned in each sentence, while the word is connected to two

Table 2. Summary of news article/comments collection from naver.

Periods of collection	Conservative media		Progressive media	
	News	Comments	News	Comments
29 October–29 November 2016	183	4511	85	5218
30 November–31 December 2016	477	10,108	116	6445
1 January–1 February 2017	48	1391	59	3526
2 February–25 February 2017	61	2106	75	5289
26 February–29 March 2017	84	2064	71	4049
30 March–14 April 2017	21	387	28	1519
Total	874	20,567	434	26,046

adjectives and/or adverbs. This means that the keyword 'accident' has higher betweenness centrality than that of 'very', 'sad' or 'tragic'.

S1. A very sad accident [it is].

S2. A sad and tragic accident [it is].

Data analysis: trust in cyber space, social cleavage and social order

The above three hypotheses are tested against the collected big data summarized in Table 2. For *H1*, we collected articles and comments posted only on the portal site, Naver, and not from the original newspaper homepage to identify the cyber interactions between progressive and conservative groups. Naver, as a free SNS server for Koreans, is a place where netizens develop their trust in cyber space amongst similar minded people without knowing their real identities. Simultaneously, they encounter opposition groups for the first time in the same cyber space leading to online confrontations and digital squabbling. Over time, two cyber communities are developed with unique intragroup keywords that identify the political spectrum of each group. In our case, these unique keywords that we will show below can distinguish progressive netizens from their conservative counterparts. For *H2* we devised an escalation index based on the number of articles that had received elevated levels of digital confrontations between conservative and progressive commentators. We statistically tested if the online escalation index has significant correlations with actual offline candlelight vigilance throughout the 22-week period. Finally, for *H3*, we observed how keywords evolved from the onset of offline confrontations to the conclusion of the political scandal when the former president and her allies were impeached and jailed. Table 3 summarizes the entire data collection results and strategies that are highlighted against the main events of each week.

Tables 2 and 3 indicate that the conservative newspaper companies have published twice the number of the total articles uploaded by the progressive news media (i.e. institutional mobilization towards social trust for and by the conservative group). In Table 4 candlelight participants peaked during the 5th week with more than 2.3 million people on the street. During this week, one of the most significant and frequent keywords that received top 100 'likes' was 'Sewol', a keyword that was neither significant nor frequent amongst conservative netizens.

Furthermore, as Table 4 and Figure 2 indicate, during this period, another keyword that had high betweenness centrality within the progressive group was 'human', a keyword that was not as significant amongst conservative netizens. In a similar vein, during Week 9 – 16 (Table 5) and Figure 3, a new keyword that surfaced in the progressive cyber discourse was 'Moon Jae-in', the current left-wing presidential candidate, who resuscitated the candlelight vigilance in the 13th and the 14th week. *H1* is therefore partially supported, as netizens are divided into two contending groups along the ideological spectrum based on their institutional trust for the conservative groups and cyber space trust for progressive groups.

Keyword network maps (Figures 2 and 3) clearly indicate divergence of two polar groups with specific betweenness centrality for each keyword. It is arguably salient that Naver therefore provides an online bridging role between progressive and conservative groups that confront each other in the cyberspace, not to mention the fact that they harness intragroup social capital and trust between conservatives or between progressives.

Table 3. Weekly data of newspaper columns on Sewol and candlelight.

Week	Start	End	Conservative reports	Progressive reports	Main events
1	29 October 2016	5 November 2016	34	30	First candlelight vigilance
2	6 November 2016	13 November 2016	40	12	Presidential approval plunges
3	14 November 2016	21 November 2016	59	22	Special prosecution starts
4	22 November 2016	29 November 2016	50	21	Drug abuse suspicion
5	30 November 2016	7 December 2016	140	33	Presidential address
6	8 December 2016	15 December 2016	150	35	Impeachment passes
7	16 December 2016	23 December 2016	87	25	Majority party splits
8	24 December 2016	31 December 2016	100	23	
9	1 January 2017	8 January 2017	14	22	1000th day of Sewol sinking
10	9 January 2017	16 January 2017	11	15	Impeachment Trial
11	17 January 2017	24 January 2017	12	12	
12	25 January, 2017	1 February 2017	11	10	
13	2 February 2017	9 February 2017	21	27	
14	10 February 2017	17 February 2017	10	12	
15	18 February 2017	25 February 2017	30	36	
16	26 February 2017	5 March 2017	11	12	
17	6 March 2017	13 March 2017	21	27	Impeachment confirmed
18	14 March 2017	21 March 2017	10	10	Sewol salvaged
19	22 March 2017	29 March 2017	42	22	
20	30 March 2017	6 April 2017	11	11	Park Geun-hye jailed
21	7 April 2017	14 April 2017	10	17	Inspection of Sewol
		Total	874	434	

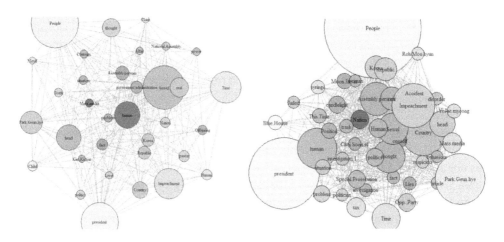

Figure 2. Keyword network map at the 5th week.
Note: Left map (progressive comments); right map (conservative comments).

To test *H2* we first calculated cyber escalation index (CEI) using the distance between the number of 'likes' and 'dislikes' for each comment. We then added weights of the three key-words of 'Sewol', 'Moon Jae-in' and 'human' to CEI. As we explained above, these three

Table 4. Major keywords in each period (Week 1–8).

Week	1	2	3	4	5	6	7	8
Progressive reports	Pres. Park People Human Sewol Nation	Pres. Park Sewol People Time Human	People Pres. Park Prosecution Sewol Special Prosecution	People Time Sewol Pres. Park Impeachment	People Sewol Time Impeachment President	Sewol People Pres. Park Human Truth	Sewol People Pres. Park Time Responsibility	Pres. Park People Sewol Nation Impeachment
Comments	1598	955	1417	1248	1257	1581	2003	1604
Conservative reports	People Pres. Park Nation Opp. Party Prosecution	People Pres. Park Human Sewol Prosecution	People Pres. Park Human Sewol Korea	People Pres. Park Sewol Time Impeachment	People Pres. Park Impeachment Assembly person Sewol	People Pres. Park Sewol Impeachment Moon Jae-in	People Hearing Pres. Park Assembly person Impeachment	People Sewol Submarine Special Prosecution Pres. Park
Comments	1243	923	881	1464	2276	3017	2129	2686
Candlelight participants	50,000	1,060,000	960,000	1,900,000	2,320,000	1,040,000	770,000	702,000

Table 5. Major keywords in each period (Week 9–16).

Week	9	10	11	12	13	14	15	16
Progressive reports	President	Sewol	Pres. Park	Sewol	Moon Jae-in	People	Special Prosecution	People
	Sewol	President	Bahn Ki-Moon	Responsibility	People	Judge	Impeachment	President
	Memory	People	Conservative	President	President	President	People	Prosecution
	People	Country	Parental League	People	Special Prosecution	Samsung	President	Sewol
	Lies	Time	Love Park Group	Time	Impeachment	Justice	Yi Jae-myeong	Rules
Comments	1061	966	883	616	2417	503	2369	1022
Conservative reports	Logic	Pres. Park	Pres. Park	Pres. Park	People	People	People	Prosecution
	Memory	Time	People	People	Pres. Park	Impeachment	Special Prosecution	Special Prosecution
	People	People	Sewol	Sewol	Impeachment	Moon Jae-in	Pres. Park	Investigation under arrest
	Pres. Park	Sewol	Black list	Impeachment	Korea	Korea	Prosecution	Wu Byeong-wu
	Lies	Impeachment	Pyo Chang-won	Responsibility	Special Prosecution	Instigation	Investigation under arrest	Park Geun-hye
Comments	2686	171	347	504	369	777	285	1044
Candlelight participants	643,380	146,700	352,400	–	425,500	806,270	844,860	1,078,130

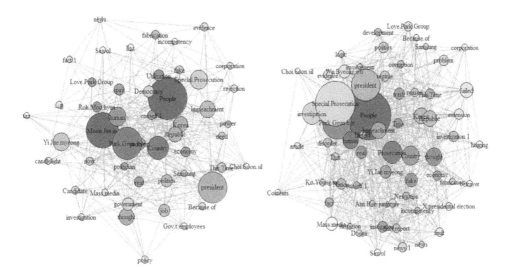

Figure 3. Keyword network map at the 15th week.
Note: Left map (progressive comments); right map (conservative comments).

keywords differentiate progressive netizens from their conservative counterparts (i.e. the importance of group identity). The weighted CEI was subsequently correlated with the actual turnouts in the candlelight vigilance for each week. The correlation result is presented in Table 6. As Table 6 demonstrates, our model of the weighted CEI explaining the vigilance turnout is significant at the 95% level ($p = 0.05$) with $R^2 = 0.498$. This further supports our assumption that trust in cyber space within one group is harnessed through keywords they share in the cyber community, which then leads to offline struggles to induce downward social mobility amongst elites.

$$CEI = (L_i - D_i) \times (\sum A_i + B_i + C_i) \times 0.33$$

where L_i = the sum of total 'likes' given to a comment during the ith week; D_i = the sum of total 'dislikes' given to a comment during the ith week; A_i, B_i, C_i = the frequency of the three keywords in each comment during the ith week; Keywords = 'Sewol', 'Moon Jae-in', 'Human'; 0.33 = keyword weights.

During the final phase of the candlelight vigilance (Table 7 and Figure 4), it is noticeable that both progressive and conservative groups highlight 'Sewol', as the former President Park had already been impeached and even imprisoned, subsiding the candlelight vigilance altogether. At this stage, the political and social order has been restored with sufficient evidence of both conservative and progressive groups ending street demonstrations. It is apparent that these groups are busy building intragroup consensus regarding the election of the next president (H3). All these can be gleaned from the fact that the size of the circle diminished with its dimmed colour, as the word's betweenness centrality decreased (Figure 4).

Table 6. Major keywords in each period (Week 17–21).

Week	17	18	19	20	21
Progressive reports	People	Sewol	Yi Jae-myeong	Sewol	Sewol
	President	Impeachment	People	People	Moon Jae-in
	Prosecution	President	Mass media	Gangnam Ward Director	Prosecution
	Sewol	Time	Prosecution	President	People
	Rules	Investigation	Moon Jae-in	Pres. election	President
Comments	963	651	1413	351	1168
Conservative reports	Prosecution	Sewol	Moon Jae-in	Sewol	Sewol
	Special prosecution	Impeachment	Pres. candidates	Moon Jae-in	Investigation under arrest
	Investigation under arrest	Chosun Daily	Yi Jae-myeong	Gangnam Ward Director	President Park
	Wu Byeong-wu	Moon Jae-in	Election	Yi Jae-myeong	Prosecution
	Park Geun-hye	Dismissal	Sewol	Salvage	Wu Byeong-wu
Comments	694	234	780	244	143
Candlelight participants	1,050,890	–	100,000	–	–

Table 7. Correlation results between CEI and candlelight turnouts.

	CEI	Candlelight turnouts
CEI	1	0.498*
Candlelight turnouts	0.498*	1

$^{*}p < 0.05$.

Findings and discussion

Using a big data analysis this contribution demonstrated how big data corroborated all three hypotheses regarding the role of a SNS service provider in harnessing social capital in South Korea. $H1$ was supported by the keyword network maps (Figures 2 and 3) during the first two phases, when different sets of keywords and their betweenness centrality ostensibly defined progressive and conservative groups in the cyber space. Naver, as a free SNS service provider in South Korea, successfully offered a free opportunity for the underrepresented people in the country to express their ideas and opinions freely for or against a newspaper article, forging two conflictual groups on the political spectrum. This supports the previous theoretical arguments that trust in cyber space is based on relational and discursive rationality (Habermas 1984; Dryzek 2005). However, it does not support Bourdieu and Wacquant (1992) elite power thesis, as he slights the importance of SNS service providers in the free market democracies. As Wang and Rowley (2012) indicated, in the East Asian context, informal trust on cyber space, not to mention offline trust within *guanxi* groups, tend to lead to actions.

$H2$ has a complicated structure of transforming online intergroup confrontations into offline political collective actions in the form of candlelight vigilance. Using a big data analysis, we found that there is a significant correlation between the intragroup keywords, which distinguish the right-wing from the left-wing, and participation in the candlelight vigilance. Based on the big data analysis about the betweenness centrality of some keywords, trust in cyber space and online confrontations between conservative and progressive SNS groups were critical factors of individual participation in the candlelight vigilance. Although the

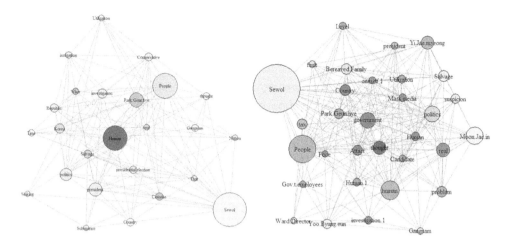

Figure 4. Keyword network map at the 19th week.
Note: Left map (progressive comments); right map (conservative comments).

limitation of the data forced us to rely on the distance between the number of 'like' and 'dislike' buttons recorded on readers' comments to measure the degree of the confrontations between the two groups, the distance weighted by three keywords that identified the left-wing SNS users was significant in predicting turnouts in the candlelight vigilance. This implies the fact that these left-wing SNS users were mobilized towards collective actions to realize the downward social mobility amongst some elite groups (Newman 1988; Nicklett and Burgard 2009; Guo 2013).

The role of the downward social mobility in forging social capital and trust in South Korea in particular and East Asia in general is obvious as it harnesses social order after both digital and offline confrontations between elite and ordinary masses subsides with the downfall of some elite groups (i.e. elite demotion for social order). Figure 4 indicates that intergroup differences in keyword sharing have substantially diminished after the arrest of the former President Park (*H3*). This supports Redding (2005) and Redding and Rowley (2017a, 2017b) for their accurate consideration of social capital as a crucial factor of social order. Our findings refined the process of restoring social order through forging social capital in cyber space.

Our findings, however, do not easily apply to China, where political democracy is few and far between, although trust in cyber space can also lead to collective actions against multi-national corporations from abroad (e.g. collective actions against Japanese MNCs during the territorial disputes between China and Japan over the Senkaku Island, or even the current ban on the importation of Korean cosmetic and cultural contents due to the deployment of the THAAD missile defence system). Our findings and models therefore can explain social capital in cyber space in Taiwan, Hong Kong, and Japan (full democracy) more than China or Singapore (limited democracy or dictatorship).

Implications for SNS service providers in East Asia

Our findings and discussions above tell us a lot about doing business in East Asia as multi-national corporations must rely on local social capital (i.e. social capital available in the hosting country) to do business. Firstly, employees in South Korea and East Asia are high end users of SNS services, as the region is proliferated by free SNS service providers. This means that SNS service providers must be able to offer free services that guarantee freedom of speech that will ensure SNS users to enjoy the process of realizing trust in cyber space amongst in-group members.

Secondly, private SNS services, where two or more conflictual groups can interact against each other, enhance communication opportunities for the opposing groups to talk out their differences and even take the matter to the street to resolve their differences. However, in the case of South Korea, it is noted that the downward social mobility amongst some elite groups was necessitated to calm down angry protesters who had successively participated in weekly rallies. Whether excessive collective actions are needed to harness social capital is questionable, especially when trust in cyber space fails to build positive social capital between groups vis-à-vis negative one such as the elite conspiracy against upward social mobility by underrepresented groups.

Thirdly, it is desirable that SNS service providers in East Asia nurture positive social capital between groups by promoting digital trust in cyber space between opposing groups. Digital campaigns that highlight achievements of both groups can potentially balance elite and non-elite groups, and would consequently enhance intergroup trust. Managerial ethics within SNS service firms is another concern to which we need to pay attention.

Finally, the lessons from the SNS service case in South Korea can be beneficial for future HR policies of hiring, nurturing and retaining a diverse group of employees to establish a new global norm of breeding social capital that engages in discursive and deliberative democracy in preference to confrontational group politics based on instrumental rationality or a 'black and white' logic. Training programmes that introduce multiple perspective approaches to a set of social and political problems that allow one to 'walk in others' shoes' to arrive at an emphatic understanding of social values (Horowitz 1985).

Limitations and conclusion

This study undertook the task of analysing South Korean social capital in cyber space, especially on its role in engendering a negative effect of social capital that deepens social cleavages and divisions along the old political lines of the left-wing and the right-wing. Using big data analyses based on the data gathered from Naver, the largest South Korean SNS service provider, we could confirm the key role Naver plays in producing the negative effect of social capital in cyber space in perpetuating Korean-style political cleavages that necessitate the social demotion of some elite groups of society in order to restore political and social order. It is predictable that the use of SNS services and social capital in cyber space will reinforce the benefit of negative social capital in bringing about the repetitive demotion of elite groups to compensate the lack of upward social mobility opportunities that undermines the underrepresented group of society.

Future studies on the relationship between elite demotion and social capital can use wider sources of big data than what has been presented in this study with more sophisticated predictive models. For example, future studies can organize better data for cyber social and political cleavages than what this study has utilized. Theoretically, future studies can focus on the theoretical implication of negative social capital and social order to generate testable hypotheses on the one hand and implantable policy implications on the other. We have constantly faced the issue of data availability in utilizing big data analysis. Furthermore, in modelling the cyber space to street demonstrations, we have also faced enormous difficulties in gathering reliable data. These need to be addressed in the future.

Disclosure statement

No potential conflict of interest was reported by the authors.

Funding

This research was supported by Basic Science Research Program and the Social Science Korea Program through the National Research Foundation of Korea funded by the Ministry of Education [grant number 2015S1A5B6036421], [grant number 2017S1A3A2067374].

ORCID

Ingyu Oh (iD) http://orcid.org/0000-0002-1645-8767

References

Baik, K. H., and S. Lee. 1997. "Collective Rent Seeking with Endogenous Group Sizes." *European Journal of Political Economy* 13 (1): 121–130.

Bourdieu, P. 1985. "The Social Space and the Genesis of Groups." *Theory and Society* 14 (6): 723–744.

Bourdieu, P. 1989. "Social Space and Symbolic Power." *Sociological Theory* 7 (1): 14–25.

Bourdieu, P. 1996. *The State Nobility: Elite Schools in the Field of Power*. Cambridge: Polity Press.

Bourdieu, P. 2005. *The Social Structures of the Economy*. Cambridge: Polity Press.

Bourdieu, P. 2011. "The Forms of Capital." In *Cultural Theory: An Anthology*, edited by I. Szeman and T. Kaposy, 81–93. Oxford: Wiley-Blackwell.

Bourdieu, P., and L. J. D. Wacquant. 1992. *An Invitation to Reflexive Sociology*. Chicago, IL: University of Chicago Press.

Cha, E., and Y. Jin. 2012. "Sosyeol Midieo wa Jeongchijeok Jipdanhaengdong Balsaeng e daehan Sogo." [A Short Study on Social Media and Political Collective Actions] *Hanguk Jeongdang Hakhoibo* 11 (2): 157–188.

Chang, S. J. 2003. "Ownership Structure, Expropriation, and Performance of Group-Affiliated Companies in Korea." *Academy of Management Journal* 46 (2): 238–253.

Cho, Y. 2001. "Dongjeok Jiphapjueui: Hanguk Jaebeolgieopeui Gieopmunhwa." [Dynamic Collectivism: Chaebol Corporate Culture in Korea] *Gukjejiyeokyeongu* 5 (1): 103–124.

Dryzek, J. S. 2005. "Deliberative Democracy in Divided Societies: Alternatives to Agonism and Analgesia." *Political Theory* 33 (2): 218–242.

Guo, S. 2013. "Economic Integration of Recent Chinese Immigrants in Canada's Second-Tier Cities: The Triple Glass Effect and Immigrants' Downward Social Mobility." *Canadian Ethnic Studies* 45 (3): 95–115.

Habermas, J. 1984. *The Theory of Communicative Action*. vol. I. Boston, MA: Beacon.

Hattori, T. 1984. "Gendai Kankoku Kigyō no Shōyū to Keiei: Zaibatsukei Kigyō o Chūsin toshite." [Ownership and Control in Modern Korean Corporations: The Case of Chaebol Corporations] *Ajia Keizai* 25 (5): 132–150.

Horowitz, I. L. 1985. *C. Wright Mills: An American Utopia*. New York: Simon and Schuster.

Jang, W. 2004. *Saibeo Keomyuniti wa Sahoigwangye eui Byeonhwa* [Changes in Social Relationships and Cyber Communities]. Seoul: Jeongbotongsin Jeongchaek Yeonguwon.

Jang, W. 2007. Saibeo Gongdongche wa Sahoijeok Jabon [Cyber Communities and Social Capital]. In *Hanguk Gyeongje/Sahoi wa Sahoijeok Jabon* [Social Capital in the Korean Economy and Society], edited by KDI. Seoul: KDI.

Ji, J. 2014. "Sewolho Chamsa eui Jeongchi Sahoihak: Shinjayujueui eui Hwansang gwa Hyeonsil." [The Political Sociology of the Sewol Calamity: The Fantasy and Reality of Neoliberalism] *Gyeongje Wa Sahoi* 104 (Winter): 14–55.

Kang, D. C. 2002. *Crony Capitalism: Corruption and Development in South Korea and the Philippines.* Cambridge: Cambridge University Press.

Kang, S. 2016. "Gujojojeong eui Jeonchijyeonjehak Bipan." [A Critique of the Political Economy of Structural Adjustment] *Inmulgwa Sasang* 218: 87–106.

Morck, R., and B. Yeung. 2004. "Family Control and the Rent-Seeking Society." *Entrepreneurship Theory and Practice* 28 (4): 391–409.

Newman, K. S. 1988. *Falling from Grace: The Experience of Downward Mobility in the American Middle Class*. New York: Free Press.

Nicklett, E. J., and S. A. Burgard. 2009. "Downward Social Mobility and Major Depressive Episodes among Latino and Asian-American Immigrants to the United States." *American Journal of Epidemiology* 170 (6): 793–801.

No, T. W. 2016. "Gieopeui Yeoyujawoni Saengjone Michineun Yeonghyange gwanhan Yeongu." [A Study on the Impact of Corporate Surplus Fund on Survival] *Jiyeok Saneop Yeongu* 39: 63–90.

Nye, J. 2004. *Soft Power: The Means to Success in World Politics*. New York: Public Affairs.

Oh, I., and H. Jun. 2016. "Economic Miracle." In *Routledge Handbook of Modern Korean History*, edited by M. Seth, 295–313. New York: Routledge.

Oh, I., and R. Varcin. 2010. "Rent-Sharing: Organizational and Technological Innovations under Military Regimes in South Korea and Turkey." *International Journal of Technology Management & Sustainable Development* 9 (2): 77–94.

Redding, G. 2005. "The Thick Description and Comparison of Societal Systems of Capitalism." *Journal of International Business Studies* 36 (2): 123–155.

Redding, G., and C. Rowley. 2017a. "Introduction: Human Capital as a Factor in Societal Progress." *Asia Pacific Business Review* 23 (2): 163–170.

Redding, G., and C. Rowley 2017b. "Conclusion: The Central Role of Human and Social Capital." *Asia Pacific Business Review* 23 (2): 299–305.

Siegel, J. 2003. "Is Political Connectedness a Paramount Investment after Liberalization? The Successful Leveraging of Contingent Social Capital and the Formation of Cross Border Strategic Alliances Involving Korean Firms and Their Global Partners (1987–2000)." *Harvard NOM Working Paper*, 3–45, Cambridge, MA.

Siegel, J. 2007. "Contingent Political Capital and International Alliances: Evidence from South Korea." *Administrative Science Quarterly* 52 (4): 621–666.

Siegel, J.I., L. Pyun, and B.Y. Cheon 2010. "Multinational Firms, Labor Market Discrimination, and the Capture of Competitive Advantage by Exploiting the Social Divide." *Harvard Business School: Strategy Unit Working Paper*, 11.

Wang, B., and C. Rowley. 2012. "Business Networks & the Emergence of Guanxi Capitalism in China: The Role of the 'Invisible Hand.'" In *Asian Business Networks in East Asia*, edited by J. Nolan, C. Rowley and M. Warner, 93–118. Oxford: Elsevier.

Wedeman, A. 1997. "Looters, Rent-Scrapers, and Dividend-Collectors: Corruption and Growth in Zaire, South Korea, and the Philippines." *The Journal of Developing Areas* 31 (4): 457–478.

The effect of technology management capability on new product development in China's service-oriented manufacturing firms: a social capital perspective

Weiwei Wu, Yexin Liu and Tachia Chin

ABSTRACT

Technology management capability (TMC) and new product development (NPD) are important for China's service-oriented manufacturers to achieve competitive advantage. In this study, TMC is conceptualized as comprising of four sub-level capabilities: searching, selecting, implementation and learning capabilities. Drawing from the theory of social capital, we hypothesize that social capital plays a role in the relationship between TMC and NPD performance. Our findings indicate that NPD performance and social capital are influenced by all the four sub-capabilities of TMC but the effect of each capability of TMC varies. Selecting capability is more significantly and positively related with NPD performance, while learning capability exerts the most significant positive effect on social capital. Moreover, our empirical findings indicate the partial mediating role of social capital in the process of TMC influencing NPD performance. This study makes a particular contribution to the literature by providing a more complete understanding of how social capital plays a role in the relationship between TMC and NPD performance. In terms of managerial implications, our results indicate that improving TMC is essential in enhancing a service-oriented manufacturing firm's NPD performance. Managers should also pay particular attention to nurturing social capital as a pathway to realize the true value of TMC.

Introduction

Emerging new technologies, new products, new markets and new management concepts are increasingly used by firms to achieve competitive advantage (Kapoor and Adner 2012; Lourdes Sosa 2013; Zaefarian et al. 2017). China's manufacturing industry is undergoing radical transformations due to mega-competition taking place on a global scale. The industry is gradually integrated with services, leading to the growth and importance of service-oriented manufacturing (Gao et al. 2011; Brax and Visintin 2017). In order to meet customers' special requirements, there is a strong need for new product development (NPD), as product innovation leads to market differentiation that could consequently create a variety of novel opportunities for manufacturers in the increasingly competitive markets (Jeong, Pae, and Zhou 2006; Matsui et al. 2007; Cao, Jiang, and Wang 2016). Nevertheless, the majority of Chinese manufacturing firms remain relatively weak in NPD performance (Guan et al. 2006; Ma et al. 2015; Chin and Liu 2016, 2015). This essentially is the biggest challenge for China's service-oriented manufacturing firms to pursue transformation and upgrading in the course of sustaining their competitiveness (DCRIC 2011).

Previous research has investigated the barriers to improve NPD performance of Chinese firms. Li (2013) argues that managerial issues are significant matters that need to be considered in the NPD performance of Chinese manufacturers. Kotabe, Jiang, and Murray (2011) suggest that managerial ability in integrating and transforming knowledge is paramount in enhancing product innovation performance. Based on a survey of senior executives from 150 large-and medium-sized Chinese manufacturers, DCRIC (2011) claims that 47% of the challenges these firms faced are related to their internal management. Chinese firms cannot rely on traditional production factors (such as low-cost labour) to compete, but instead must enhance the efficiency and effectiveness of managing technologies (DCRIC 2011). Many Chinese firms have had poor innovation and competitive performance because of the lack of management skills and their failure to cultivate technology management capability (TMC). Despite TMC being expected to influence NPD, there have been limited studies investigating the impact of TMC on NPD performance.

Adopting the knowledge-based view, the process of TMC in influencing NPD performance is closely aligned with knowledge acquisition, assimilation, transformation and exploitation (Cetindamar, Phaal, and Probert 2009). Guan et al. (2006) show that Chinese firms are used to spend a large portion of their innovation costs on the acquisition of technological equipment from world-renowned multinational enterprises (MNEs), but had largely overlooked the importance of building interpersonal trust and cooperation with these MNEs (Redding 2005; Rowley and Harry 2010; Rowley and Redding 2014). Such cooperation and trusting relationships are the foundations of social capital (Kim, Im, and Slater 2013; Kwon and Adler 2014; Suseno and Pinnington 2018), which could facilitate the acquisition and utilization of technological knowledge. Indeed, firms do not face difficulties in the transfer of hardware blueprints, product specifications and pricing lists, but they find it more challenging to transfer the intangible 'know-how'. Chinese firms should not merely cultivate TMC, but they need to further develop social capital to foster more social interactions, communications and reciprocity between firms when transferring technologies and know-how in order to maintain their creativity and innovation (Camps and Marques 2014). Thus, social capital may play a significant role in the relationship between TMC and NPD performance. However, current literature has not extensively examined this important role of social capital in building a firm's TMC and its NPD performance, in which this study seeks to explore.

This study is a response to the call of Rowley and Redding (2014) to focus on the processes within firms that can create competitive advantage. In this study, we provide valuable insights into the literature in several ways. First, we empirically test the relationship between TMC and NPD performance, given that most previous studies had merely implied the effects of TMC on NPD. Second, we examine the potential influences of TMC on social capital. This has interestingly not been extensively explored in previous studies (Gaimon, Hora, and Ramachandran 2017). Third, we indicate the mediating role of social capital in the process of TMC affecting NPD performance, which expands our understanding of the link between TMC and product innovation. Our findings are of interest to decision makers in China's service-oriented manufacturing firms by highlighting the importance of TMC and social capital for NPD performance, which is consequently important in exploring relevant innovation creation issues in China's service-oriented manufacturing firms.

Literature review

TMC

Technology can be seen as the embodiment and deployment of technical and scientific knowledge that leads to the creation of goods and services. Technology management can be traced back to the early 1970s under such labels as research and development (R&D) management, innovation management, engineering management or strategic management (Drejer 1997). Firms have to implement an overall strategy for effectively managing technology. Technology management, therefore, is critical to firms' competitiveness because it is related to the strategic dimension and significant value of technology (Phaal, Paterson, and Probert 1998). Cetindamar, Phaal, and Probert (2009) have explored the topic of technology management through the lens of dynamic capabilities and presented a technology management framework with an emphasis on the development and exploitation of technological capabilities. They argue that TMC is a kind of dynamic capability that defines the way in which a firm generates and deploys its existing resources, and where it obtains new resources. In short, TMC can be viewed as the combination of routines and processes which are developed, deployed and protected for managing technology in the most efficient way to achieve long-term profit (Díaz-Díaz, Aguiar-Díaz, and De Saá-Pérez 2008). It is worth noting that TMC appears to be more vital to service-oriented manufacturers than to traditional manufacturers as TMC adds the value of producers' service offerings to the total prices of tangible goods (Gebauer et al. 2012; Zhen 2012). TMC can strengthen the value creation process since it is a process of effective integration and utilization of existing technological resources with business requirements. For example, when selling high-tech products, it would serve as an added value if firms provide professional consulting and training services that usually require a high level of TMC.

Various scholars have explored the structure and elements of TMC. For instance, Gregory, Probert, and Cowell (1996) identify five generic processes of TMC, namely identification, selection, acquisition, exploitation and protection. Levin and Barnard (2008) outline a technology management framework consisting of four categories: producing scientific and technological knowledge, transforming knowledge into working artifacts, linking artifacts with user requirements and providing organizational support. All these management processes seem linear, but Cotec (1998) identifies a nonlinear process of TMC that includes five key activities – scan, focus, resource, implement, and learn, and innovation can happen in any of the five key activities. Cotec's (1998) study may be the first that incorporates learning as an important component of TMC. Since then, the importance of learning has been widely recognized (Drejer 1997). For example, Cetindamar, Phaal, and Probert (2009, 2016) propose that TMC activities include learning from the development and exploitation of technologies, and they argue that learning forms a critical part of TMC as it embeds technologies into organizational processes and human resources.

In view of our study on service-oriented manufacturers, we regard TMC as a firm's dynamic capability of planning, developing and exploiting technological capabilities to improve firms' competitiveness. More specifically, in our model, TMC involves searching inside and outside the firm, selecting valuable information to make strategic plans, and implementing these plans, with all of these activities being connected by learning. Thus, we propose that there are four sub-level capabilities of TMC, namely searching capability, selecting capability, implementation capability and learning capability.

Searching capability

Searching is an important aspect of TMC for ensuring a better fit between the firm's internal needs and external conditions. Firms search their internal and external environments to gather and process signals about their strengths, weaknesses, while identifying opportunities and threats. The key elements of searching capability include R&D environmental monitoring, business unit environmental monitoring, corporate environmental monitoring and technological capability monitoring (Cotec 1998; Levin and Barnard 2008).

Selecting capability

Selecting capability highlights the importance of understanding the specificities of technologies and its impact on the firm's functions. As such, this capability is about the firm committing resources to activities related to the strategic management of technology portfolios (Cetindamar, Phaal, and Probert 2016). Searching capability results in the acquisition of complex information, and knowing how to interpret signals that are most likely to impact the firm's competitiveness. The key elements of selecting capability include R&D strategy, R&D portfolio evaluation, R&D funding, post-project audit, technology roadmapping, product line planning, product portfolio evaluation, feasibility study, technology need assessment and new business unit development (Gregory, Probert, and Cowell 1996; Levin and Barnard 2008).

Implementation capability

Implementation capability involves resourcing and executing the decisions made in the selection process. Various kinds of activities are implemented to foster product innovation (Gregory, Probert, and Cowell 1996; Cetindamar, Phaal, and Probert 2009). The key elements of implementation capability include intellectual property management, project execution, technology transfer, technology adaptation, post-project support, performance management, technology alliance management and personnel management (Levin and Barnard 2008).

Learning capability

Learning capability suggests the need for the firm to reflect on previous capabilities, review its experience of success and failure, and learn on how to adapt, manage, and capture relevant knowledge from its past experience. Learning can be captured from the technology management process in two ways: by developing an improved technological capability, and by developing a more effective management process of technological change (Cotec 1998). Thus, there are two types of learning in technology management: technological learning in order to capture and accumulate technological competence and organizational learning to develop organizational routines for managing the process of technological change (Cotec 1998). Key elements in learning capability include structured and challenging reflection on the process, conceptualizing, experimentation and capturing of previous experience (Cotec 1998).

Our model thus aims to provide a more comprehensive understanding of the TMC concept by encompassing all core activities relevant to our research setting. The proposed TMC model appears to be more feasible and pragmatic, as it incorporates these four sub-capabilities, which can be used by any firms.

Social capital

The notion of social capital has been discussed extensively in the literature since the mid-1980s. Social capital is gaining prominence as a concept that provides a foundation for describing and characterizing a firm's set of relationships (Inkpen and Tsang 2005; Cuevas-Rodríguez, Cabello-Medina, and Carmona-Lavado 2014), as it argues that the networks of firm relationships constitute a valuable resource for firm development (Adler and Kwon 2002; Suseno and Pinnington 2017). Social capital can be conceptualized as the actual and potential resources provided by and derived from firms' social relations. We follow a narrow view in which the notion of social capital is confined to describing firms' social relationships.

A great majority of studies have proposed that social capital entails beneficial outcomes (e.g. Florin, Lubatkin, and Schulze 2003; Zahra 2010; Maurer, Bartsch, and Ebers 2011; Chin and Liu 2015; Chin et al. 2017; Suseno and Pinnington 2017). For example, Yli-Renko, Autio, and Sapienza (2001), employing a sample of 180 entrepreneurial high-technology ventures, point out that social capital facilitates external knowledge acquisition in key customer relationships. Florin, Lubatkin, and Schulze (2003), in their longitudinal study of 275 US ventures that went public, find that social capital provides ventures with a durable source of competitive advantage by leveraging the productivity of their resource base. Zahra (2010) shows how social capital enables family firms to assemble the resources (especially knowledge) necessary for successful adaptation.

The importance of social capital as a determinant of innovation has received much attention (Landry, Amara, and Lamari 2002; Alguezaui and Filieri 2010). From knowledge based view, innovation is considered as a process with its implementation resting upon knowledge resources (Leiponen and Helfat 2010). The social network created by social capital can establish rich communication channels and increase the social interactions. This consequently creates opportunities for knowledge acquisition from both internal and external sources to support innovation activities (Molina-Morales and Martínez-Fernández 2010; Maurer, Bartsch, and Ebers 2011). For example, social capital has been generally perceived as the resources that can be derived from a set of ties to achieve specific goals (Suseno and Pinnington 2017, 2018). Many researchers prove that social capital can stimulate intra-organizational knowledge sharing for the generation of new ideas (Manning 2010; Cuevas-Rodríguez, Cabello-Medina, and Carmona-Lavado 2014). In addition, social capital can also facilitate the creation of inter-organizational networks, which may facilitate firms to access unavailable knowledge and further improve their innovation capabilities (Wu 2008; Martínez-Cañas, Sáez-Martínez, and Ruiz-Palomino 2012).

While service-oriented manufacturing business requires more complex processes to integrate goods and services and therefore involves more value co-creation activities with suppliers and customers (Lin, Pekkarinen, and Ma 2015; Chin et al. 2017, 2016), it is imperative for manufacturing firms to nurture social capital to enhance cooperation and coordination among business stakeholders. Such a service culture is more likely to help manufacturers in fostering guanxi-based social capital that enhances the establishment of trust and networks (Redding 2005; Rowley and Redding 2014). In short, social capital is indeed a valuable asset that stems from accessing various resources available through social relationships (Krause, Handfield, and Tyler 2007; Pérez-Luño et al. 2011).

NPD performance

Product innovation is a critical component of China's manufacturing firms to bring innovative products to market ahead of their competitors. As such, NPD is important for firms. Existing research has highlighted that NPD performance is a multidimensional construct (Hsu and Fang 2009; Lazzarotti, Manzini, and Mari 2011), with various indicators to measure NPD performance (see Table 1).

As shown in Table 1, we argue that NPD is related to the efficient balance and control of time, cost, quality and profit margins, as well as the effective maintenance of coordination with suppliers, customers and all related stakeholders. Viewed from this angle, relative to traditional manufacturers, service-oriented firms are more obliged to cope with far more complicated interpersonal relationships within and outside organizations in NPD processes, with service operations needing better communicative competences for performing service-related tasks (Tao et al. 2017). The synergistic value-creation mechanism between production and service is believed to guide China's manufacturing firms to design more modern, comprehensive solutions and to propel continuous product innovation to cater to ever-changing customer demands (Gao et al. 2011). As such, it is particularly critical to discuss the TMC-NPD associations in the context of service-oriented manufacturing in China's context.

Table 1. The measures of NPD performance.

Researchers	Indexes
Souder (1988)	(1) NPD cycle; (2) NPD cost; (3) prototype development proficiency; (4) design change frequency; (5) the technology performance of R&D; (6) the commercialization performance of R&D; (7) market effects
Calantone, Schmidt, and Song (1996)	(1) the ratio of investment (ROI); (2) the investment growth rate (GROI); (3) ratio of sales (ROS); (4) sales growth rate (GROS); (5) market share and growth rate
Song and Parry (1997)	(1) overall profit; (2) new product sales compared with competitors; (3) profit rate for new product compared with competitors; (4) new product success compared with the expected profit
Atuahene-Gima and Ko (2001)	(1) market share; (2) sales and customer use; (3) sales growth; (4) profit objectives
Liu, Chen, and Tsai (2005)	(1) new product life cycle; (2) new product sales and profits; (3) time to market for new product
Wang (2009)	(1) quality and speed to market; (2) number of major customer; (3) market share rate; (4) widening customer choice and expectation; (5) flexibility; (6) number of new products or processes; (7) number of patent; (8) fee of research; (9) index of productivity; (10) trademark; (11) information system; (12) competitive priorities of responsiveness; (13) capability of employees; (14) output merit of employees; (15) skill training of employees

Hypotheses development

TMC and NPD performance

NPD is the process of transforming business opportunities into tangible products (Jeong, Pae, and Zhou 2006; Rauniar and Rawski 2012) while TMC is the managerial knowledge embedded in the organization that is available to support the realization of product innovation (Díaz-Díaz, Aguiar-Díaz, and De Saá-Pérez 2008; Wu et al. 2014). TMC addresses the effective identification, selection, acquisition, exploitation and protection of technological resources needed to facilitate product innovation (Cetindamar, Phaal, and Probert 2009), and it can ensure technological resources are effectively linked to product innovation requirements (Gaimon 2008). Therefore, it can be inferred that TMC has an impact on NPD performance.

More specifically, the searching capability of TMC deals with acquiring technology information (Kostoff 2012). It highlights that firms with strong searching capability can quickly identify new technological trends, respond to technology changes and master the state-of-art technologies, which may enable them to better understand the market and its dynamics. The technology information obtained by searching capability serves as the foundation of NPD strategy formulation (Cooper and Edgett 2010), which is the critical factor of successful undertaking NPD projects. After acquiring new technological information from external sources, the selecting capability of TMC helps to interpret the exact meaning of the acquired knowledge, identifies how new and prior knowledge interacts, and incorporates novel knowledge into knowledge base (Li et al. 2012). The integration of this accumulated knowledge as part of the NPD process can help firms to develop attractive new product concept (Martín-de Castro et al. 2013), which is important for the introduction of new products. Form resource-based view, successful NPD requires the use and redistribution of technological resources (Kim, Shin, and Min 2016). The implementation capability of TMC is concerned with appropriately distributing and effectively embedding technological resources within the NPD process (Wu, Liu, and Yu 2016). This implementation capability also offers supportive routines to employ various technological resources (Levin and Barnard 2008; Oerlemans, Knoben, and Pretorius 2013; Phaal, Farrukh, and Probert 2013), which ensures the achievement of NPD performance. Finally, the learning capability of TMC highlights the importance of recording information from past product development projects, and this consequently influences performance (Sherman, Berkowitz, and Souder 2005). Firms possessing learning capability can accumulate experiences from the NPD procedure (Nguyen, Chen, and De Cremer 2017), by integrating extant knowledge with different methods (Kim and Atuahene-Gima 2010). This means that learning capability increases the possibility of developing a structured NPD process, which may accelerate the strategic use of resources for NPD performance. We therefore hypothesize:

H1: TMC and NPD performance are significantly and positively related.

H1a: Searching capability is significantly and positively related to NPD performance.

H1b: Selecting capability is significantly and positively related to NPD performance.

H1c: Implementation capability is significantly and positively related to NPD performance.

H1d: Learning capability is significantly and positively related to NPD performance.

TMC and social capital

TMC is directly relevant to acquisition, assimilation and transformation of technological resources embedded in the internal and external network into the NPD process (Badawy 2009; Cetindamar, Phaal, and Probert 2009), demonstrating the close correlation between TMC and social capital. Following this logic, the sub-capabilities of TMC – searching capability, selecting capability, implementation capability and learning capability all exert impact on social capital. Searching capability monitors the external environment which includes establishing routines for the systematic scanning of existing and emerging technologies. Searching capability also involves developing an awareness of the technological information which are, or may be, important to the business (Wu, Liu, and Yu 2016). In the scanning process, it is important for organizations to utilize their searching capability to develop reliable and effective communication channels within and across organizational boundaries, as a source of social capital. Selecting capability involves the choice of technological information that should be supported and promoted (Shehabuddeen, Probert, and Phaal 2006). Selecting capability further enables firms to establish frequent communication within the organization in order to gather ideas and select useful information, which facilitates social interactions. Implementation capability invokes cross-functional integration (Wu, Liu, and Yu 2016), which may promote the development of social ties. This may facilitate collaborative behaviours and collective action, and thus develops connections among actors and a common set of goals for the organization. Learning capability is also important to the development of social capital. The organizational learning process consists of the acquisition, dissemination and use of knowledge (Bhatti, Larimo, and Coudounaris 2016). The learning mechanisms may have a positive impact on social capital by increasing the internal group cohesion and co-ordination (Sun and Anderson 2010). Moreover, learning capability also facilitates the external interactions with the external environment for technology transfers and R&D collaboration (Huikkola, Ylimäki, and Kohtamäki 2013). We therefore hypothesize:

H2: TMC and social capital are significantly and positively related.

H2a: Searching capability is significantly and positively related to social capital.

H2b: Selecting capability is significantly and positively related to social capital.

H2c: Implementation capability is significantly and positively related to social capital.

H2d: Learning capability is significantly and positively related to social capital.

The role of social capital

Combining the technology management and social capital literatures with NPD theory leads to the assertion that social capital plays an important role in the relationship between TMC and NPD performance. NPD is a complex activity, which requires new knowledge being applied to commercial ends (Cankurtaran, Langerak, and Griffin 2013). Firms can search and select internal and external technological knowledge across boundaries, and reinterpret and transform the acquired knowledge through effective TMC (Wu, Liu, and Yu 2012, 2016). This is important since NPD requires knowledge flow to perform useful actions to solve problems related to concept development, technological development and commercial development (Frankort 2016). In the process of TMC generating technological knowledge, social capital provides first mover benefits in terms of the level of technological knowledge that is available and/or the timeliness with which it is available (Maurer, Bartsch, and Ebers 2011).

Furthermore, in order to achieve successful NPD performance, firms should combine internal and external sources of technological knowledge (Prabhu, Chandy, and Ellis 2005). TMC establishes the close ties to build social capital that is characterized by mutual feelings of attachment and trust (Prashantham and Dhanaraj 2010; Suseno and Pinnington 2017, 2018). The network relationships established by TMC facilitate firms to exploit existing internal knowledge and also explore external technological knowledge beyond firm-specific competencies. Consequently, firms investing in TMC are more likely to have broader social networks, and thereby tend to outperform competitive rivals in their product innovation activities (Chiang and Hung 2010).

In addition, NPD also needs coordination to enhance formal and informal communication since product innovation activities are executed in the different functional groups. TMC can coordinate the activities that constitute the product innovation process and provide the infrastructure for supporting functional integration (McFadyen and Cannella 2004). In this way, TMC facilitates and leverages interaction relationships by reducing the transaction costs through social capital, which consequently improves the efficiency of the development of new products. We therefore hypothesize that:

H3: Social capital mediates the effects of TMC on NPD performance.

Methods

Sample

Based on the literature and background as discussed above, we designed a structured and closed-type questionnaire that asked respondents to rate their business units on TMC, social capital and NPD performance. The questionnaire was first developed in English and then translated into Chinese. In order to ensure accuracy, the Chinese version was subsequently retranslated into English by a third party. We carefully checked the two versions of English questionnaire and agreed that there was no substantial difference between them in the meanings of the items. Moreover, to detect potential problems in the questionnaire, a pretest was run with a small sub-sample of 20 respondents, including professors and managers who are familiar with innovation management field. After the pre-test, the questionnaire was revised again to make sure that there were no problems for the respondents in completing it.

We sent the questionnaire to 150 Chinese service-oriented manufacturing firms. We asked senior managers to complete the questionnaire since senior managers have a more comprehensive understanding of TMC, social capital and NPD performance. Completed questionnaires were returned in sealed envelopes or as e-mail file attachments. 130 firms responded to this questionnaire. Of these responses, 122 were valid (after eliminating those cases with missing data). This sample was sufficient to allow statistical analysis at the firm level.

Measures

The survey questionnaire comprises four parts. The first three parts assess TMC, social capital and NPD performance, respectively, using a 5-point Likert scale with 1 = strongly disagree, 3 = neutral and 5 = strongly agree. The fourth part of the questionnaire is related to various descriptive information about each firm.

We designed scale measures to assess the four capabilities of TMC. By reorganizing the routines from Levin and Barnard's (2008) technology management framework, we developed 3 items to assess searching capability, 10 items to assess selecting capability, and 7 items to assess implementation capability. We also used four items that describe technology management adapted from Cotec's (1998) study, to assess learning capability. The measurement items of TMC are shown in Table 2.

In addition, we used the scale from Maurer and Ebers (2006) and Inkpen and Tsang (2005) to measure the social capital. A sample item is 'The team members of NPD project communicate very often with each other'. Drawing from previous research, we developed three items to assess NPD performance: the NPD cycle (NPDP1) (Liu, Chen, and Tsai 2005; Souder 1988), the return on investment (NPDP2) (Calantone, Schmidt, and Song 1996; Song and Parry 1997) and the market share (NPDP3) (Souder 1988; Calantone, Schmidt, and Song 1996; Atuahene-Gima and Ko 2001). These items were assessed for each firm relative to its competitors.

We also included two control variables, namely firm size (FS) and type of industry (TOI). It is important to control for FS, measured by number of employees, because of the impact a firm's employees as its resources can influence the firm's NPD performance (Hitt, Hoskisson, and Kim 1997; Swan and Allred 2003; Devaraj, Hollingworth, and Schroeder 2004). TOI is an important control variable because of the influence it exerts on TMC (Wu et al. 2010). The respondents in this study were from high-technology and non-high-technology industries, which were controlled for in our model using dummy variables for each industry type.

Reliability, validity and common method bias

We calculated Cronbach's α coefficient for each construct. The Cronbach's α values of TMC, social capital and NPD performance are 0.786, 0.772, 0.793, respectively, indicating that the constructs have acceptable reliability.

The questionnaire was formed based on an extensive review of previous research. We also asked a panel of our pilot study respondents, i.e. professors and managers in our pre-test stage, to review the indicators and the scope of the content of the questionnaire. They verified that the indicators and the contents of the questionnaire accurately represent the measurement objective, thus establishing the content validity.

We performed confirmatory factor analysis (CFA) to check the unidimensionality of the constructs using AMOS 16.0 with maximum likelihood estimation. A measurement model included all of our proposed constructs, and each item was allowed to load only on its proposed construct. The results of this assessment showed that χ^2/degrees of freedom = 2.683, $p < 0.01$; goodness of fit index = 0.935; comparative fit index = 0.920; normed fit index = 0.876 and root mean square error of approximation = 0.052, indicating that it was a very good model fit. Convergent validity, the extent to which the measurement items represent the

Table 2. The measurement index of TMC.

Construct	Items
Searching capability (SHC) adapted from Levin and Barnard (2008)	My firm scans the external environment, including technologies, competitors, suppliers, customers, regulators, etc. (SHC1)
	My firm analyzes its technological capability, including technologies, patents, copyrights, trademarks, standards, etc. (SHC2)
	My firm investigates the market and technical feasibility of an idea (SHC3)
Selecting capability (STC) adapted from Levin and Barnard (2008)	My firm chooses creative process to develop new product/process (STC1)
	My firm plans the progression of technology to be developed by R&D (STC2)
	My firm determines what technologies current and future customers want (STC3)
	My firm develops a plan for future direction of product line/platform (STC4)
	My firm evaluates portfolio of R&D projects to achieve desired balance along different dimensions (STC5)
	My firm develops its plan and budget (STC6)
	My firm determines the role of various technologies in business units (STC7)
	My firm determines if a programme/project should be funded (STC8)
	My firm determines how to fund R&D efforts (STC9)
	My firm determines when a new set of products/technologies/markets warrant the formation of a new business unit (STC10)
Implementation capability (IC) adapted from Levin and Barnard (2008)	My firm designs, staffs, and manages projects (IC1)
	My firm shifts ownership of artefact and accompanying knowledge (IC2)
	My firm absorbs and adapts a technical artefact and accompanying knowledge (IC3)
	My firm provides supports to adopters of technology (IC4)
	My firm measures and manages performance (IC5).
	My firm identifies, develops and manages strategic partnerships and consortia (IC6)
	My firm manages intellectual property (patents, copyright, trademarks, and standards) (IC7)
Learning capability (LC) adapted from Cotec (1998)	My firm capture experience honestly (LC1)
	My firm makes the structured and challenging reflection on technology management process (LC2)
	My firm captures and codifies the lessons learned into frameworks and eventually procedures to build on lessons learned (LC3)
	My firm has the willingness to try and manage things differently next time, to see if the lessons learned are valid (LC4)

construct, was confirmed as each path loading was greater than twice its associated standard error.

Discriminant validity was tested through inter-factor correlations. All inter-factor correlations were reasonably low and within an acceptable range. A more rigorous test of discriminant validity was carried out by checking the average variance extracted (AVE). AVE was calculated through the square root of the average communality and confirmed because the square root of the AVE was greater than all other cross-loadings, ranging between 0.716 and 0.783, as shown in Table 3.

Table 3. Interfactor correlations.

Factors	1	2	3	4	5	6
Searching capability (1)	0.726					
Selecting capability (2)	0.235***	0.762				
Implementation capability (3)	0.213***	0.322***	0.783			
Learning capability (4)	0.282***	0.226***	0.358***	0.716		
Social capital (5)	0.223***	0.218***	0.211***	0.402***	0.756	
NPD performance (6)	0.142***	0.313***	0.227***	0.249**	0.343***	0.761

Note: Square-root AVE of the corresponding construct is displayed in the diagonal.
Significance levels: ***$p < 0.01$.

Table 4. The regression analysis of the relationships among TMC, social capital and NPD performance.

Model	Model 1	Model 2
Dependent variables	NPD performance	Social capital
Independent variables		
SHC	0.221**	0.262**
STC	0.332***	0.247**
IC	0.241**	0.233**
LC	0.263**	0.321***
Control variables		
TOI	0.126	0.153
FS	0.097	0.106

Significance levels: **$p < 0.05$, ***$p < 0.01$.

We used Harman's (1967) one-factor test to examine common method bias. The rationale behind the test is that if common method bias is a serious problem in the data, then all the measures would tend to load on a single factor when both the independent and dependent variables are entered into factor analysis. The results showed a six-factor structure, which explained 78% of the variance. No single factor was apparent in the unrotated factor structure, with the first factor accounting for about 24% of the total variance. Thus, a single factor did not emerge; nor there was a general factor accounting for the majority of the covariance in the variables. These results suggest that common method bias is not a significant problem in the data-set.

Results

We tested the hypotheses using SPSS 20.0 to run multiple regression analysis. The results for H1 and H2 are shown in Table 4, and the results for H3 are shown in Table 5.

The relationship between TMC and NPD performance

In Model 1, searching capability, selecting capability, implementation capability and learning capability are the independent variables and NPD performance the dependent variable. All four capabilities of TMC are significant and positively related to NPD performance, thus supporting all of H1 (H1a–H1d). Model 1 further shows that selecting capability is more significantly related with NPD performance ($\beta = 0.332$, $p < 0.01$), compared with selecting capability ($\beta = 0.221$, $p < 0.05$), implementation capability ($\beta = 0.247$, $p < 0.05$) and learning

Table 5. The multiple-regression analysis results.

Model	Model 3	Model 4	Model 5
Dependent variables	NPD performance	Social capital	NPD performance
Independent variables			
TMC	0.896***	0.606***	0.372**
Social capital			0.519***
Control variables			
TOI	0.083**	0.213	0.102**
FS	0.093	0.188	0.094

Significance levels: **$p < 0.05$, ***$p < 0.01$.

capability ($\beta = 0.263$, $p < 0.01$). This implies the comparative importance of selecting capability to NPD performance.

The relationship between TMC and social capital

In Model 2, searching capability, selecting capability, implementation capability and learning capability are the independent variables and social capital is the dependent variable. All four capabilities of TMC are significant and positively related to social capital, thus supporting all of H2 (H2a–H2d). Learning capability ($\beta = 0.321$, $p < 0.01$) in comparison to searching capability ($\beta = 0.262$, $p < 0.05$), selecting capability ($\beta = 0.247$, $p < 0.05$) and implementation capability ($\beta = 0.233$, $p < 0.05$) has the most significant and the greatest influence on social capital. This implies a greater importance of learning capability to social capital in comparison to the effects of the other three sub-capabilities of TMC on social capital.

The role of social capital in the relationship between TMC and NPD performance

Following the procedure of Baron and Kenny (1986), we employed multiple regression analysis to test whether social capital plays a mediating role in the relationship between TMC and NPD performance. First, we analyzed the relationship between TMC and NPD performance (Model 3). Second, we analyzed the relationship between TMC and social capital (Model 4). Then, social capital was entered into Model 5, and the significance of the coefficients was examined.

Like Model 1, the results for Model 3 confirm that TMC has a significant positive effect on NPD performance when TMC is the only variable. When social capital is entered into this model in Model 5, both TMC and social capital have significant positive effects on NPD performance. In comparing the coefficients for TMC in Models 3 and Model 5, we find that the direct effect of TMC on NPD performance decreases when social capital is incorporated ($\beta = 0.896$ decreases to $\beta = 0.372$). Moreover, the effect of TMC on social capital and the effect of social capital on NPD performance are significant. These results indicate that social capital mediates the effect of TMC on NPD performance.

We also used the Sobel test to examine the statistical significance of the indirect relationship between TMC and NPD performance through social capital. The result of the Sobel test statistic (t) is 3.772, with the one-tailed probability being 0.0001626 and the two-tailed probability being 0.0003183. This indicates that social capital indeed plays an intermediary role in the relationship between TMC and NPD performance. Thus, H3 is supported.

Discussion

Our results show that TMC has a significant and positive effect on NPD performance, confirming that TMC is an important capability that should be incorporated in the product innovation process of firms. One of our respondents, a successful service-oriented manufacturer in China, is a sample case that illustrates the importance of TMC for NPD. Since its inception, the firm has focused on improving TMC, such as scanning and choosing word-leading hydroelectric technologies, implementing distribution and incentive regulations. The firm has accumulated more than fifty years of TMC, providing it with a solid foundation to consistently implement successful product innovations (Wu, Yu, and Wu 2012).

Our study further indicates that the four sub-capabilities of TMC – searching capability, selecting capability, implementation capability and learning capability – all exert positive and significant effects on both NPD performance and social capital. However, the effectiveness of each sub-capability differs. Selecting capability is more significantly related to NPD performance because it deals with strategic issues (Levin and Barnard 2008; Cetindamar, Phaal, and Probert 2009). Selecting capability requires the firm to choose strategic analyses to identify the strengths and weaknesses of firms. The evaluation of the firm's internal strengths and weaknesses creates a solid foundation for product innovation strategy and product innovation plan. Learning capability has the most significant and greatest influences on social capital, and it provides the basis for the development of social capital. Learning capability accumulates relevant organizational success by reinforcing intra- and inter-organizational social interactions. As such, firms with high level of learning capability may leverage their past experience to bring the organization's members together around a shared vision internally (Akgün et al. 2007) and promote strategic alliances externally (Li et al. 2014). Following this argument, we found that learning capability greatly accelerates the development of social capital.

Our findings also shed lights on the role social capital plays in the process of TMC in influencing NPD performance. Our results indicate that TMC can directly and indirectly affect NPD performance through social capital, suggesting that Chinese service-oriented manufacturing firms should strengthen their TMC and social capital simultaneously to achieve better NPD performance. With some traditional product-focused technological capabilities becoming redundant and obsolete (Motohashi and Yun 2007), we argue that it is necessary for Chinese service-oriented manufacturing firms to develop their capabilities for newer innovative products. In this context, the transformation of industry requires firms to emphasize more on TMC as well as social capital (Gebauer, Gustafsson, and Witell 2011). Social capital should therefore be viewed as a key resource that can enable firms to develop TMC and further facilitate NPD. In other words, social capital is needed to develop technological competences that may be better developed by service-oriented manufacturing firms to attain a competitive advantage.

Although this study presents several important points regarding the effect of TMC on NPD from social capital perspective, it also suffers from some limitations. We only incorporate social capital as a mediator in analyzing the relationship between TMC and NPD performance. Thus, our research model can be advanced by investigating the mediating effects of other types of capital such as human capital and cultural capital on the TMC-NPD relationships.

In addition, other environmental characteristics, such as technological turbulence (Gaimon, Hora, and Ramachandran 2017), may potentially have an impact on TMC, social capital, and NPD performance. Future studies could therefore explore various other environmental characteristics, which would provide a more comprehensive interpretation of our research results.

Another opportunity for future research is by considering research samples from other countries. The sample used in this study was taken only from China. However, different countries may have different TM practices (Choi et al. 2012); for example, the U.S. has a comparative advantage in project management while Spain focuses on intellectual property, and these different practices may lead to different results. Future research can therefore be conducted in other countries to further contribute to our understanding of how TMC is associated with NPD performance across different countries.

Implications

The study offers several theoretical contributions. First, this study provides theoretical grounds and empirical evidence for positing the influence of TMC on NPD performance. In particular, our results indicate that TMC is an antecedent of NPD performance. We also verify that each of the four sub-capabilities of TMC – searching capability, selecting capability, implementation capability and learning capability – has different impacts on NPD performance. The examination of each of these sub-capabilities of TMC on NPD performance through incorporating social capital perspective has not been extensively addressed in previous studies (Cetindamar, Phaal, and Probert 2009; Wu, Yu, and Wu 2012). In this way, our study provides a distinctive potential for firms to capture values from TMC in order to stimulate NPD performance.

Second, this study contributes to the social capital literature by demonstrating the effect of TMC on social capital. Prior social capital studies have been primarily focused on investigating social networks (Arregle et al. 2007; Alguezaui and Filieri 2010), with TMC rarely being mentioned. Our study theoretically and empirically confirms that TMC has a significant positive effect on social capital, and that social capital is further influenced by all four sub-capabilities of TMC. This contributes to the social capital theory by uncovering an important new direction on how firms develop social capital and technology management.

Third, this study identifies the mediating role of social capital in the relationship between TMC and NPD performance, which expands our understanding of how TMC affects NPD performance. This also provides an important supplement to the technology management research. Although previous research provides hints on the influence of TMC on innovation, our study confirms such assertion by showing that social capital indeed plays an important role. By examining the mediating role of social capital, this study reveals the underlying mechanism of the TMC-NPD performance relationship.

As for the managerial implications, this study provides new insights into the technology management practices of Chinese service-oriented manufacturing. In a service-oriented industry, technology management and the delivery of service offerings must closely interact (Santamaría, Jesús Nieto, and Miles 2012). Our findings highlight the importance of TMC in modern manufacturing systems, such that firms with stronger TMC are more likely to achieve better NPD performance. Firms should thus strengthen their TMC by simultaneously promoting their searching, selecting, implementation and learning capabilities. Our results further show that selecting capability has a stronger relationship to NPD performance than the other three capabilities and thus technology managers should place more emphasis to this aspect of TMC. We have also indicated that firms can develop their selecting capability through developing information interpretation, identifying key signals, and designing strategies and plans.

This study has demonstrated that a partial effect of TMC on NPD performance is exerted through social capital. This implies that managers should pay particular attention to fostering the firm's social capital so as to maximize the outcomes of their TMC efforts. Most importantly, in order to obtain the benefits from TMC, it is worth noting that managers should emphasize the linkage between TMC and social capital, with a special focus on learning capability because this capability has a more significant relationship with social capital than the other three sub-capabilities of TMC.

Conclusion

In recent years, technology management research has attracted increasing attention in academic discussions and practical applications. However, there has been a scarcity of research examining the influence of TMC on NPD performance in China's service-oriented manufacturing. To fill this research gap, the current research examines the impact of TMC on NPD performance, and further explores the mediating effect of social capital. Overall, our study demonstrates that TMC is an important antecedent of NPD and social capital, and each of the four sub-capabilities of TMC – searching capability, selecting capability, implementation capability and learning capability, exerts significant impacts on NPD performance and social capital. The outcomes of this study further offer contributions to the technology management literature, and provide interesting directions for future studies.

Disclosure statement

No potential conflict of interest was reported by the authors.

Funding

This work was supported by the National Natural Science Foundation of China (grant numbers 71472055, 71272175), National Social Science Foundation of China (grant number 16AZD0006), National Science Foundation for Post-doctoral Scientists of China (grant numbers 201104424, 2012M520697), Heilongjiang Philosophy and Social Science Research Project (grant number 14B105) and the Project sponsored by SRF for ROCS, SEM.

References

Atuahene-Gima, K., and A. Ko. 2001. "An Empirical Investigation of the Effect of Market Orientation and Entrepreneurship Orientation Alignment on Product Innovation." *Organization Science* 12: 54–74. doi:10.1287/orsc.12.1.54.10121.

Adler, P. S., and S. W. Kwon. 2002. "Social Capital: Prospects for a New Concept." *Academy of Management Review* 27 (1): 17–40. doi:10.5465/AMR.2002.5922314.

Akgün, A. E., H., Keskin. J. C., Byrne, and S. Aren. 2007. "Emotional and Learning Capability and their Impact on Product Innovativeness and Firm Performance." *Technovation* 27 (9): 501–513. doi:10.1016/j.technovation.2007.03.001.

Alguezaui, S., and R. Filieri. 2010. "Investigating the Role of Social Capital in Innovation: Sparse Versus Dense Network." *Journal of Knowledge Management* 14 (6): 891–909. doi:10.1108/13673271011084925.

Arregle, J. L., M. A. Hitt, D. G. Sirmon, and P. Very. 2007. "The Development of Organizational Social Capital: Attributes of Family Firms." *Journal of Management Studies* 44 (1): 73–95. doi:10.1111/j.1467-6486.2007.00665.x.

Badawy, A. M. 2009. "Technology Management Simply Defined: A Tweet Plus Two Characters." *Journal of Engineering and Technology Management* 26 (4): 219–224. doi:10.1016/j.jengtecman.2009.11.001.

Baron, R. M., and D. A. Kenny. 1986. "The Moderator–Mediator Variable Distinction in Social Psychological Research: Conceptual, Strategic, and Statistical Considerations." *Journal of Personality and Social Psychology* 51 (6): 1173–1182. doi:10.1037/0022-3514.51.6.1173.

Bhatti, W. A., J. Larimo, and D. N. Coudounaris. 2016. "The Effect of Experiential Learning on Subsidiary Knowledge and Performance." *Journal of Business Research* 69 (5): 1567–1571. doi:10.1016/j.jbusres.2015.10.018.

Brax, S. A., and F. Visintin. 2017. "Meta-Model of Servitization: The Integrative Profiling Approach." *Industrial Marketing Management* 60 (1): 17–32. doi:10.1016/j.indmarman.2016.04.014.

Cankurtaran, P., F. Langerak, and A. Griffin. 2013. "Consequences of New Product Development Speed: A Meta-Analysis." *Journal of Product Innovation Management* 30 (3): 465–486. doi:10.1111/jpim.12011.

Cao, J., Z. Jiang, and K. Wang. 2016. "Customer Demand Prediction of Service-Oriented Manufacturing Incorporating Customer Satisfaction." *International Journal of Production Research* 54 (5): 1303–1321. doi:10.1080/00207543.2015.1067377.

Calantone, R. J., J. B. Schmidt, and X. M. Song. 1996. "Controllable Factors of New Product Success: A Cross-National Comparison." *Marketing Science* 15 (4): 341–358. doi:10.1287/mksc.15.4.341.

Camps, S., and P. Marques. 2014. "Exploring How Social Capital Facilitates Innovation: The Role of Innovation Enablers." *Technological Forecasting and Social Change* 88 (10): 325–348. doi:10.1016/j.techfore.2013.10.008.

Cetindamar, D., R. Phaal, and D. Probert. 2009. "Understanding Technology Management as a Dynamic Capability: A Framework for Technology Management Activities." *Technovation* 29 (4): 237–246. doi:10.1016/j.technovation.2008.10.004.

Cetindamar, D., R. Phaal, and D. Probert. 2016. *Technology Management: Activities and Tools*. Palgrave Macmillan.

Chiang, Y. H., and K. P. Hung. 2010. "Exploring Open Search Strategies and Perceived Innovation Performance from the Perspective of Inter-Organizational Knowledge Flows." *R&D Management* 40 (3): 292–299. doi:10.1111/j.1467-9310.2010.00588.x.

Chin, T., and R. H. Liu. 2015. "Understanding Labor Conflicts in Chinese Manufacturing: A Yin-Yang Harmony Perspective." *International Journal of Conflict Management* 26 (3): 288–315. doi:10.1108/IJCMA-09-2014-0074.

Chin, T., and R. H. Liu. 2016. "Critical Management Issues in China's Socio-Economic Transformation: Multiple Scientific Perspectives to Strategy and Innovation." *Chinese Management Studies* 11 (1): 12–18. doi:10.1108/CMS-01-2017-0007.

Chin, T., R. H. Liu, and X. Yang. 2016. "'Reverse Internationalization' in Chinese Firms: A Study of How Global Startup OEMs Seek to Compete Domestically." *Asia Pacific Business Review* 22 (2): 201–219.

Chin, T., R. H. Liu, D. J. Yang, L. Y. Hu, and Y. Yang. 2017. "Effects of Dynamic Core Competences on Own Brand Strategy in Reverse Internationalization." *Journal of Management Science* 30 (2): 27–38. doi:10.3969/j.issn.1672-0334,2017.02.003.

Choi, D. G., Y. Lee, M. Jung, and H. Lee. 2012. "National Characteristics and Competitiveness in MOT Research: A Comparative Analysis of Ten Specialty Journals, 2000–2009." *Technovation* 32 (1): 9–18. doi:10.1016/j.technovation.2011.09.004.

Cooper, R. G., and S. J. Edgett. 2010. "Developing a Product Innovation and Technology Strategy for Your Business." *Research-Technology Management* 53 (3): 33–40. doi:10.1080/08956308.2010.11657629.

Cotec. 1998. *Temaguide: A Guide to Technology Management and Innovation for Companies*. Brussels: Research Report for Innovation Programme of European Communities.

Cuevas-Rodríguez, G., C. Cabello-Medina, and A. Carmona-Lavado. 2014. "Internal and External Social Capital for Radical Product Innovation: Do They Always Work Well Together?" *British Journal of Management* 25 (2): 266–284. doi:10.1111/1467-8551.12002.

DCRIC. 2011. "Where is China's manufacturing industry going?". Deloitte China Manufacturing Competitiveness Study 2011.

Devaraj, S., D. G. Hollingworth, and R. G. Schroeder. 2004. "Generic Manufacturing Strategies and Plant Performance." *Journal of Operations Management* 22 (3): 313–333. doi:10.1016/j.jom.2004.03.001.

Díaz-Díaz, N. L., I. Aguiar-Díaz, and P. De Saá-Pérez. 2008. "The Effect of Technological Knowledge Assets on Performance: The Innovative Choice in Spanish Firms." *Research Policy* 37 (9): 1515–1529. doi:10.1016/j.respol.2008.06.002.

Drejer, A. 1997. "The Discipline of Management of Technology, Based on Considerations Related to Technology." *Technovation* 17 (5): 253–265. doi:10.1016/S0166-4972(96)00107-1.

Florin, J., M. Lubatkin, and W. Schulze. 2003. "A Social Capital Model of High-Growth Ventures." *Academy of Management Journal* 46 (3): 374–384. doi:10.2307/30040630.

Frankort, H. T. W. 2016. "When Does Knowledge Acquisition in R&D Alliances Increase New Product Development? The Moderating Roles of Technological Relatedness and Product-Market Competition." *Research Policy* 45 (1): 291–302. doi:10.1016/j.respol.2015.10.007.

Gaimon, C. 2008. "The Management of Technology: A Production and Operations Management Perspective." *Production and Operations Management* 17 (1): 1–11. doi:10.3401/poms.1070.0007.

Gaimon, C., M. Hora, and K. Ramachandran. 2017. "Towards Building Multidisciplinary Knowledge on Management of Technology: An Introduction to the Special Issue." *Production and Operations Management* 26 (4): 567–578. doi:10.1111/poms.12644.

Gao, J., Y. L. Yao, V. C. Y. Zhu, L. Y. Sun, and L. Lin. 2011. "Service-Oriented Manufacturing: A New Product Pattern and Manufacturing Paradigm." *Journal of Intelligent Manufacturing* 22 (3): 435–446. doi:10.1007/s10845-009-0301-y.

Gebauer, H., A. Gustafsson, and L. Witell. 2011. "Competitive Advantage Through Service Differentiation by Manufacturing Companies." *Journal of Business Research* 64 (12): 1270–1280. doi:10.1016/j.jbusres.2011.01.015.

Gebauer, H., G. J. Ren, A. Valtakoski, and J. Reynoso. 2012. "Service-Driven Manufacturing: Provision, Evolution and Financial Impact of Services in Industrial Firms." *Journal of Service Management* 23 (1): 120–136. doi:10.1108/09564231211209005.

Gregory, M. J., D. R. Probert, and D. R. Cowell. 1996. "Auditing Technology Management Processes." *International Journal of Technology Management* 12 (3): 306–319. doi:10.1504/IJTM.1996.025497.

Guan, J. C., C. K. Mok, R. C. M. Yam, K. S. Chin, and K. F. Pun. 2006. "Technology Transfer and Innovation Performance: Evidence from Chinese Firms." *Technological Forecasting and Social Change* 73 (6): 666–678. doi:10.1016/j.techfore.2005.05.009.

Harman, H. H. 1967. *Modern Factor Analysis*. Chicago: University of Chicago Press.

Hitt, M. A., R. E. Hoskisson, and H. Kim. 1997. "International Diversification: Effects on Innovation and Firm Performance in Product-Diversified Firms." *Academy of Management Journal* 40 (4): 767–798. doi:10.2307/256948.

Hsu, Y. H., and W. Fang. 2009. "Intellectual Capital and New Product Development Performance: The Mediating Role of Organizational Learning Capability." *Technological Forecasting and Social Change* 76 (5): 664–677. doi:10.1016/j.techfore.2008.03.012.

Huikkola, T., J. Ylimäki, and M. Kohtamäki. 2013. "Joint Learning in R&D Collaborations and the Facilitating Relational Practices." *Industrial Marketing Management* 42 (7): 1167–1180. doi:10.1016/j.indmarman.2013.07.002.

Inkpen, A. C., and E. W. K. Tsang. 2005. "Social Capital, Networks, and Knowledge Transfer." *Academy of Management Review* 30 (1): 146–165. doi:10.5465/AMR.2005.15281445.

Jeong, I., J. H. Pae, and D. S. Zhou. 2006. "Antecedents and Consequences of the Strategic Orientations in New Product Development: The Case of Chinese Manufacturers." *Industrial Marketing Management* 35 (3): 348–358. doi:10.1016/j.indmarman.2005.06.010.

Kapoor, R., and R. Adner. 2012. "What Firms Make vs. What They Know: How Firms' Production and Knowledge Boundaries Affect Competitive Advantage in the Face of Technological Change." *Organization Science* 23 (5): 1227–1248. doi:10.1287/orsc.1110.0686.

Kim, N., and K. Atuahene-Gima. 2010. "Using Exploratory and Exploitative Market Learning for New Product Development." *Journal of Product Innovation Management* 27: 519–536. doi:10.1111/j.1540-5885.2010.00733.x.

Kim, N., S. Im, and S. F. Slater. 2013. "Impact of Knowledge Type and Strategic Orientation on New Product Creativity and Advantage in High-Technology Firms." *Journal of Product Innovation Management* 30 (1): 136–153. doi:10.1111/j.1540-5885.2012.00992.x.

Kim, N., S. Shin, and S. Min. 2016. "Strategic Marketing Capability: Mobilizing Technological Resources for New Product Advantage." *Journal of Business Research* 69 (12): 5644–5652. doi:10.1016/j.jbusres.2016.03.072.

Kostoff, R. N. 2012. "Literature-Related Discovery and Innovation – Update." *Technological Forecasting and Social Change* 79 (4): 789–800. doi:10.1016/j.techfore.2012.02.002.

Kotabe, M., C. X. W. Jiang, and J. Y. Murray. 2011. "Managerial Ties, Knowledge Acquisition, Realized Absorptive Capacity and New Product Market Performance of Emerging Multinational Companies: A Case of China." *Journal of World Business* 46 (2): 166–176. doi:10.1016/j.jwb.2010.05.005.

Krause, D. R., R. B. Handfield, and B. B. Tyler. 2007. "The Relationships Between Supplier Development, Commitment, Social Capital Accumulation and Performance Improvement." *Journal of Operations Management* 25 (2): 528–545. doi:10.1016/j.jom.2006.05.007.

Kwon, S. W., and P. S. Adler. 2014. "Social Capital: Maturation of a Field of Research." *Academy of Management Review* 39 (4): 412–422. doi:10.5465/amr.2014.0210.

Landry, R., N. Amara, M. Lamari. 2002. "Does Social Capital Determine Innovation? To What Extent?" *Technological Forecasting and Social Change* 69 (7): 681–701. doi:10.1016/S0040-1625(01)00170-6.

Lazzarotti, V., R. Manzini, and L. Mari. 2011. "A Model for R&D Performance Measurement." *International Journal of Production Economics* 134 (1): 212–223. doi:10.1016/j.ijpe.2011.06.018.

Leiponen, A., and C. E. Helfat. 2010. "Innovation Objectives, Knowledge Sources, and the Benefits of Breadth." *Strategic Management Journal* 31 (2): 224–236. doi:10.1002/smj.807.

Levin, D. Z., and H. Barnard. 2008. "Technology Management Routines that Matter Technology Managers." *International Journal of Technology Management* 41 (1–2): 228–237. doi:10.1504/IJTM.2008.015982.

Li, L. 2013. "The Path to Made-in-China: How this was Done and Future Prospects." *International Journal of Production Economics* 146 (1): 4–13. doi:10.1016/j.ijpe.2013.05.022i.

Li, Q., P. Maggitti, K. Smith, P. Tesluk, and R. Katila. 2012. "Top Management Attention to Innovation: The Role of Search Selection and Intensity in New Product Introductions." *Academy of Management Journal* 56 (3): 893–916. doi:10.5465/amj.2010.0844.

Li, Y., H. Chen, Y. Liu, and M. W. Peng. 2014. "Managerial Ties, Organizational Learning, and Opportunity Capture: A Social Capital Perspective." *Asia Pacific Journal of Management* 31 (1): 271–291. doi:10.1007/s10490-012-9330-8.

Lin, Y., S. Pekkarinen, and S. Ma. 2015. "Service-Dominant Logic for Managing the Logistics-Manufacturing Interface: A Case Study." *The International Journal of Logistics Management* 26 (1): 195–214. doi:10.1108/IJLM-08-2013-0095.

Liu, P. L., W. C. Chen, and C. H. Tsai. 2005. "An Empirical Study on the Correlation Between the Knowledge Management Method and NPD Strategy on Product Performance in Taiwan's Industries." *Technovation* 25 (6): 637–644. doi:10.1016/j.technovation.2003.11.001.

Lourdes Sosa, M. 2013. "Decoupling Market Incumbency from Organizational Prehistory: Locating the Real Sources of Competitive Advantage in R&D for Radical Innovation." *Strategic Management Journal* 34 (2): 245–255. doi:10.1002/smj.2012.

Ma, Z., M. Yu, C. Gao, J. Zhou, and Z. Yang. 2015. "Institutional Constraints of Product Innovation in China: Evidence from International Joint Ventures." *Journal of Business Research* 68 (5): 949–956. doi:10.1016/j.jbusres.2014.09.022.

Manning, P. 2010. "Explaining and Developing Social Capital for Knowledge Management Purposes." *Journal of Knowledge Management* 14 (1): 83–99. doi:10.1108/13673271011015589.

Martín-de Castro, G., M. Delgado-Verde, J. E. Navas-López, and J. Cruz-González. 2013. "The Moderating Role of Innovation Culture in the Relationship Between Knowledge Assets and Product Innovation." *Technological Forecasting and Social Change* 80 (2): 351–363. doi:10.1016/j.techfore.2012.08.012.

Martínez-Cañas, R., F. J. Sáez-Martínez, and P. Ruiz-Palomino. 2012. "Knowledge Acquisition's Mediation of Social Capital-Firm Innovation." *Journal of Knowledge Management* 16 (1): 61–76. doi:10.1108/13673271211198945.

Matsui, Y., R. Filippini, H. Kitanaka, and O. Sato. 2007. "A Comparative Analysis of New Product Development by Italian and Japanese Manufacturing Companies: A Case Study." *International Journal of Production Economics* 110 (1–2): 16–24. doi:10.1016/j.ijpe.2007.02.007.

Maurer, I., V. Bartsch, and M. Ebers. 2011. "The Value of Intra-organizational Social Capital: How it Fosters Knowledge Transfer, Innovation Performance, and Growth." *Organization Studies* 32 (2): 157–185. doi:10.1177/0170840610394301.

Maurer, I., and M. Ebers. 2006. "Dynamics of Social Capital and Their Performance Implications: Lessons from Biotechnology Start-ups." *Administrative Science Quarterly* 51 (2): 262–292. doi:10.2189/asqu.51.2.262.

McFadyen, M. A., and A. A. Cannella. 2004. "Social Capital and Knowledge Creation: Diminishing Returns of the Number And Strength of Exchange Relationships." *Academy of Management Journal* 47 (5): 735–746. doi:10.2307/20159615.

Molina-Morales, F. X., and M. T. Martínez-Fernández. 2010. "Social Networks: Effects of Social Capital on Firm Innovation." *Journal of Small Business Management* 48 (2): 258–279. doi:10.1111/j.1540-627X.2010.00294.x.

Motohashi, K., and X. Yun. 2007. "China's Innovation System Reform and Growing Industry and Science Linkages." *Research Policy* 36 (8): 1251–1260. doi:10.1016/j.respol.2007.02.023.

Nguyen, B., J. Chen, and D. De Cremer. 2017. "When New Product Development Fails in China: Mediating Effects of Voice Behaviour and Learning from Failure." *Asia Pacific Business Review* 23 (4): 559–575. doi:10.1080/13602381.2017.1339455.

Oerlemans, L. A. G., J. Knoben, and M. W. Pretorius. 2013. "Alliance Portfolio Diversity, Radical and Incremental Innovation: The Moderating Role of Technology Management." *Technovation* 33 (6–7): 234–246. doi:10.1016/j.technovation.2013.02.004.

Pérez-Luño, A., C. C. Cabello Medina, A. C. Carmona Lavado, and G. C. Cuevas Rodríguez. 2011. "How Social Capital and Knowledge Affect Innovation." *Journal of Business Research* 64 (12): 1369–1376. doi:10.1016/j.jbusres.2011.01.014.

Phaal, R., C. J. Paterson, and D. R. Probert. 1998. "Technology Management in Manufacturing Business: Process and Practical Assessment." *Technovation* 18 (8): 541–589. doi:10.1016/S0166-4972(98)00026-1.

Phaal, R., C. Farrukh, and D. R. Probert. 2013. *Technology Management and Roadmapping at the Firm Level*. Berlin Heidelberg: Springer.

Prabhu, J. C., R. K. Chandy, and M. E. Ellis. 2005. "The Impact of Acquisitions on Innovation: Poison Pill, Placebo, or Tonic?" *Journal of Marketing* 69 (1): 114–130. doi:10.1509/jmkg.69.1.114.55514.

Prashantham, S., and C. Dhanaraj. 2010. "The Dynamic Influence of Social Capital on the International Growth of New Ventures." *Journal of Management Studies* 47 (6): 967–994. doi:10.1111/j.1467-6486.2009.00904.x.

Rauniar, R., and G. Rawski. 2012. "Organizational Structuring and Project Team Structuring in Integrated Product Development Project." *International Journal of Production Economics* 135 (2): 939–952. doi:10.1016/j.ijpe.2011.11.009.

Redding, G. 2005. "The Thick Description and Comparison of Societal Systems of Capitalism." *Journal of International Business Studies* 36 (2): 123–155. doi:10.1057/palgrave.jibs.8400129.

Rowley, C., and G. Redding. 2014. "Building Human and Social Capital in Pacific Asia." *Asia Pacific Business Review* 18 (3): 295–301. doi:10.1080/13602381.2011.591655.

Rowley, C., and W. Harry. 2010. *Managing People Globally: An Asian Perspective*. Oxford: Chandos Publishing.

Santamaría, L., M. J. Jesús Nieto, and I. Miles. 2012. "Service Innovation in Manufacturing Firms: Evidence from Spain." *Technovation* 32 (2): 144–155. doi:10.1016/j.technovation.2011.08.006.

Shehabuddeen, N., D. Probert, and R. Phaal. 2006. "From Theory to Practice: Challenges in Operationalising a Technology Selection Framework." *Technovation* 26 (3): 324–335. doi:10.1016/j.technovation.2004.10.017.

Sherman, J. D., D. Berkowitz, and W. E. Souder. 2005. "New Product Development Performance and the Interaction of Cross-Functional Integration and Knowledge Management." *Journal of Product Innovation Management* 22 (5): 399–411. doi:10.1111/j.1540-5885.2005.00137.x.

Song, X. M., and M. E. Parry. 1997. "A Cross-National Comparative Study of New Product Development Processes: Japan and the United States." *Journal of Marketing* 61 (2): 1–18. doi:10.2307/1251827.

Souder, W. E. 1988. "Managing Relations Between R&D and Marketing in New Product Development Projects." *Journal of Product Innovation Management* 5 (1): 6–19. doi:10.1016/0737-6782(88)90029-X.

Sun, P. Y., and M. H. Anderson. 2010. "An Examination of the Relationship Between Absorptive Capacity and Organizational Learning, and a Proposed Integration." *International Journal of Management Reviews* 12 (2): 130–150. doi:10.1111/j.1468-2370.2008.00256.x.

Suseno, Y., and A. H. Pinnington. 2018. "The Significance of Human Capital and Social Capital: Professional–Client Relationships in the Asia Pacific." *Asia Pacific Business Review* 24 (1): 72–89. doi:10.1080/13602381.2017.1281641.

Suseno, Y., and A. H. Pinnington. 2017. "Building Social Capital and Human Capital for Internationalization: The Role of Network Ties and Knowledge Resources." *Asia Pacific Journal of Management*. https://link.springer.com/article/10.1007/s10490-017-9541-0.

Swan, K. S., and B. B. Allred. 2003. "A Product and Process Model of the Technology-Sourcing Decision." *Journal of Product Innovation Management* 20 (6): 485–496. doi:10.1111/1540-5885.00044.

Tao, F., Y. Cheng, L. Zhang, and A. Y. Nee. 2017. "Advanced Manufacturing Systems: Socialization Characteristics and Trends." *Journal of Intelligent Manufacturing* 28 (5): 1079–1094. doi:10.1007/s10845-015-1042-8.

Wang, W. P. 2009. "Evaluating New Product Development Performance by Fuzzy Linguistic Computing." *Expert Systems with Applications* 36 (6): 9759–9766. doi:10.1016/j.eswa.2009.02.034.

Wu, W. P. 2008. "Dimensions of Social Capital and Firm Competitiveness Improvement: The Mediating Role of Information Sharing." *Journal of Management Studies* 45 (1): 122–146. doi:10.1111/j.1467-6486.2007.00741.x.

Wu, W. W., T. Li, B. Yu, and J. Wang. 2014. "Technological Capability and Technology Management: Which Dominates the Development of China's Telecommunications Industry?" *Chinese Management Studies* 8 (2): 180–200. doi:10.1108/CMS-02-2014-0019.

Wu, W. W., D. P. Liang, B. Yu, and Y. Yang. 2010. "Strategic Planning for Management of Technology of China's High Technology Enterprises." *Journal of Technology Management in China* 5 (1): 6–25. doi:10.1108/17468771011032769.

Wu, W. W., Y. X. Liu, and B. Yu. 2016. "Technology Management for New Product Development." *Diversity of Managerial Perspectives from Inside China*, 129–145. Singapore: Springer.

Wu, W. W., B. Yu, and C. Wu. 2012. "How China's Equipment Manufacturing Firms Achieve Successful Independent Innovation: The Double Helix Mode of Technological Capability and Technology Management." *Chinese Management Studies* 6 (1): 160–183. doi:10.1108/17506141211213915.

Yli-Renko, H., E. Autio, and H. J. Sapienza. 2001. "Social Capital, Knowledge Acquisition, and Knowledge Exploitation in Young Technology-Based Firms." *Strategic Management Journal* 22 (6–7): 587–613.

Zaefarian, G., S. Forkmann, M. Mitręga, and S. C. Henneberg. 2017. "A Capability Perspective on Relationship Ending and Its Impact on Product Innovation Success and Firm Performance." *Long Range Planning* 50 (2): 184–199. doi:10.1016/j.lrp.2015.12.023.

Zahra, S. A. 2010. "Harvesting Family Firms' Organizational Social Capital: A Relational Perspective." *Journal of Management Studies* 47 (2): 345–366. doi:10.1111/j.1467-6486.2009.00894.x.

Zhen, L. 2012. "An Analytical Study on Service-Oriented Manufacturing Strategies." *International Journal of Production Economics* 139 (1): 220–228. doi:10.1016/j.ijpe.2012.04.010.

Beyond 'know-what' and 'know-how' to 'know-who': enhancing human capital with social capital in an Australian start-up accelerator

Pi-Shen Seet, Janice Jones, Lloyd Oppelaar and Graciela Corral de Zubielqui

ABSTRACT

This study investigates the enhancement of human capital with social capital in a start-up accelerator and how this integration affects the entrepreneurial learning experience. In particular, it examines the relative importance of the three components 'know-what', 'know-how' and 'know-who'. The study involved thematic analysis of semi-structured interviews with participants in an Australian start-up accelerator that is delivered using ideas such as Design Thinking, the Business Model Canvas and Lean Start-up methodology. We find that although the programme emphasised 'know-what' and 'know-how', 'know-who' was most significant for participant learning. The results indicate that mentors and experts were especially helpful in shaping learning and in developing entrepreneurial networks. Moreover, our results show that the processes of 'know-what', 'know-how' and 'know-who' are interrelated – by knowing 'who', participants learnt 'what' and 'how to' through social learning. The research contributes to entrepreneurial learning theory and application particularly in the Asia Pacific context, by providing evidence that 'know-who' closes the learning loop for 'know-what' and 'know-how' as 'know-who' can actually provide entrepreneurs with the means to enhance their entrepreneurial self-efficacy.

Introduction

Given the rapid increase in start-ups and venture capital in recent times, there has been an emergence of new entities in entrepreneurial ecosystems that try to offer services to help budding and new entrepreneurs (Miller and Bound 2011). One of these entities is the start-up accelerator, also referred to as a start-up factory (Miller and Bound 2011) or seed accelerator (Hochberg 2016), which is an organization that delivers entrepreneurial education programmes and other start-up support and networking services to help entrepreneurs rapidly learn the lessons and avoid mistakes of managing and growing start-ups, especially in the early stages of venture development. However, while start-up accelerators have received much attention, they have received little research scrutiny (Hathaway 2016). Furthermore, they are often misunderstood or mistakenly grouped with other entities that work with early stage ventures (e.g. incubators, angels, and early stage venture capitalists). Yet, unlike incubators and providers of formal entrepreneurship education courses, start-up accelerators do not just focus on providing entrepreneurship education or low-cost infra-structure. They also aim to accelerate enterprises by integrating nascent entrepreneurs and start-ups into a network or ecosystem.

Building on rapid growth of start-up accelerators in the USA like Y Combinator and AngelPad which helped accelerate the growth of companies like AirBnB, Dropbox, Postmates and Vungle, other countries in the world have quickly adopted the accelerator model (Sepulveda 2012; Stross 2013). In the Asia Pacific region, Australia was an early adopter of the start-up accelerator model with the Melbourne Accelerator Programme that started in 2010. By 2017, there were about 30 start-up accelerators across different states, with a num-ber starting overseas branches in cities around the Asia Pacific region (Bliemel et al. 2016). Recognizing the need for SME and start-up development, in the 2012 APEC Leaders' Declaration, APEC leaders endorsed the APEC Start-up Accelerator (ASA) initiative which facilitates member countries to establish platforms for building capacities for start-ups and young entrepreneurs (Shen 2014). Since then, as part of the ASA initiative, APEC member states have been active in hosting various start-up activities, like Chinese Taipei (APEC Start-up Accelerator Leadership Summit), Indonesia (Seminar on the Dynamics of SME), Malaysia (Global Entrepreneurship Summit), Peru (Start-up APEC Conference II), Russia (Young Entrepreneurship Network) and Korea (APEC Start-up Conference) (Shen 2014).

In the Asia Pacific, start-up accelerators have been especially helpful in complementing other entrepreneurship education and development initiatives. For example, Malaysia launched its Higher Education Institute Entrepreneurship Foundation (HEIEF) in 2010 to create high-quality talent with the intellectual attributes and entrepreneurship values required to achieve its New Economy Model by 2020 (MOHE 2010). Although start-up accel-erators only began supplementing other entrepreneurship education programmes and incubator facilities from about 2012 onwards, this has helped contribute to university grad-uates engaging directly with entrepreneurial activities with 1114 graduates in 2011 growing to 1273 in 2012 and accelerating to 2387 in 2013, and 4060 in 2014 (Othman and Nasrudin 2016). Similarly, it is estimated that the number of students exposed to entrepreneurship knowledge and skills development through structured programmes had increased by 30 per cent in 2014 (Norfadhilah 2014). Thus, start-up accelerators are vital in supporting entre-preneurship for economic growth, which is particularly important to sustain the economic sustainability of the Asia Pacific region.

The rapid proliferation of start-up accelerators has also meant that they are viewed by other industries as organizations to learn from. In particular, accelerators have been seen as a means for some industries that are seeking to transform themselves, for example, the manufacturing sector in their efforts to transition to servitization by innovating capabilities and processes to shift from selling products to selling integrated products and services that deliver value in use. In this way, industries are transformed to be more service-oriented in order to capture more value from the value chain (Baines et al. 2009; Lightfoot, Baines, and

Smart 2013). The emphasis of servitization is on leveraging on the knowledge or intellectual capital among manufacturers which forms the basis of significant potential value. It is also to develop innovative business models, enabling companies to move up the value chain and exploit higher value business activities (Roos, Bainbridge, and Jacobsen 2001; Roos, Pike, and Fernstrom 2005). Setting up their service divisions as spin-offs based on models of start-up accelerators has enabled many manufacturing firms to rapidly transform into servitization (Roos 2012, 2015), which is important in the increasingly competitive market.

Since the 1990s, organizations that deliver entrepreneurship education have grown in number, size and scope in Australia (Daly 2013) and also globally. Many of these programmes use a variety of pedagogical techniques to teach participating entrepreneurs a broad spectrum of content (Maritz and Brown 2013) despite little evidence on the efficacy of these programmes (Kuratko 2005; Rae 2012). The result is that such programmes may confuse potential entrepreneurs and negatively affect the overall impact of entrepreneurship education (Pittaway and Cope 2007). Consequently, the majority of the organizations offering these programmes may do nothing to enhance entrepreneurship skills and motivation (O'Connor 2013). Furthermore, there is a lack of consensus as to what, if any, course or training components are most effective in providing for entrepreneurial learning, in this emerging field (Alberti, Sciascia, and Poli 2004; Solomon, Duffy, and Tarabishy 2002). Furthermore, most entrepreneurship education courses tend to educate 'about' entrepreneurship rather than educating 'for' entrepreneurship (Kirby 2004). Therefore, our research is intended to contribute to a better understanding of entrepreneurship education in the context of start-up accelerators in terms of what should be taught and how it can be better delivered (Alberti, Sciascia, and Poli 2004; Gibb and Cotton 1998; Matlay 2009; Pittaway and Cope 2007; Bygrave 1993).

It is the ability to combine the learning components from a properly delivered entrepreneurship education programme with appropriate mentoring and relevant industry connections that purportedly help these start-up accelerators not only incubate new entrepreneurs but actually accelerate their development. In so doing, start-up accelerators attempt to combine the three components of entrepreneurial learning that Gibb (1993, 1997) has labelled 'know-what', 'know-how' and 'know-who'. 'Know-what' and 'know-how' can be understood in terms of developing knowledge and experience, important aspects of human capital. 'Know-who' can be understood in terms of developing ties or networks, which is an aspect of social capital. Research on the relationship between management and organizational performance has found that effective practices centre around the ability to integrate development of human capital (skills, experience and knowledge of employees) (Lepak and Snell 1999) with that of social capital (knowledge that exists in groups and networks) (Sung-Choon, Morris, and Snell 2007).

Therefore, the objective of this study is to examine the nature of entrepreneurial learning in terms of the extent to which they develop human capital ('know-what' and 'know-how') and social capital ('know-who') in start-up accelerators that offer a unique entrepreneurship learning experience that combines formal entrepreneurship education with other components like mentoring. The research contributes to previous literature by exploring two major dimensions of the 'black box': (1) how human capital is developed, by examining what content is taught and what processes are used in the entrepreneurship education component of start-up accelerators, and (2) if and how social capital adds value to the process of entrepreneurial learning. This is especially relevant in the Asia-Pacific context in response to calls for more research into these aspects (Redding and Rowley 2017) whereby both human capital and social capital play important roles in the business systems by working together to achieve something greater than the sum of the individual components (Redding and Rowley 2017).

Thus, while much of the research examining human capital and social capital in entrepreneurship education in the Asia Pacific region is limited by the use of student samples (Sun et al. 2017), this research contributes to entrepreneurial learning theory by providing evidence that social capital or 'know-who' is just as important as the human capital development aspects of 'know-what' and 'know-how'. This is because 'know-who' can provide nascent entrepreneurs with the means to better access 'know-what' and 'know-how' (Gibb 1997) to accelerate growth in their start-up ventures.

We find that although the emphasis of the programme was on the human capital aspects of 'know-what' (e.g. rapid prototyping) and 'know-how' (e.g. how to develop a business model), the participants found that the 'know-who' or social capital component was most significant in their learning. Furthermore, our results show that 'know-what', 'know-how' and 'know-who' are interrelated – by knowing 'who', participants learnt 'what' and 'how to'. In particular, mentors and experts were able to help improve entrepreneurial learning by integrating classroom-based content with real-world connections and networks.

Literature review

Start-up accelerators and entrepreneurship education

Start-up accelerators offer limited duration (about three months on average) cohort-based programmes that incorporate entrepreneurship education programmes and mentorship which conclude with a 'demo day' where the entrepreneurs pitch to groups of qualified investors or the public (Hochberg 2016). While they are similar to traditional business incubators, their fixed duration nature combined with intensive entrepreneurship education programmes and mentorship is claimed to develop ventures that survive better outside of an incubator environment (Cohen 2013). Table 1 below summarizes the difference between start-up accelerators and incubators (Cohen 2013).

Much of the formal knowledge and expertise in start-up accelerators is delivered through structured entrepreneurship education programmes by mainly experienced entrepreneurs to the members of the accelerators (Fishback et al. 2007; Radojevich-Kelley and Hoffman 2012). Fayolle, Gailly, and Lassas-Clerc (2006, 702) defined entrepreneurship education programmes as 'any pedagogical program or process of education for entrepreneurial attitudes and skills, which involves developing personal qualities'. However, following the lessons of the bursting of the dot-com bubble in the early 2000s, which were reinforced in the Global Financial Crisis in 2007, there was a realization of a need to move beyond pedagogy to include more mentoring and guidance for nascent ventures, with the intention of reducing high failure rates (O'Connell 2011).

Table 1. Start-up accelerators vs. traditional incubators.

	Start-up accelerators	Incubators
Duration	Fixed short term (3 months average)	Fixed long term (1–5 years)
Selection	Competitive, cyclical	Non-competitive
Education	Formal	Ad hoc
Mentorship	Intense, by self and others	Minimal, as needed

Start-up accelerators adopted this approach whereby 'their primary goal is to increase the quantity and quality of entrepreneurs, influence entrepreneurial behaviour, entrepreneurial tendency and entrepreneurial outcomes' (Matlay 2009, 382). Besides formal mentoring, start-up accelerators also offer many (planned and unplanned) networking opportunities for participants, including with peers and mentors, who might be successful entrepreneurs, graduates of the accelerator, early stage investors or even corporate executives (Cohen 2013; Miller and Bound 2011). Start-up accelerators aim to increase both the quantity and quality of entrepreneurs in the ecosystem by attracting and motivating potential entrepreneurs and by influencing their behaviour (what they do and how they do it) through the development of both human capital and social capital.

However, Maritz and Brown (2013) and Cohen (2013) lament that despite the proliferation of start-up accelerators and entrepreneurship education providers, little is known about what is actually learnt in these programmes and how effective the teaching or delivery of these initiatives are. They call for research into the 'illumination of the black box of entrepreneurship education programs' and a better understanding of the interrelated parts of learning on these programmes and the relationships between them. This gap is not new: more than a decade previously, Gibb and Cotton (1998) argued that there was considerable conceptual confusion regarding what entrepreneurship education is e.g. what it does and should teach, how it should teach it and what it aims to and accomplishes. Little has explored on this aspect since the early study by Gibb and Cotton (1998), particularly in the context of start-up accelerators the Asia Pacific region.

Human capital and the development of 'know-what' and 'know-how'

Human capital theory suggests that organizations with more human capital (i.e. the combination of knowledge, skills and abilities of human resources) will generally secure superior outcomes (Becker 1964; Hatch and Dyer 2004), especially when the organization's focus is on innovation (Felício, Couto, and Caiado 2014). In the context of highly knowledge-intensive and competitive industries, it has been argued that these human capital elements are especially significant for start-ups and smaller firms as they provide the overall intellectual capital that enable them to sustain their competitive advantage (Youndt, Subramaniam, and Snell 2004). However, how human capital contributes to the process of innovation has eluded most researchers (Marvel and Lumpkin 2007) with a lack of research especially in understanding this phenomenon among new ventures (Freel 2005).

Two key characteristics, knowledge and experience, underpin human capital theory (Becker 1964). Cater and Cater (2009) found that human capital was a factor that explained performance differences in firms in general but most studies have found that this was especially more pronounced among smaller and newer firms. Shrader and Siegel (2007)'s longitudinal study of high-technology ventures found that for small, technology-based new ventures, human capital in the form of the quality of employees was the most important determinant for success because employees with more human capital (i.e. more education and experience) help firms implement new technologies more effectively (Wright et al. 2007). In terms of innovation, many researchers argue that human capital may play an even larger role in the future because of the rapidly increasing knowledge-intensive activities (Bosma et al. 2004; Tharenou and Seet 2014; Corral Corral de Zubielqui et al. 2015; Jones and Corral de Zubielqui 2017; Honig 2001).

In a comprehensive meta-analysis of research spanning three decades on the relationship between human capital and entrepreneurial success, Unger et al. (2011) find a significant but small relationship between human capital and success, especially among smaller and younger firms. In particular, they found that the relationship was higher for knowledge/skills as compared to experience and suggest that there seems to be a bias in existing research which focuses mainly on the management competencies and experience of the lead entrepreneur (Zacharakis and Dale Meyer 2000). They also pointed to the need to move away from the individual level of understanding the relationship of human capital to outcomes, and to shift research on human capital away from a static view of entrepreneurship to a process view. In terms of skills, there is a need to 'explicate the processes that lead to acquisition of knowledge and skills' (Unger et al. 2011, 353). Some researchers have begun responding to this, for example, in the understanding of the effect of entrepreneurship education on innovation and other outcomes (Martin, McNally, and Kay 2013). Our research responds to that call by moving beyond merely content learning to understanding how some of the newer delivery techniques will help in the human capital development process of participants in start-up accelerators.

'Know-what' and 'know-how' as important aspects of entrepreneurial learning capture the human capital development component of what knowledge participants actually learn or receive from entrepreneurship education. However, unlike formal education, there is little uniformity in entrepreneurship education offerings; this is commonly considered to be related to the fact that entrepreneurship is an emerging field (Alberti, Sciascia, and Poli 2004; Solomon, Duffy, and Tarabishy 2002). It is recognized that most entrepreneurship education courses educate 'about' entrepreneurship rather than educating 'for' entrepreneurship (Kirby 2004). Only rarely do they focus on developing the skills, attributes and behaviour of the successful entrepreneur (Alberti, Sciascia, and Poli 2004). While they have the roots mainly in North America and Europe, these approaches are also generalizable to the Asia Pacific context as they share a 'common quest' of creating entrepreneurs (Kelley and Thomas 2011). In light of this, the study takes the definition offered by (Alberti, Sciascia, and Poli 2004, 7) that content learning is 'any form of knowledge or education offered by the program pertaining to both "about" and "for" entrepreneurship, that is the teaching of theory, history, skills, attributes and behaviour'.

The content of formal entrepreneurship education can be divided into two forms: traditional and contemporary. Traditional methods generally refer to a more analytical and prescriptive approach to entrepreneurship whereas contemporary methods refer to a more design and experientially based approach (Nielsen and Pia 2015; Osterwalder 2004). Table 2 summarizes the traditional components of 'know-what' and 'know-how' in entrepreneurship education. We briefly outline these traditional components – entrepreneurial self-efficacy (ESE), skills and finance – below.

Self-efficacy refers to 'people's beliefs about their capabilities to exercise control over their own activities and over events that affect their lives' (Bandura 1991, 257). One focus of many providers of entrepreneurship education traditionally has been to try to change the beliefs and attitudes of the entrepreneurs towards such behaviour and finally developing their self-efficacy or belief that they could do or master the behaviour that they were required to do (Bandura 1991; Fayolle and Gailly 2008; Rae 2012). Entrepreneurship educators have also

Table 2. Traditional content.

Type	Reference
Entrepreneurial self-efficacy	Bandura (1991)
	Ajzen (1991)
	Fayolle and Gailly (2008)
	Rae (2012)
Entrepreneurial skills	Rondstadt, Vesper, and McMullen (1988)
• Business planning	Hills (1988)
• Business law	Bygrave (1997)
• Marketing	Gibb (1997)
• Production	Rae (1997)
• Product design	Gorman, Hanlon, and King (1997)
	Jack and Anderson (1999)
	Fiet (2001a, 2001b)
	Honig and Karlsson (2004)
	Kuratko (2004, 2005)
Entrepreneurial finance	Ronstadt, Vesper, and McMullan (1988)
	Cohen and Levinthal (1990)
	Shepherd and Zacharakis (2001)
	Kuratko (2005)
	Dimov and Shepherd (2005)
	Rae (2012)

traditionally focused on the development of entrepreneurial skills within the framework of a business plan (Hills 1988; Honig 2004). These skills relate to selling, marketing, developing a customer base, developing a product and areas of business law such as intellectual property and confidentiality (Bygrave 1993; Kuratko 2004; Kuratko 2005; Rae 2012; Ronstadt, Vesper, and McMullan 1988). Among these skills, traditional programmes teach entrepreneurs about entrepreneurial finance, and the need to access financing for ventures (Cohen and Levinthal 1990; Shepherd and Zacharakis 2001; Ronstadt, Vesper, and McMullan 1988).

There have been many limitations discussed in relation to traditional methods of entrepreneurship education including: their inability to enable and prepare the entrepreneur for the speed of change, dynamism, non-sequential nature, unpredictability, complexity and level of technological influence within the entrepreneurial landscape (Neck and Greene 2011). Indeed, traditional methods have not been satisfactory in preparing or providing the entrepreneur with the required skills, behaviours, attitudes and tools to survive in this environment (Fritscher and Pigneur 2009). Neck and Greene (2011) claim that traditional approaches to entrepreneurship education are based on a world of yesterday, a world where precedent was the foundation for future action and where history often did predict the future. Although the core of entrepreneurship is the identification and exploitation of opportunities (Shane and Venkataraman 2000), the majority of providers of entrepreneurship education adopt a more traditional approach and assume the opportunity has already been identified.

'Know-what' and 'know-how': contemporary perspectives

In response to these issues, contemporary methods of entrepreneurship education have been developed that purportedly allow the entrepreneur to be more dynamic in the development of a venture, with the methods enabling increased pivoting, whereby entrepreneurs change directions but stay grounded in what they've learned (Ries 2011) and adapt in the creation phase to make the most of opportunities as they arise and to respond to barriers as they eventuate (Eisenmann, Ries, and Dillard 2012). Contemporary methods have also been developed in order to encompass a greater use of technology and experiential processes to reflect the unpredictable nature of entrepreneurship, equipping and educating the entrepreneur for their industry conditions (Pittaway 2004).

The majority of this new content has typically been centred on Design Thinking (DT), the Business Model Canvas (BMC) and the Lean Start-up Approach (LSA). Table 3 illustrates as the types of contemporary content and the predominant authors who are central to the debate on the merit in providing valuable entrepreneurial learning for entrepreneurs undergoing entrepreneurship education.

DT in entrepreneurship focuses on the reconstruction and solution of problems rather than analysis of the problems (Johansson and Woodilla 2009). DT allows entrepreneurs to exploit opportunities in uncertain environments (Neck and Greene 2011). Building on DT and the lack of consensus within the field as to the legitimacy and benefit of business planning especially after the bursting of the dot-com bubble and the Global Financial Crisis, Osterwalder (2012) developed a more modern approach to business planning in the form of Business Model Ontology. In essence, its development and that of the BMC is an attempt to address the problem that the business planning process is an attractive and powerful learning process, but that a disproportionate amount of time is spent honing secondary research skills rather than actually taking smart action in the real world.

The LSA is very closely related to DT and the BMC and they are usually deployed in unison. The LSA is a hypothesis-driven approach to evaluating entrepreneurial opportunity. Entrepreneurs translate their vision into falsifiable business model hypotheses, then test the hypotheses using a series of 'minimum viable products', each of which represents the smallest set of features/activities needed to rigorously validate a concept (Eisenmann, Ries, and Dillard 2012). Validation is therefore also a key component of the LSA, where the participants develop a minimal viable product and then validate its worth and the various assumptions regarding it. Based on the validation feedback, entrepreneurs must then decide whether to persevere with their business model; 'pivot' by changing some model elements, or abandon the start-up. Figure 1 depicts the relationship between DT, the LSA and the BMC.

Analytical thinking is largely different to DT and is the basis for traditional forms of entrepreneurship education. This is reflected by Brown (2005) who describes that traditionally entrepreneurs are trained to think analytically (like social and natural scientists), suggesting that analytical thinking is good for analysis, cutting things apart and extrapolating and predicting from the past into the future, which is appropriate for approaches such as business planning (Fiet 2001a; Honig 2004). However, Brown (2005) suggests that it is not very good for trying to envision a new future and figuring out a way to change it. He proposes that DT is rooted in optimism, and the goal to get something done and to bring it to the marketplace. However, as illustrated by Figure 1 there is an overlap of analytical thinking and design

Table 3. Contemporary content.

Type	Reference
Design thinking	Neck (2014)
Business model canvas	Osterwalder (2004)
Lean start-up approach	Eisenmann, Ries, and Dillard (2012)
Validation	Rae (2012)

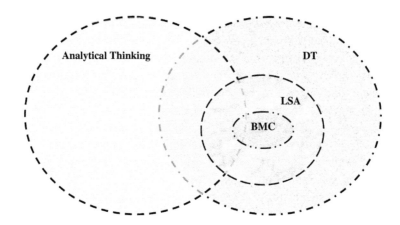

Figure 1. Relationship of contemporary content.

thinking. The LSA and BMC predominantly are based on DT, but also have relationship to analytical thinking. This is evident when comparing the traditional business plan and contemporary BMC; there are inherent similarities and also differences between the two due to one being primarily analytical and the other being primarily design oriented.

However, despite the fact that Design Thinking, the Business Model Canvas and Lean Start-up Approach are becoming increasingly prevalent within entrepreneurship education offerings (Blank 2013; Eisenmann, Ries, and Dillard 2012; Neck and Greene 2011; Osterwalder 2004, 2012), there is very little empirical research investigating their actual value and benefits vis-à-vis traditional content. Therefore, a gap exists in the research to explore the benefit of these contemporary perspectives of 'know-what' and 'know-how' in enhancing entrepreneurial learning, which is what this research aims to address.

Social capital and the development of 'know-who': the missing catalyst

The newer, more contemporary approaches to delivering entrepreneurial learning also move beyond content or traditional human capital development to include networking and other aspects of social capital development (Bridge 2014). An important part of the Lean Start-up Approach is for entrepreneurs to get direct feedback from potential customers or key informants in the value chain, as opposed to traditional means of desktop research or market research surveys. Part of this comes from using networks to 'co-create' new products or services (Zijdemans and Tanev 2014).

Rae (2012) suggests that entrepreneurs who learn how to validate assumptions by reaching out to wider network and gaining feedback from key stakeholders in order to validate the hypothesis and assumptions (e.g. what customers are interested in and prepared to pay for production such as costs and availability and venture management) are relatively more successful in getting started as these assumptions were often found to be over-optimistic and had to be revised.

In entrepreneurship research, the term 'network' generally describes a mix of informal and formal relationships. This includes people and organizations that are linked through formal and social interactions (Kiss and Danis 2008) whereby formal relationships are often underpinned by informal, inter-personal relationships among members of different organizations (Perkmann and Walsh 2007). In the entrepreneurial context, networks allow start-ups to access and utilize external resources to overcome resource constraints so as to better facilitate survival and growth (Madhok 2002; BarNir and Smith 2002), and thereby minimizing some disadvantages of their 'smallness' and 'newness' (Aldrich and Auster 1986; BarNir and Smith 2002). Because of technological developments like the Internet, early stage ventures are increasingly relying on relationships rather than 'arms-length' in transactional market links (Chesbrough 2003; Cooke, Heidenreich, and Braczyk 2004; Seely-Brown and Duguid 2001).

Among entrepreneurs, networks and contacts with other people are social sources of opportunity-relevant information which can then be acted on by the owner-manager (Ozgen and Baron 2007). Social networks have been found to be important in opportunity recognition (Singh 2000) and the larger the entrepreneur's or owner-manager's social networks, the more opportunities they recognize (Dufays and Huybrechts 2014; Singh et al. 1999; Stam, Arzlanian, and Elfring 2014; Greve and Salaff 2003). This is especially relevant in highly communitarian societies in the Asia Pacific region (Ahmad and Seet 2009; Zhao and Lu 2016; Seet 2007).

In spite of the recognition that social capital is an important component in entrepreneurship (Gedajlovic et al. 2013), much of the research in entrepreneurship education has focused on human capital e.g. Business Model Canvas (Breuer 2013) or team learning (Harms 2015). Hence, there is a gap in terms of a deeper understanding of the roles of social capital like mentoring, which this research attempts to contribute to in the context of start-up accelerators.

Research method

The exploratory nature of the study led to a qualitative research design to 'illuminate the black box' of entrepreneurship education by specifically examining in detail the human capital and social capital aspects of entrepreneurial learning within a start-up accelerator that uses contemporary Design Thinking methods. The study used in-depth semi-structured interviews to explore the perceptions and experiences of start-up accelerator participants. The use of in-depth interviews enables a more nuanced exploration of a complex matter (Rubin and Rubin 2011). The opportunity for participants to engage in a discussion with the researcher, and for the researcher to probe responses mean that issues can be explored in detail. It also allows for richer understanding of the delivery of entrepreneurial learning content and this method of data collection is supported by other studies in the field which have used the same collection technique (Sullivan 2000; Man and Lau 2005).

Access to learning blogs that the participants were encouraged to complete was also provided. The purpose of these blogs was to allow the participants to discuss and self-reflect upon what they had learnt in the programme. This provided an additional source of data that facilitated triangulation.

Sample

The sample comprised participants of a start-up accelerator run by a South Australian university that involved both student entrepreneurs and new entrepreneurs from the surrounding council areas. Driven by manufacturing, South Australia – a state in Australia – experienced significant population and economic growth above the national average after the Second World War till the 1970s. However, since then, with the movement of manufacturing offshore (Beer 1998), the shift of 'head office' activity to Melbourne and Sydney (O'Connor and Stimson 1995), the collapse of the South Australian State Bank in the 1990s (Walmsley and Weinand 1997) and the severe nation-wide drought in the 2000s negatively impacting on the driest state in the driest continent (Rutherfurd and Finlayson 2011), and most recently, the closure of manufacturing facilities in the automotive sector (e.g. Mitsubishi and Holden) as well as production/distribution facilities in the retail sector (e.g. Coca Cola), have negatively impact the South Australian economy (Clibborn, Lansbury, and Wright 2016). In 2014, South Australia began focusing on building an entrepreneurial ecosystem as part of its industrial transformation strategy (O'Connor and Reed 2015). Exploratory research mapping the South Australian entrepreneurial ecosystem shows a significant increase in networking and start-up events, co-working spaces, incubators and accelerators (Bliemel et al. 2016). The vibrancy of the entrepreneurial ecosystem in Adelaide, besides creating local impact, has had wider network effects and has led to the assistance of development of accelerators in the Asia Pacific region (e.g. ThincLab Singapore; Lindsay 2012).

Theoretical sampling was used as the goal was not to generalize to the wider population but to theory. The sample was designed to achieve a balance between those who had no experience (students) and those that had some experience (new entrepreneurs). In total, 20 semi-structured interviews of participants were conducted. The interview questions covered the following aspects:

- expectations of entrepreneurs prior to the programme,
- questions relating to what and how they learnt during the programme, and
- questions pertaining to the expectations of the participant being met.

In terms of the learning blogs, only four participants completed them and triangulation was only possible for the results of these four participants.

As can be seen in Table 4, out of the 20 participants interviewed, 14 had completed the programme and 6 were in the final stages of the programme. The sample comprised more males (15 vs. 5 females), which is common in most start-up accelerators and formal entrepreneurship education programmes. For a university-supported start-up accelerator, there was a relatively low number of students in the sample, with there being 15 non-students and 5 students. This is in contrast to the mainstream entrepreneurship education programmes or courses that are run in universities for their students which are made up entirely of university students. This is also in line with the practice that start-up accelerators need to be open to all but at the same time be competitive in terms of entry (Hochberg 2016). Hence, in the selection criteria, applicants, including students, were asked for their motivations for joining the start-up accelerator, with one of the sub-criteria being whether they were planning to start/grow their own ventures. The sample obtained from the start-up accelerator may be more appropriate and reflective of the real world of entrepreneurship whereby the majority of entrepreneurs are not just going to be students from university but people of all different ages from all different avenues of life. The majority of the entrepreneurs were also new entrepreneurs; this was deliberate as the programme chosen was created for nascent or beginner entrepreneurs.

Table 4. Participant profiles.

Participant	Gender	Completed program	Experience
E1	F	Y	No – Student
E2	M	Y	No – Student
E3	F	Y	No
E4	F	Y	No
E5	M	Y	Yes – Founder of previous businesses
E6	M	Y	Medium – Been involved with start-ups
E7	M	Y	Yes – Been involved starting and managing other start-ups
E8	M	Y	No
E9	M	Y	Medium – Run unrelated business
E10	M	Y	Medium – career experience in industry
E11	M	Y	No – Student
E12	M	Y	No
E13	F	Y	No
E14	M	Y	No
E15	M	N – Current	Yes – Manages business and been involved in starting new ventures
E16	M	N – Current	No
E17	M	N – Current	No
E18	F	N – Current	No
E19	M	N – Current	Yes – Started new ventures before
E20	M	N – Current	No

Analysis

Interviews were transcribed and checked for accuracy. As much as possible, interviews were written to a pre-determined structure covering a consistent range of issues to allow easier analysis across interviews. Individual transcripts were initially analysed with themes or patterns coded. Thereafter, these were combined across the entire interview data and overarching themes identified. Coding occurred inductively (Saldana 2009) in order to draw out the main themes and patterns. The findings from the interviews are presented under three headings:

- Know-what: Business Model Canvas;
- Know-how: Lean Start-up Approach; and
- Know-who: Mentors, Experts, Peers, Potential Customers and Key Stakeholders

Discussion of results

Know-what: business model canvas (BMC)

As can be seen from Table 5, much of the content that the participants were looking for when entering the programme was provided by the BMC. As respondent E15 states, the BMC provided a structure and outline for the participants in regard to what they needed to do in order to create a business: 'I found that having something like the Business Model Canvas has given me a framework I can apply on a lot of things, I didn't have the knowledge of how to apply in that specific order or quite so simply.' For example, it taught the participants the need to develop revenue streams, discern partnerships and conduct customer validation.

Participants found that the BMC was actionable and design oriented, enabling the participants to apply or test the various components of their business and adapt these

Table 5. Business model canvas.

Interviewee	Interviewees' quotes
E11	'I have a much broader idea of how it's all going to come together and taking action to pull it about and put it together again.'
E18	'It goes back to that business model canvas, everything within that I am just honing in on and unpacking. You know how to identify the right channels, who the target market is, who they look like, how to personify them, the archetype of that person, linking values to the value proposition and to the customer segment, recognising that there is different customer segments and different revenue models. It's an invaluable process for me.'
E10	'With the business model canvas and going through it in such a formulaic way, each week they'd focus on a particular aspect and the problem with that is that everyone had actually come in to this in varying levels and some people were individuals some people were groups and I had something already developed. So, different people, different points and each week you're expected to do their concentrated on a particular aspect and that didn't match up with everyone.'

components based on the feedback received. Respondent E18 said, 'For me, to be able to do, you know, countless canvasses, it constantly changes depending on who I speak to but it helps me to really understand what my concept [is] so much more, like thoroughly.' It appears to have made the business plan more adaptable to enable entrepreneurs to make the most of opportunities as they arise; it also appears to give a clearer picture of the necessary components of a venture.

Although the majority of the participants found the provision of the BMC to be beneficial, some of the participants found its highly structured approach to be problematic (Table 5). This is evident from respondent E12, who states that 'I already had an idea, I had a business plan and a working prototype so I was further along the path and so the program wasn't entirely geared towards where I was with my project, it was more geared towards somebody at an earlier stage with an idea.' This meant that the BMC may be less applicable to individuals who began the programme further along the entrepreneurial learning process or who had specific, perhaps highly complex areas of particular difficulty, like licensing for example. This may suggest that the BMC is aimed at and more applicable to entrepreneurs who were looking to start or who were at the very beginning of the business creation process, rather than entrepreneurs who already had a product, business or prototype made and functioning.

Know how: lean start-up approach (LSA)

Through the LSA, participants were first taught how to develop a minimal viable product and second, the need to engage with customers and key stakeholders.

As shown in Table 6, learning the need for, and how to develop, a minimal viable product (MVP) provided the entrepreneurs with the ability to more easily move forward and progress the development of their business idea.

Prior to the programme, many participants struggled with the issue of their ideas and proposed businesses being too big, restricting or crippling their development due to cost or complexity. This is reflected in the following quote from participant E8: '... What I had done before the start-up accelerator program was built here, add here and expand it, the next thing, it's unworkable and unmanageable and more importantly not something that you or I could do tomorrow.' The LSA and MVP made the idea or venture actionable, and the

Table 6. Minimal viable product.

Interviewee	Interviewees' quotes
E4	'Definitely the minimum viable product, so that is getting the base idea up and running as quickly as possible so you can get that real world feedback. A lot of people spend a lot of time and money producing something and then they put it out there and it doesn't take. So it is important to get that really simple base idea and get the feedback and work on it and go from there.'
E1	'We realised we had to make it smaller and get our minimal viable product out there and selling it to people, and that wasn't possible with our original idea, it was just way to big and way to complex.'
E5	'The minimal viable product and talking to customers is the core of the lean start-up approach, and then looking at all the different kinds of revenue streams and types of partnerships you can have and the different structures of the company you can have.'

Table 7. Validation.

Interviewee	Interviewees' quotes
E6	'I think the main thing would definitely be a cheaper way to validate the business model. That's the first thing I got, there's a lot of different ways you can find out if the model is right. The second is when I'm starting a business it is all based on assumptions and I need to do validate those assumptions, that is what the EEP taught me.'
E8	'Rather than learning from experience the whole process has been accelerated into 12 weeks and I could validate all assumptions about my business model in 12 weeks.'

participants could actually move forward with its development as they could test it through showing potential customers and stakeholders, and develop it based on this feedback.

Responses also indicate that participants were looking for the programme to teach them how to validate whether or not their idea was a viable business proposition (Table 7). This is illustrated by respondent E13: 'It validated that it was a business idea and program that would or could be successful, it validated for me that I could do it'. Participants also appeared to learn that they needed to and could validate the assumptions they held about their business before actually building the product, as illustrated by respondent E6: 'During the start-up accelerator program I realised that I can actually test all my assumptions and test exactly what customers want before I actually build the product. That was the biggest thing that I took away from the program.'

Know-who: potential customers and key stakeholders

Despite the start-up accelerator focusing on delivering contemporary content, many of the participants highlighted the 'people' aspect of their learning experience, namely their mentors, the experts that were involved in the programme, and the interactions with potential customers and key stakeholders. Many of the participants expressed a feeling of working in isolation prior to the programme and described themselves as having a tendency to ruminate, be indecisive and inactive. The participants identified that their confidence increased during the programme and that they found themselves going to events and talking to people that they would not have done prior to the programme. We examine this theme in more detail below.

Mentors

Mentors were found to be one of the predominant and most beneficial learning outcomes of the programme as well as one of the main processes of learning. The start-up accelerator introduced and connected the participants to mentors that they needed to know and work with, mentors that they would not have had access to, or known how to access outside of the programme.

The participants often described working with or learning from their mentors as the 'best' or 'most valuable' means of learning offered by the programme (Table 8). This value was predominantly derived from the real world experience of the mentors. Respondent E9 demonstrates this point: 'The mentors, having had been very successful in their own businesses have some ideas about what you can and can't do and they straighten you out.' The participants valued the opportunities to ask questions and receive advice based on the prior experience of their mentors.

The second pattern to emerge was the guidance provided by, and the ability of, the mentors in steering participants in the right direction, developing their ESE and helping them to alter their entrepreneurial behaviour. According to respondent E18: 'My mentor has led me to speak to different people which has led to bigger things and people and places and events that I would never have known about if it wasn't for her.' Similarly, respondent E9 states: 'Where the mentors come in really handy is they say, "Look, here is your idea, go see this printer because he will be able to help you with the printing," for instance; or "go see the Harvey World Travel guy because he will be interested in what you are doing."'

Learning through the mentors was also evident as the participants received advice, information, problem solving, feedback, emotional support and further connections to various individuals, groups and activities that they had not known about or had access to prior to the programme and their mentor relationship. This is in line with existing literature by Hegarty (2006) which identifies the advantages of mentorship coming from the knowledge which is derived from being able to ask questions and receive practical advice as well as seeing and hearing someone who has gone through an entrepreneurial process and experienced failures and successes.

Effective mentorship was found to be a key driver in regard to the development of ESE and entrepreneurial behaviour, with mentors being able to provide advice, motivation and emotional support for entrepreneurial risk taking and behaviour (St-Jean and Mathieu 2015; Hoang and Antoncic 2003; Ahsan et al. 2018). The mentors helped develop ESE and change entrepreneurial behaviour by motivating, encouraging and directing the participants, telling them 'to do this', 'go see this person, they may be able to help', 'or go see this person, they will be interested'.

Table 8. Mentors and mentorship.

Interviewee	Interviewees' quotes
E3a	'Making networks and contacts and being able to pick the brains of people who have been there and done that, and getting their insights. That was the most valuable part, people who knew about entrepreneurship and who have been there and were able to give me really sound advice.'
E2	'Mentors that were there or mentors and professionals that were there each week they were probably the key learning resources providing professional experience and advice on problems that we were having.'
E3b	'... Getting onto our personal mentors a lot earlier would have been good as it took a while and the selection of the mentors to match personality as well as the project and the expertise of the mentors ...'

Experts

The start-up accelerator introduced the participants to experts with the knowledge and expertise who could help the participants learn about and perform skills that they were lacking in. This included providing access to law and design students and experts in fields such as marketing, search engine optimization and production, that the participants did not have access to outside of the programme. Many of the participants found this to be one of the most valuable outcomes of the programme.

Prior to the programme, many of the participants stated that they did not know where to begin in looking for this kind of expertise (e.g. who to contact), let alone specifically what they needed to have done, as illustrated in Table 9. Respondent E3 highlights this point:

> There is a lot of basic advice that I got that I didn't know, like starting a website, I didn't know how to do that. There is a lot of things involved that I didn't have or hadn't thought of, I didn't know how or where to start or who to look for. The advice I got on how to do it cheaper and better through getting contacts was all really, really good. I feel like I have contacts and know where to start looking.

This aligns with existing research which find that an effective entrepreneurship education programme should introduce nascent entrepreneurs to people who might be able to facilitate their success, such as expert practitioners (Miles et al. 2017; St-Jean and Mathieu 2015). The participants expressed that this would be an invaluable learning outcome as similar to the mentors, they did not have access to, or know how to access these contacts. The participants were seeking to be connected to 'experts' (St-Jean et al. 2017) who could assist them with the development of a website or logo, the drafting a confidentiality statement, provide them with advice regarding intellectual property, search engine optimization, production, different manufacturing techniques and marketing.

Not only did the experts provide or teach these areas of expertise, they also, in line with research by (Hoang and Antoncic 2003), connected the participants to further networks of skilled individuals that could be of use to the participants and their ventures. The degree of importance and value the participants were discovered to place on these networks provides credence to Gibb (1997) and other research in the Asia Pacific context (Batjargal and Liu 2004; Zhao, Frese, and Giardini 2010) that success in entrepreneurship is dependent not only on knowledge but the network of individuals with whom the entrepreneur is connected.

Although the programme brought in some experts, there was still demand from the participants for the provision of further access to individuals with these particular areas of

Table 9. Experts.

Interviewee	Interviewees' quotes
E10a	'The other thing I found valuable and helpful is that they brought specialists in, for example; in Law or SEO and design. Especially for the people who weren't so techy or design focussed.'
E15	'It's always its good having people there I made some new connections in regard to IP so that's been some really good value and input I've got so far.'
E12	'it was useful in introducing me to a couple useful people in the community that could help with legal matters and that sort of thing which is useful.'
E9	'With the TAFE programs you get some of this MVP happening via website development which is really good. But having said that the process still is very piece mill … … it gets cut off to quickly and you have to hand that process on to another group and it then takes some time for that group to get their head around what they were doing.'
E10b	'… Whereas if this program had a marketing person come in and all those different skill sets and were willing to do that you would actually pump out some teams that would have a bit of sound business knowledge, know how to market, test a product or idea …'

skill, knowledge and expertise. As shown by respondent E12: 'I would have liked more intensive focus on certain things such as exposure to people who assist with registering a trade mark or how to write a contract ... If there had just been a person there who could have sat down and said this is what you need to do to write a privacy policy for your website.'

Peers

The third group of people identified that the participants wanted to be connected to and learn from, were the other participants (Kacperczyk 2013; Sosa 2011). The participants had wanted to work and learn more collaboratively with their fellow participants (Table 10). This is what Lévesque, Minniti, and Shepherd (2009, p 551) defined as collaborative learning, which is 'the process of learning through participation and cooperation with people.' Where this varies from social learning is that it is participative, and not purely observational.

We found that the participants wanted to learn collaboratively and that the use of this learning process would have been an area of significant improvement for the programme. The importance the participants attach to being able to work with other nascent entrepreneurs and learn from them reflects the literature by Pittaway and Cope (2007) who propose that collaborative learning between nascent entrepreneurs can significantly increase their learning and preparedness for the entrepreneurial environment. The reason for this as noted by Clements and Moore (2009), is that it helps participants deal with uncertainty and ambiguity and problems in a real world environment, creating more emotional exposure in the programme and hence preparing them for the entrepreneurial environment in which they will operate.

The lone entrepreneurs who were not working in teams in the start-up accelerator expressed the desire to be able to work collaboratively with other entrepreneurs and people. The reason for this is that they thought it would provide them with access to the insight and skills of other people that are different from their own and that it would increase their level of motivation and confidence (ESE), thus increasing the chances of a venture's creation and survival. This sentiment is reflected in the research by Blank (2013) which finds that entrepreneurial teams as opposed to lone entrepreneurs are more likely to successfully start and manage new ventures.

Potential customers and key stakeholders

The participants also described the learning received from the customers and key stakeholders as practical knowledge and information specific to their individual business. Respondent E6 illustrates this point: 'Each week I had to talk to customers and so that was the process in which I learnt a lot about what they want and what I can do as a business. To

Table 10. Peers.

Interviewee	Interviewees' quotes
E2	'Learning from our peers was valuable as these people were in the same situation as us and they had the same problems as us. Also, they were getting out of the building and some were getting really good results and getting really far down the track really fast.'
E4	'The peers, you learn from them but it also sets the benchmark and pushes you a bit more to achieve what your trying to achieve, it's not competition but it keeps you up to speed. Being held accountable each week for having done the homework and progressing your idea, it kind of pushed you forward and forced you to move forward. I think if you're by yourself you can just linger on things for a long time'

Table 11. Potential customers and stakeholders.

Interviewee	Interviewees' quotes
E2	'The way we learnt the most was probably getting out there and talking to people, that was the biggest thing. All the other mediums, the videos, mentors and peers pushed us to doing this.'
E20	'I would say talking to the customer. Yeah. Before being in the program I was in my own head, what it was going to be like and creating, I wasn't basing it on feedback, it was kind of the other way around. You have to start from the customer.'
E12	'It forces you on a week to week basis to go well who is your customer? Are they really who you think they are? So just going through the process is helpful. It actually forced you to get out and challenge or test your assumptions about what your customers want or what they need or who they are were challenged by talking about it with the group then talking with customers.'

learn more about the business idea, it is definitely talking to customers.' Participants received knowledge and information regarding what they could offer their customers, how much their customers would pay for their product or service, what their customers really wanted and needed, where changes needed to be made to their product or service and what did their customer understand and not understand about their business (Table 11). Prior to the programme, participants stated that they did not understand the need for or know how to engage with potential customers/stakeholders, nor were they engaging with potential customers and stakeholders. This led to participants building their ventures on the basis of their own assumptions, instead of basing it on customer and stakeholder information. Participants stated that they had wasted time and, in some instances, money on ideas which, had they used ESE, could have been identified very quickly as having little value.

Participants referred to their idea or business before the programme as 'just being in their own head' – they made up their own assumptions about what was real and correct, what would work and what would not work. None of these preconceptions were based on customer or supplier feedback and interacting with potential customers and suppliers tested the assumptions the participants held about their business by providing them with new knowledge, as evidenced by respondent E12 in Table 11.

The participants revealed a theme that learning to speak to their potential customers and stakeholders enabled them to learn and discern based on real data who their customers really might be, what their customers really wanted and needed and how they might provide value for their customers, with a number reflecting that engaging with potential customers and stakeholders will now be their first point of call for any future ideas.

Summary: enhancing 'know-what' and 'know-how' with 'know-who'

A key finding from this study is that while the contemporary 'know-what' and 'know-how' in the form of Design Thinking, the Business Model Canvas and Lean Start-up Approach is well received by start-up accelerator participants, it was the 'know-who' component that really enhanced their entrepreneurial learning experiences. To that end, this study reinforces earlier research that found enhanced learning coming from the knowledge which comes from seeing and hearing from someone who has gone through an entrepreneurial process and experienced failures and success, and the opportunity to ask questions and receive practical advice (Hegarty 2006). It also reinforces the importance of social capital (Gedajlovic et al. 2013) that can act as a key driver or catalyst in regard to bridging learning to the development of ESE and entrepreneurial behaviour (Hoang and Antoncic 2003).

From the study, it can be seen that it is 'know-who' that closes the learning loop with 'know-what' and 'know-how' for entrepreneurs (Argyris 2002; Hampden-Turner 1993). The learning of 'know-who' has a positive impact on the development of 'know-how' through social learning theory which advances that learning occurs when an individual is motivated to perform by observing experienced people and imitating them (Bandura 1977). For example, the interactions with experts allow the start-up accelerator participants to learn about the practice of entrepreneurship and the advice and information from them, plus their successful or failed entrepreneurial experiences help start-up accelerator participants to have a better understanding of what needs to be done or avoided to develop their entrepreneurial ventures more successfully (i.e. 'know-how') (Stokes, Wilson, and Wilson 2010). The mentors also help change entrepreneurial behaviour by motivating, encouraging and directing the participants. 'Know-who' also has a positive impact on the development of 'know-what'. In particular, it is through the interactions with potential customers and key informants in the value chain that allow participants to have key insights into what customers are really looking for and this will allow them to change their product or business model quickly instead of investing too much time and resources in unviable ideas (Eisenmann, Ries, and Dillard 2012). Put together, social capital through 'know-who' enhances the human capital of 'know-what' and 'know-how' by developing the capacity of participants to problem solve, motivate themselves and develop a higher level of entrepreneurial self-efficacy and emotional support for entrepreneurial risk taking and behaviour. This is also applicable in the Asia Pacific context with relationships and networks being perceived as critical in facilitating entrepreneurship and creating value (Zhao, Frese, and Giardini 2010).

Limitations and future research

Our study has two noticeable limitations. First, it is based on a relatively small sample of start-up accelerator participants and as such, this research does not aim to produce results that are universally applicable. Further, it does not cover other stakeholders as part of the start-up accelerator (for example, the directors, mentors, instructors, and experts) as the focus was on understanding what and how the participants in the start-up accelerator learnt from their own perspectives and accounts. Future research should examine the phenomenon among larger samples of different types of start-up accelerator participants and stakeholders.

Second, the process of learning is an ongoing one which may have different outcomes at different stages of the entrepreneurial journey. The interviews and blogs only captured a moment in time, albeit with retrospective bias. Also, any learning that actually took place would be based on the subjective opinion and perception of the participants. That is, do they think or feel that they learnt something, how do they think or feel that they learnt it and what do they think they have learnt. We did not examine the tangible or quantifiable measure of this learning. While the research found that the amount of benefit and development the participants perceive themselves to have gained from learning and completing the programme in the start-up accelerator was positive, whether or not the contemporary approaches to entrepreneurship education in the start-up accelerator will ultimately lead to increased entrepreneurial success is unknown. To really see how the participants put their 'know-what', 'know-how' and 'know-who' into practice, further ongoing contact will be needed and future research would benefit from longitudinal studies.

Conclusion

The study's objective was to examine the extent and nature of entrepreneurial learning in terms of the extent to which they develop human capital ('know-what' and 'know-how') and social capital ('know-who') in start-up accelerators.

Overall, the study shows that the processes of 'know-what', 'know-how' and 'know-who' are interrelated – by knowing 'who', participants learnt 'what' and 'how to'. The research therefore makes the important contribution to entrepreneurial learning theory by shining a bit of light into 'the black box of entrepreneurship education' by providing evidence of that 'know-who' is just as important as 'know-what' and 'know-how' as 'know-who' can actually provide entrepreneurs with the means to access 'know-what' and 'know-how'. The study also answers calls for more research on actual entrepreneurs as opposed to students undergoing entrepreneurship education courses in higher education institutions (Robinson, Huefner, and Keith Hunt 1991; Seet and Seet 2006).

Any form of entrepreneurial learning leading to developing ESE has been emphasized by various researchers on the basis that increasing desirable entrepreneurial behaviour would increase the likelihood of success, particularly in being able to identify, validate and take advantage of entrepreneurial opportunities (Chandler and Jansen 1997; Karlsson and Moberg 2013). The study contributes to entrepreneurial learning research and practice by showing that in the context of a start-up accelerator that is implementing contemporary entrepreneurial education methods (which incorporate ideas like the Business Model Canvas, the Lean Start-up Approach and mentoring), the combination of human capital and social capital is a powerful catalyst for developing Entrepreneurial Self-Efficacy. It therefore finds evidence that start-up accelerators, by closing the learning loop and using social learning techniques, are responding to earlier critiques of entrepreneurship education that note that effective entrepreneurial learning programmes must show students 'how' to behave entrepreneurially (Ronstadt 1987; St-Jean et al. 2017). In particular, it reinforces the issues raised by Rae (2012) and Fayolle and Gailly (2008) that programmes that developed ESE enable the participants to engage with potential stakeholders and acquire this kind of data instead of ruminating or being inactive, which may result in those participants' ventures being relatively more successful in getting started and surviving.

Up until the early 2000s, entrepreneurship education was largely confined to North America (Katz 2003). However, since then, given the success of early internet start-ups driven by the development of the Internet, entrepreneurship education programmes have grown rapidly in many parts of the world, and has experienced phenomenal expansion in the Asia Pacific (Kelley and Thomas 2011; Seet and Seet 2006; Norasmah and Norfadhilah 2016; Matlay 2016). Among the various innovations in entrepreneurship education, start-up accelerators were formed as a response to address the high attrition and other errors that emerged from the dot-com bubble and the Global Financial Crisis (Haines 2014a). As noted in the introduction, start-up accelerators have been multiplying in numbers across many Asia Pacific countries (Shen 2014). Just as the Lean Start-up Approach proposes pivoting towards a successful business model, the various Asia Pacific countries will iterate their models of start-up accelerators to adapt to local, culturally specific conditions (Haines 2014b; Solesvik, Westhead, and Matlay 2014), as they learn from mistakes among countries that have started early like Australia (Maritz, Jones, and Shwetzer 2015). For example, while the Techstars accelerator worked well in the USA and in the UK, the lack of supportive foreign visas and minimal ongoing government support stymied the growth of imitative models like ANZ Innovyz Start in Australia (Bliemel et al. 2016). In places like Singapore and Taiwan, strong government promotion and investment in start-up accelerators have seen many start-ups being put through these schemes but the limited size of domestic markets has led to many being unable to overcome the 'valley of death' (Moore 1999; Shen 2014). Regardless of this, research on what makes accelerators in Australia and other Asian countries successful has found significant similarities in that, in terms of supporting entrepreneurial ventures, venture success is highly contingent on them being able to leverage on the relationships or social capital that they have within the entrepreneurial ecosystem (Bliemel et al. 2016; Vanhonacker, Zweig, and Chung 2006; Shen 2014).

A recent study among New Zealand start-up accelerators show that start-up accelerators can be excellent platforms for authentic learning for nascent entrepreneurs (Miles et al. 2017) but the authors also noted that there was a need for context specific research to examine whether start-up accelerators also helped develop specific entrepreneurial competencies like the ability to develop, harness, and leverage human, organizational, social, and economic capital. This research attempts to contribute to better understanding that link. Time will tell but hopefully, if the phenomenon of start-up accelerators continues to develop these techniques of growing both human and social capital in the Asia Pacific, there will be fewer entrepreneurial failures and more successful innovative ventures in the region in the future. Not only that, the ability to successfully do so will also spill-over onto other players in the service sector that are closely watching and experimenting e.g. manufacturing firms that are planning to rapidly servitize in order to capture more value higher up the value chain.

Disclosure statement

No potential conflict of interest was reported by the authors.

References

Ajzen, Icek. 1991. "The Theory of Planned Behavior." *Organizational Behavior and Human Decision Processes* 50 (2): 179–211. doi:10.1016/0749-5978(91)90020-T.

Ahmad, Noor Hazlina, and Pi-Shen Seet. 2009. "Understanding Business Success through the Lens of SME Founder-Owners in Australia and Malaysia." *International Journal of Entrepreneurial Venturing* 1 (1): 72–87.

Ahsan, Mujtaba, Congcong Zheng, Alex DeNoble, and Martina Musteen. 2018. "From Student to Entrepreneur: How Mentorships and Affect Influence Student Venture Launch." *Journal of Small Business Management* 56 (1): 76–102. doi:10.1111/jsbm.12362.

Alberti, Fernando, Salvatore Sciascia, and Alberto Poli. 2004. "Entrepreneurship Education: Notes on an Ongoing Debate." Paper presented at the Proceedings of the 14th Annual IntEnt Conference, University of Napoli Federico II, Italy.

Aldrich, Howard, and Ellen R. Auster. 1986. "Even Dwarfs Started Small: Liabilities Ofage and Size and Their Strategic Implications." *Research in Organizational Behavior* 8: 165–186.

Argyris, Chris. 2002. "Double-Loop Learning, Teaching, and Research." *Academy of Management Learning & Education* 1 (2): 206–218. doi:10.5465/AMLE.2002.8509400.

Baines, T. S., H. W. Lightfoot, O. Benedettini, and J. M. Kay. 2009. "The Servitization of Manufacturing: A Review of Literature and Reflection on Future Challenges." *Journal of Manufacturing Technology Management* 20 (5): 547–567. doi:10.1108/17410380910960984.

Bandura, Albert. 1977. *Social Learning Theory*. Englewood Cliffs, NJ: Prentice-Hall.

Bandura, Albert. 1991. "Social Cognitive Theory of Self-Regulation." *Organizational Behavior and Human Decision Processes* 50 (2): 248–287. doi:10.1016/0749-5978(91)90022-L.

BarNir, Anat, and Ken A. Smith. 2002. "Interfirm Alliances in the Small Business: The Role of Social Networks." *Journal of Small Business Management* 40 (3): 219–232. doi:10.1111/1540-627X.00052.

Batjargal, Bat, and Mannie Liu. 2004. "Entrepreneurs' Access to Private Equity in China: The Role of Social Capital." *Organization Science* 15 (2): 159–172. doi:10.1287/orsc.1030.0044.

Becker, Gary S. 1964. *Human Capital*. Chicago, IL: Chicago University Press.

Beer, Andrew. 1998. "Immigration and Slow-Growth Economies: The Experience of South Australia and Tasmania." *Australian Geographer* 29 (2): 223–240. doi:10.1080/00049189808703216.

Blank, Steve. 2013. "Why the Lean Start-up Changes Everything." *Harvard Business Review* 91 (5): 63–72.

Bliemel, Martin J, Ricardo G. Flores, Saskia de Klerk, Morgan P. P. Miles, Bianca Costa, and Pedro Monteiro. 2016. "The Role and Performance of Accelerators in the Australian Startup Ecosystem." *UNSW Business School Research Paper (2016MGMT03)*.

Bosma, Niels, Mirjam van Praag, Roy Thurik, and Gerrit de Wit. 2004. "The Value of Human and Social Capital Investments for the Business Performance of Startups." *Small Business Economics* 23 (3): 227–236.

Breuer, Henning. 2013. "Lean Venturing: Learning to Create New Business through Exploration, Elaboration, Evaluation, Experimentation, and Evolution." *International Journal of Innovation Management* 17 (3): 1340013. doi:10.1142/s1363919613400136.

Bridge, Simon. 2014. "Exploring the Nature of Social Capital to Facilitate Its Inclusion in Enterprise Education." *Education + Training* 56 (8/9): 839–851. doi:10.1108/ET-04-2014-0043.

Brown, T. 2005. "Strategy by Design." *Fast Company* 95: 52–54.

Bygrave, William D. 1993. "Theory Building in the Entrepreneurship Paradigm." *Journal of Business Venturing* 8 (3): 255–280. doi:10.1016/0883-9026(93)90031-Y.

Bygrave, William D. 1997. *The Portable MBA in Entrepreneurship*. 2nd ed. The Portable MBA Series. New York: J. Wiley & Sons.

Cater, Toma, and Barbara Cater. 2009. "(in)Tangible Resources as Antecedents of a Company's Competitive Advantage and Performance." *Journal for East European Management Studies* 14 (2): 186–209.

Chandler, Gaylen N., and Erik Jansen. 1997. "Founder Self-Efficacy and Venture Performance: A Longitudinal Study." *Academy of Management Proceedings* 1997 (1): 98–102. doi:10.5465/ambpp.1997.4980945.

Chesbrough, H. W. 2003. *Open Innovation: The New Imperative for Creating and Profiting from Technology*. Cambridge, MA: Harvard Business School Press.

Clements, B. and S. Moore 2009. *SPEED Final Report by the LEAD Institution*. Wolverhampton: Institute for Innovation and Enterprise, The University of Wolverhampton.

Clibborn, Stephen, Russell D. Lansbury, and Chris F. Wright. 2016. "Who Killed the Australian Automotive Industry: The Employers, Government or Trade Unions?" *Economic Papers: A Journal of Applied Economics and Policy* 35 (1): 2–15. doi:10.1111/1759-3441.12127.

Cohen, Susan. 2013. "What Do Accelerators Do? Insights from Incubators and Angels." *Innovations: Technology, Governance, Globalization* 8 (3–4): 19–25.

Cohen, Wesley M., and Daniel A. Levinthal. 1990. "Absorptive Capacity: A New Perspective on Learning and Innovation." *Administrative Science Quarterly* 35 (1): 128–152. doi:10.2307/2393553.

Cooke, P., M. Heidenreich, and H. Braczyk. 2004. *Regional Innovation Systems: The Role of Governance in a Globalised World*. London: Routledge.

Corral de Zubielqui, Graciela, Janice Jones, Pi-Shen Seet, and Noel Lindsay. 2015. "Knowledge Transfer between Actors in the Innovation System: A Study of Higher Education Institutions (HEIS) and SMES." *Journal of Business & Industrial Marketing* 30 (3/4): 436–458. doi:10.1108/JBIM-07-2013-0152.

Daly, P. 2013. *Towards a City of Entrepreneurs: The Emergence of Adelaide as a Recognised Start-up Community*. Adelaide City Council.

Dimov, Dimo P., and Dean A. Shepherd. 2005. "Human Capital Theory and Venture Capital Firms: Exploring 'Home Runs' and 'Strike Outs'." *Journal of Business Venturing* 20 (1): 1–21. doi:10.1016/j.jbusvent.2003.12.007.

Dufays, Frédéric, and Benjamin Huybrechts. 2014. "Connecting the Dots for Social Value: A Review on Social Networks and Social Entrepreneurship." *Journal of Social Entrepreneurship* 5 (2): 214–237. doi:10.1080/19420676.2014.918052.

Eisenmann, Thomas R, Eric Ries, and Sarah Dillard. 2012. "Hypothesis-Driven Entrepreneurship: The Lean Startup." *Harvard Business School Entrepreneurial Management Case No. 812-095*.

Fayolle, Alain, and Benoit Gailly. 2008. "From Craft to Science: Teaching Models and Learning Processes in Entrepreneurship Education." *Journal of European Industrial Training* 32 (7): 569–593. doi:10.1108/03090590810899838.

Fayolle, Alain, Benoît Gailly, and Narjisse Lassas-Clerc. 2006. "Assessing the Impact of Entrepreneurship Education Programmes: A New Methodology." *Journal of European Industrial Training* 30 (9): 701–720. doi:10.1108/03090590610715022.

Felício, J. Augusto, Eduardo Couto, and Jorge Caiado. 2014. "Human Capital, Social Capital and Organizational Performance." *Management Decision* 52 (2): 350–364. doi:10.1108/MD-04-2013-0260.

Fiet, James O. 2001a. "The Theoretical Side of Teaching Entrepreneurship." *Journal of Business Venturing* 16 (1): 1–24. doi:10.1016/S0883-9026(99)00041-5.

Fiet, James O. 2001b. "The Pedagogical Side of Entrepreneurship Theory." *Journal of Business Venturing* 16 (2): 101–117. doi:10.1016/S0883-9026(99)00042-7.

Fishback, Bo, Christine Gulbranson, Robert Litan, Lesa Mitchell, and Marisa Porzig. 2007. "Finding Business 'Idols': A New Model to Accelerate Start-Ups. Ewing Marion Kauffman Foundation." C. Scott Dempwolf, Jennifer Auer and Michelle D'Ippolito (2014), Innovation Accelerators: Defining Characteristics Among Startup Assistance Organizations, SBA (Small Business Administration), Optimal Solutions Group, LLC. Dinah Adkins (2011), What are the new seed or venture accelerators.

Freel, Mark S. 2005. "Patterns of Innovation and Skills in Small Firms." *Technovation* 25 (2): 123–134. doi:10.1016/S0166-4972(03)00082-8.

Fritscher, Boris, and Yves Pigneur. 2009. "Supporting Business Model Modelling: A Compromise between Creativity and Constraints." Paper presented at the TAMODIA.

Gedajlovic, Eric, Benson Honig, Curt B. Moore, G. Tyge Payne, and Mike Wright. 2013. "Social Capital and Entrepreneurship: A Schema and Research Agenda." *Entrepreneurship Theory and Practice* 37 (3): 455–478. doi:10.1111/etap.12042.

Gibb, Allan A. 1993. "Enterprise Culture and Education: Understanding Enterprise Education and Its Links with Small Business, Entrepreneurship and Wider Educational Goals." *International Small Business Journal* 11 (3): 11–34. doi:10.1177/026624269301100301.

Gibb, Allan A. 1997. "Small Firms' Training and Competitiveness. Building upon the Small Business as a Learning Organisation." *International Small Business Journal* 15 (3): 13–29. doi:10.1177/0266242697153001.

Gibb, A. A., and J. Cotton. 1998. "Entrepreneurship in Schools and College Education–Creating the Leading Edge." Paper presented at the Background paper to the conference to be held at the Department of Trade and Industry Conference Centre.

Gorman, Gary, Dennis Hanlon, and Wayne King. 1997. "Some Research Perspectives on Entrepreneurship Education, Enterprise Education and Education for Small Business Management: A Ten-Year Literature Review." *International Small Business Journal* 15 (3): 56–77. doi:10.1177/0266242697153004.

Greve, Arent, and Janet W. Salaff. 2003. "Social Networks and Entrepreneurship." *Entrepreneurship Theory and Practice* 28 (1): 1–22. doi:10.1111/1540-8520.00029.

Haines, Julia Katherine. 2014a. "Emerging Innovation: The Global Expansion of Seed Accelerators." Paper presented at the Proceedings of the companion publication of the 17th ACM conference on Computer supported cooperative work & social computing.

Haines, Julia Katherine. 2014b. "Iterating an Innovation Model: Challenges and Opportunities in Adapting Accelerator Practices in Evolving Ecosystems." Paper presented at the Ethnographic Praxis in Industry Conference Proceedings.

Hampden-Turner, C. 1993. "Dilemmas of Strategic Learning Loops." In *Strategic Thinking : Leadership and the Management of Change : Symposium : Revised Selected Papers*, edited by John Hendry, Gerry Johnson and Julia Newton, 327–346. Chichester: Wiley.

Harms, Rainer. 2015. "Self-Regulated Learning, Team Learning and Project Performance in Entrepreneurship Education: Learning in a Lean Startup Environment." *Technological Forecasting and Social Change* 100 (Supplement C): 21–28. doi:10.1016/j.techfore.2015.02.007.

Hatch, Nile W., and Jeffrey H. Dyer. 2004. "Human Capital and Learning as a Source of Sustainable Competitive Advantage." *Strategic Management Journal* 25 (12): 1155–1178. doi:10.1002/smj.421.

Hathaway, Ian. 2016. "Accelerating Growth: Startup Accelerator Programs in the United States." *Advanced Industry Series* (81).

Hegarty, Cecilia. 2006. "It's Not an Exact Science: Teaching Entrepreneurship in Northern Ireland." *Education + Training* 48 (5): 322–335. doi:10.1108/00400910610677036.

Hills, G. E. 1988. "Variations in University Entrepreneurship Education: An Empirical Study of an Evolving Field." *Journal of Business Venturing* 3: 109–122.

Hoang, Ha, and Bostjan Antoncic. 2003. "Network-Based Research in Entrepreneurship: A Critical Review." *Journal of Business Venturing* 18 (2): 165–187. doi:10.1016/S0883-9026(02)00081-2.

Hochberg, Yael V. 2016. "Accelerating Entrepreneurs and Ecosystems: The Seed Accelerator Model." *Innovation Policy and the Economy* 16 (1): 25–51. doi:10.1086/684985.

Honig, Benson. 2001. "Human Capital and Structural Upheaval: A Study of Manufacturing Firms in the West Bank." *Journal of Business Venturing* 16 (6): 575–594. doi:10.1016/S0883-9026(99)00060-9.

Honig, Benson. 2004. "Entrepreneurship Education: Toward a Model of Contingency-Based Business Planning." *Academy of Management Learning & Education* 3 (3): 258–273. doi:10.5465/amle.2004.14242112.

Honig, Benson, and Tomas Karlsson. 2004. "Institutional Forces and the Written Business Plan." *Journal of Management* 30 (1): 29–48. doi:10.1016/j.jm.2002.11.002.

Jack, Sarah L., and Alistair R. Anderson. 1999. "Entrepreneurship Education within the Enterprise Culture: Producing Reflective Practitioners." *International Journal of Entrepreneurial Behavior & Research* 5 (3): 110–125. doi:10.1108/13552559910284074.

Johansson, Ulla, and Jill Woodilla. 2009. "Towards an Epistemological Merger of Design Thinking, Strategy and Innovation." Paper presented at the 8th European Academy of Design Conference.

Jones, Jane, and Graciela Corral de Zubielqui. 2017. "Doing Well by Doing Good: A Study of University-Industry Interactions, Innovationess and Firm Performance in Sustainability-Oriented Australian SMEs." *Technological Forecasting and Social Change* 123 (Supplement C): 262–270. doi:10.1016/j.techfore.2016.07.036.

Kacperczyk, Aleksandra J. 2013. "Social Influence and Entrepreneurship: The Effect of University Peers on Entrepreneurial Entry." *Organization Science* 24 (3): 664–683. doi:10.1287/orsc.1120.0773.

Karlsson, Tomas, and Kåre Moberg. 2013. "Improving Perceived Entrepreneurial Abilities through Education: Exploratory Testing of an Entrepreneurial Self Efficacy Scale in a Pre-Post Setting." *The International Journal of Management Education* 11 (1): 1–11. doi:10.1016/j.ijme.2012.10.001.

Katz, Jerome A. 2003. "The Chronology and Intellectual Trajectory of American Entrepreneurship Education: 1876–1999." *Journal of Business Venturing* 18 (2): 283–300. doi:10.1016/S0883-9026(02)00098-8.

Kelley, Donna, and Hugh Thomas. 2011. *Entrepreneurship Education in Asia*. Cheltenham: Edward Elgar.

Kirby, David A. 2004. "Entrepreneurship Education: Can Business Schools Meet the Challenge?" *Education + Training* 46 (8/9): 510–519. doi:10.1108/00400910410569632.

Kiss, Andreea N., and Wade M. Danis. 2008. "Country Institutional Context, Social Networks, and New Venture Internationalization Speed." *European Management Journal* 26 (6): 388–399. doi:10.1016/j.emj.2008.09.001.

Kuratko, Donald F. 2004. "Entrepreneurship Education in the 21st Century: From Legitimization to Leadership." In *USASBE National Conference Proceedings* 16: 45–60.

Kuratko, Donald F. 2005. "The Emergence of Entrepreneurship Education: Development, Trends, and Challenges." *Entrepreneurship: Theory & Practice* 29 (5): 577–597.

Lepak, David P., and Scott A. Snell. 1999. "The Human Resource Architecture: Toward a Theory of Human Capital Allocation and Development." *The Academy of Management Review* 24 (1): 31–48. doi:10.2307/259035.

Lévesque, Moren, Maria Minniti, and Dean Shepherd. 2009. "Entrepreneurs' Decisions on Timing of Entry: Learning from Participation and from the Experiences of Others." *Entrepreneurship Theory and Practice* 33 (2): 547–570. doi:10.1111/j.1540-6520.2009.00303.x.

Lightfoot, Howard, Tim Baines, and Palie Smart. 2013. "The Servitization of Manufacturing: A Systematic Literature Review of Interdependent Trends." *International Journal of Operations & Production Management* 33 (11/12): 1408–1434. doi:10.1108/IJOPM-07-2010-0196.

Lindsay, Noel. 2012. "Avatars Not Just for Movies." *Public Administration Today* (31): 19.

Madhok, A. 2002. "Reassessing the Fundamentals and beyond: Ronald Coase, the Transaction Cost and Resource-Based Theories of the Firm and the Institutional Structure of Production." *Strategic Management Journal* 23: 535–550.

Man, Thomas W. Y., and Theresa Lau. 2005. "The Context of Entrepreneurship in Hong Kong: An Investigation through the Patterns of Entrepreneurial Competencies in Contrasting Industrial Environments." *Journal of Small Business and Enterprise Development* 12 (4): 464–481. doi:10.1108/14626000510628162.

Maritz, Alex, and Christopher R. Brown. 2013. "Illuminating the Black Box of Entrepreneurship Education Programs." *Education + Training* 55 (3): 234–252. doi:10.1108/00400911311309305.

Maritz, Alex, Colin Jones, and Claudia Shwetzer. 2015. "The Status of Entrepreneurship Education in Australian Universities." *Education + Training* 57 (8/9): 1020–1035. doi:10.1108/ET-04-2015-0026.

Martin, Bruce C., Jeffrey J. McNally, and Michael J. Kay. 2013. "Examining the Formation of Human Capital in Entrepreneurship: A Meta-Analysis of Entrepreneurship Education Outcomes." *Journal of Business Venturing* 28 (2): 211–224. doi:10.1016/j.jbusvent.2012.03.002.

Marvel, Matthew R., and G. T. Lumpkin. 2007. "Technology Entrepreneurs' Human Capital and Its Effects on Innovation Radicalness." *Entrepreneurship Theory and Practice* 31 (6): 807–828. doi:10.1111/j.1540-6520.2007.00209.x.

Matlay, Harry. 2009. "Entrepreneurship Education in the UK: A Critical Analysis of Stakeholder Involvement and Expectations." *Journal of Small Business and Enterprise Development* 16 (2): 355–368. doi:10.1108/14626000910956100.

Matlay, H. 2016. "Entrepreneurship Education in Asia." *Education + Training* 58 (7/8): 899–900. doi:10.1108/ET-06-2016-0104.

Miles, Morgan P., Huibert de Vries, Geoff Harrison, Martin Bliemel, Saskia de Klerk, and Chick J. Kasouf. 2017. "Accelerators as Authentic Training Experiences for Nascent Entrepreneurs." *Education + Training* 59 (7/8): 811–824. doi:10.1108/ET-01-2017-0007.

Miller, Paul, and Kirsten Bound. 2011. *The Startup Factories: The Rise of Accelerator Programmes to Support New Technology Ventures*. Nesta.

MOHE. 2010. *Development of Higher Education Institute Entrepreneurship Foundation*. Putrajaya: Ministry of Higher Education Malaysia.

Moore, Geoffrey A. 1999. *Crossing the Chasm*. 2nd ed. Oxford: Capstone.

Neck, Heidi M., and Patricia G. Greene. 2011. "Entrepreneurship Education: Known Worlds and New Frontiers." *Journal of Small Business Management* 49 (1): 55–70. doi:10.1111/j.1540-627X.2010.00314.x.

Neck, Heidi M. 2014. *Teaching Entrepreneurship: A Practice-Based Approach*. Cheltenham: Edward Elgar Pub.

Nielsen, Suna Løwe, and Stovang Pia. 2015. "DesUni: University Entrepreneurship Education through Design Thinking." *Education + Training* 57 (8/9): 977–991. doi:10.1108/ET-09-2014-0121.

Norasmah, Othman, and Nasrudin Norfadhilah. 2016. "Entrepreneurship Education Programs in Malaysian Polytechnics." *Education + Training* 58 (7/8): 882–898. doi:10.1108/ET-11-2014-0136.

Norfadhilah, Nasrudin. 2014. "Penilaian Pencapaian Objektif Program Pembudayaan Keusahawanan (PPK) Di Politeknik Malaysia." Universiti Kebangsaan.

O'Connor, Allan. 2013. "A Conceptual Framework for Entrepreneurship Education Policy: Meeting Government and Economic Purposes." *Journal of Business Venturing* 28 (4): 546–563. doi:10.1016/j.jbusvent.2012.07.003.

O'Connell, B. 2011. "Start X: Training Ground for Stanford's Best and Brightest." *Kauffman Foundation*.

O'Connor, A., and G. Reed. 2015. *South Australia's Entrepreneurial Ecosystem: Voice of the Customer Research Report', Report Prepared for the SA Government Department of State Development by the Entrepreneurship*. Commercialisation and Innovation Centre (ECIC), University of Adelaide.

O'Connor, Kevin B., and Robert John Stimson. 1995. *The Economic Role of Cities: Economic Change and City Development, Australia 1971–1991*. Australian Government Pub. Service.

Osterwalder, Alexander. 2004. "The Business Model Ontology – A Proposition in a Design Science Approach." Doctoral Thesis, University of Lausanne, Lausanne, Switzerland.

Osterwalder, Alexander. 2012. "Business Model Canvas: A Simple Tool for Designing Innovative Business Models." *Forbes Magazine*.

Othman, Norasmah, and Norfadhilah Nasrudin. 2016. "Entrepreneurship Education Programs in Malaysian Polytechnics." *Education + Training* 58 (7/8): 882–898. doi:10.1108/ET-11-2014-0136.

Ozgen, Eren, and Robert A. Baron. 2007. "Social Sources of Information in Opportunity Recognition: Effects of Mentors, Industry Networks, and Professional Forums." *Journal of Business Venturing* 22 (2): 174–192. doi:10.1016/j.jbusvent.2005.12.001.

Perkmann, M., and K. Walsh. 2007. "University-Industry Relationships and Open Innovation: Towards a Research Agenda (Review Article)." *International Journal of Management Reviews* 9: 259–280.

Pittaway, L. A. 2004. "Simulating Entrepreneurial Learning: Assessing the Utility of Experiential Learning Designs." *Lancaster University Management School Working Paper*, 1–33.

Pittaway, Luke, and Jason Cope. 2007. "Entrepreneurship Education: A Systematic Review of the Evidence." *International Small Business Journal* 25 (5): 479–510.

Radojevich-Kelley, Nina, and David Lynn Hoffman. 2012. "Analysis of Accelerator Companies: An Exploratory Case Study of Their Programs, Processes, and Early Results." *Small Business Institute Journal* 8 (2): 54–70.

Rae, David M. 1997. "Teaching Entrepreneurship in Asia: Impact of a Pedagogical Innovation." *Entrepreneurship, Innovation and Change* 6 (3): 193–227.

Rae, David. 2012. "Action Learning in New Creative Ventures." *International Journal of Entrepreneurial Behavior & Research* 18 (5): 603–623. doi:10.1108/13552551211253955.

Redding, Gordon, and Chris Rowley. 2017. "Conclusion: The Central Role of Human and Social Capital." *Asia Pacific Business Review* 23 (2): 299–305. doi:10.1080/13602381.2017.1289033.

Ries, Eric. 2011. *The Lean Startup: How Today's Entrepreneurs Use Continuous Innovation to Create Radically Successful Businesses*. Crown Books.

Robinson, Peter B., Jonathan C. Huefner, and H. Keith Hunt. 1991. "Entrepreneurial Research on Student Subjects Does Not Generalize to Real World Entrepreneurs." *Journal of Small Business Management* 29 (2): 42–50.

Ronstadt, R.. 1987. "The Educated Entrepreneurs: A New Era of Entrepreneurial Education is Beginning." *American Journal of Small Business* 11 (4): 37–54.

Ronstadt, Robert, Karl H. Vesper, and W. Ed. McMullan. 1988. "Entrepreneurship: Today Courses, Tomorrow Degrees?" *Entrepreneurship Theory and Practice* 13 (1): 7–13. doi:10.1177/104225878801300102.

Roos, G. 2012. *Manufacturing into the Future*. Adelaide: Adelaide Thinkers-in-Residence Office, Government of South Australia.

Roos, Göran. 2015. "Servitization as Innovation in Manufacturing – A Review of the Literature." In *The Handbook of Service Innovation*, edited by Renu Agarwal, Willem Selen, Göran Roos and Roy Green, 403–435. London: Springer.

Roos, G., A. Bainbridge, and K. Jacobsen. 2001. "Intellectual Capital Analysis as a Strategic Tool." *Strategy & Leadership* 29 (4): 21–26.

Roos, G., S. Pike, and L. Fernstrom. 2005. *Managing Intellectual Capital in Practice*. London: Routledge.

Rubin, Herbert J., and Irene S. Rubin. 2011. *Qualitative Interviewing: The Art of Hearing Data*. Los Angeles, CA: Sage.

Rutherfurd, I. A. N., and Brian Finlayson. 2011. "Whither Australia: Will Availability of Water Constrain the Growth of Australia's Population?" *Geographical Research* 49 (3): 301–316. doi:10.1111/j.1745-5871.2011.00707.x.

Saldana, Johnny. 2009. *The Coding Manual for Qualitative Researchers*. London: SAGE Publications.

Seely-Brown, J., and P. Duguid. 2001. "Knowledge and Organization: A Social-Practice Perspective." *Organization Science* 12 (2): 198–213.

Seet, Pi-Shen. 2007. "Reconciling Entrepreneurial Dilemmas – A Case Study of a Huaqiao (华侨) Entrepreneur in China." *Journal of Asia Entrepreneurship and Sustainability* 3 (3): 75–97.

Seet, Pi-Shen, and Lip-Chai Seet. 2006. "Changing Entrepreneurial Perceptions and Developing Entrepreneurial Competencies through Experiential Learning: Evidence from Entrepreneurship Education in Singapore's Tertiary Education Institutions." *Journal of Asia Entrepreneurship and Sustainability* 2 (2): 162–191.

Sepulveda, Fernando. 2012. "The Difference between a Business Accelerator and a Business Incubator?" *Inc. Web*, 31.

Shane, Scott, and S. Venkataraman. 2000. "The Promise of Entrepreneurship as a Field of Research." *Academy of Management Review* 25 (1): 217–226.

Shen, Joan. 2014. "Recent Development on Start-up Acceleration and Business Continuity Planning in APEC Region." *Editorial Statement*, 21.

Shepherd, D. A., and A. Zacharakis. 2001. "Speed to Initial Public Offering of VC-Backed Companies." *Entrepreneurship Theory and Practice* 25: 59.

Shrader, Rod, and Donald S. Siegel. 2007. "Assessing the Relationship between Human Capital and Firm Performance: Evidence from Technology-Based New Ventures." *Entrepreneurship Theory and Practice* 31 (6): 893–908. doi:10.1111/j.1540-6520.2007.00206.x.

Singh, Robert Paul. 2000. *Entrepreneurial Opportunity Recognition through Social Networks*. New York: Garland Publishing.

Singh, Robert P., Gerald E. Hills, G. T. Lumpkin, and Ralph C. Hybels. 1999. *The Entrepreneurial Opportunity Recognition Process: Examining the Role of Self-Perceived Alertness and Social Networks*. Paper presented at the Academy of Management Proceedings.

Solesvik, Marina, Paul Westhead, and Harry Matlay. 2014. "Cultural Factors and Entrepreneurial Intention: The Role of Entrepreneurship Education." *Education + Training* 56 (8/9): 680–696. doi:10.1108/ET-07-2014-0075.

Solomon, George T., Susan Duffy, and Ayman Tarabishy. 2002. "The State of Entrepreneurship Education in the United States: A Nationwide Survey and Analysis." *International Journal of Entrepreneurship Education* 1 (1): 65–86.

Sosa, Manuel E. 2011. "Where Do Creative Interactions Come from? The Role of Tie Content and Social Networks." *Organization Science* 22 (1): 1–21. doi:10.1287/orsc.1090.0519.

Stam, Wouter, Souren Arzlanian, and Tom Elfring. 2014. "Social Capital of Entrepreneurs and Small Firm Performance: A Meta-Analysis of Contextual and Methodological Moderators." *Journal of Business Venturing* 29 (1): 152–173. doi:10.1016/j.jbusvent.2013.01.002.

St-Jean, Étienne, and Cynthia Mathieu. 2015. "Developing Attitudes toward an Entrepreneurial Career through Mentoring: The Mediating Role of Entrepreneurial Self-Efficacy." *Journal of Career Development* 42 (4): 325–338. doi:10.1177/0894845314568190.

St-Jean, Étienne, Maripier Tremblay, Frank Janssen, Jacques Baronet, Christophe Loué, and Aziz Nafa. 2017. "May Business Mentors Act as Opportunity Brokers and Enablers among University Students?" *International Entrepreneurship and Management Journal* 13 (1): 97–111. doi:10.1007/s11365-016-0397-4.

Stokes, David, Nicholas Wilson, and Nick Wilson. 2010. *Small Business Management and Entrepreneurship*. Cengage Learning EMEA.

Stross, Randall. 2013. *The Launch Pad: Inside Y Combinator*. London: Penguin.

Sullivan, Robert. 2000. "Entrepreneurial Learning and Mentoring." *International Journal of Entrepreneurial Behavior & Research* 6 (3): 160–175. doi:10.1108/13552550010346587.

Sun, Hongyi, Choi Tung Lo, Bo Liang, and Yuen Ling Belle Wong. 2017. "The Impact of Entrepreneurial Education on Entrepreneurial Intention of Engineering Students in Hong Kong." *Management Decision* 55 (7): 1371–1393. doi:10.1108/MD-06-2016-0392.

Sung-Choon, Kang, Shad S. Morris, and Scott A. Snell. 2007. "Relational Archetypes, Organizational Learning, and Value Creation: Extending the Human Resource Architecture." *The Academy of Management Review* 32 (1): 236–256. doi:10.2307/20159290.

Tharenou, Phyllis, and Pi-Shen Seet. 2014. "China's Reverse Brain Drain." *International Studies of Management & Organization* 44 (2): 55–74. doi:10.2753/IMO0020-8825440203.

Unger, Jens M., Andreas Rauch, Michael Frese, and Nina Rosenbusch. 2011. "Human Capital and Entrepreneurial Success: A Meta-Analytical Review." *Journal of Business Venturing* 26 (3): 341–358. doi:10.1016/j.jbusvent.2009.09.004.

Vanhonacker, W. R., D. Zweig, and S. F. Chung. 2006. Transnational or social capital? Returnee versus local entrepreneurs. *China's Domestic Private Firms: Multidisciplinary Perspectives on Management and Performance.*

Walmsley, D. J., and H. C. Weinand. 1997. "Is Australia Becoming More Unequal?" *Australian Geographer* 28 (1): 69–88. doi:10.1080/00049189708703181.

Wright, Mike, Keith M. Hmieleski, Donald S. Siegel, and Michael D. Ensley. 2007. "The Role of Human Capital in Technological Entrepreneurship." *Entrepreneurship Theory and Practice* 31 (6): 791–806. doi:10.1111/j.1540-6520.2007.00202.x.

Youndt, Mark A., Mohan Subramaniam, and Scott A. Snell. 2004. "Intellectual Capital Profiles: An Examination of Investments and Returns*." *Journal of Management Studies* 41 (2): 335–361. doi:10.1111/j.1467-6486.2004.00435.x.

Zacharakis, Andrew L., and G. Dale Meyer. 2000. "The Potential of Actuarial Decision Models: Can They Improve the Venture Capital Investment Decision?" *Journal of Business Venturing* 15 (4): 323–346.

Zhao, Hongxin, and Jiangyong Lu. 2016. "Contingent Value of Political Capital in Bank Loan Acquisition: Evidence from Founder-Controlled Private Enterprises in China." *Journal of Business Venturing* 31 (2): 153–174. doi:10.1016/j.jbusvent.2015.12.002.

Zhao, Xiang-yang, Michael Frese, and Angelo Giardini. 2010. "Business Owners' Network Size and Business Growth in China: The Role of Comprehensive Social Competency." *Entrepreneurship & Regional Development* 22 (7–8): 675–705. doi:10.1080/08985620903171376.

Zijdemans, Erik, and Stoyan Tanev. 2014. "Conceptualizing Innovation in Born-Global Firms." *Technology Innovation Management Review* 4 (9): 5–10.

Conclusion: future directions for research on social capital and the services industry

Yuliani Suseno and Chris Rowley

ABSTRACT

This collection aimed to provide a broader picture of the implications of social capital in service-oriented firms. In this piece, we identify trends for future research on social capital with a focus on the services industry, an important sector of the economy. We focus on three future directions: the internationalization of service firms, social capital for service-oriented social enterprises and public policy programmes to create social capital, particularly in the context of Asia Pacific. We then identify how the contributions to this collection are related to these future directions to encourage more confirmatory work in this dynamic field of research and practice on social capital in service-oriented firms in the Asia Pacific region.

Introduction

In this collection, we sought to address the relevance of social capital in the context of service-oriented firms in the Asia Pacific region. Social capital is about resources and network ties embedded in social structures and relationships (Nahapiet and Ghoshal 1998; Kwon and Adler 2014). Social capital is important in business relationships between providers and their clients (Suseno and Pinnington 2018) and is, therefore, particularly pertinent in the context of service-oriented firms. The contributions presented in our collection draw us into a more extensive debate over the issue of social capital in terms of the different research approaches to social capital – either egocentric or sociocentric – and the creation and outcomes of social capital. However, despite the wealth of literature on social capital spanning different levels of analysis, from individuals (e.g. Gubbins and Garavan 2015), organizational (e.g. Lins, Servaes, and Tamayo 2017) and societal (e.g. Aldrich and Meyer 2015), what is still missing is the broader picture of the implications of social capital in the context of service-oriented firms.

The focus of our work here is to identify trends for future research on social capital in service-oriented firms. This also indicates the implications for theory and theory development and business and management practice of social capital and service firms via the trio of areas of internationalization, social entrepreneurship and policy programmes.

Social capital and the internationalization of service firms

Service firms have traditionally relied on local regulations and institutions and were delivered chiefly to serve their local and regional communities. However, the service industry is growing and internationalizing remarkably faster than manufacturing industries (Simon and Welsh 2010; Gallouj et al. 2015; Suseno and Pinnington 2017a, 2017b), partly due to the firms' lower requirements for capital investment. Indeed, 'few companies in non-service sectors can boast the same geographical spread and … since the 1990s manufacturing multinationals have been focused on downsizing and outsourcing their operations rather than on expanding their international footprint' (Boussebaa and Morgan 2015, 71). The term 'internationalization' refers to the geographical reach of businesses into foreign markets while adapting (or localizing) to culturally related issues. It is frequently an incremental process as 'a means to *augment* a firm's resource base by (internal) *exploration* of existing knowledge through organizational learning, and (external) access to complementary knowledge' (Meyer, Wright, and Pruthi 2009, 558).

The internationalization of service firms is bounded within the following factors. First, the internationalization of service firms could be the result of domestic clients bringing with them their service providers to provide for their international work. Service firms often need to remain close to their clients to build knowledge through continuous interactions with their clients (Cheung, Mirza, and Leung 2008; Abdelzaher 2012). Suseno and Pinnington (2018) outline that social capital facilitates knowledge acquisition from clients. Contractor, Kundu, and Hsu (2003) gave the example of market research, advertising and financial services as professional service firms that follow their clients abroad.

There are instances where firms are only able to successfully compete in international markets through the assistance of third parties, such as agents, institutions and partners, to minimize their liability of newness or foreignness and risks in foreign countries (e.g. Johanson and Vahlne 2009; Zhou and Guillén 2015; Renko et al. 2016). For example, firms that internationalize to foreign markets may lack local knowledge which may put them at a disadvantage in comparison to domestic competitors. This problem applies to both manufacturing and service firms. Thus, social capital is required when firms internationalize as these firms need to develop and maintain beneficial network relationships that may enable them to compete in those markets. The bonds that firms have with their domestic clients that have internationalized may help these firms to further build their social capital in those markets. In turn, such social capital may enable the firms to find partners who are trustworthy (Child, Rodrigues, and Frynas 2009), acquire foreign market knowledge and financial resources (Lindstrand, Melén, and Nordman 2011) and also increase international opportunity exploitation (Prashantham and Floyd 2012; Lindstrand and Hånell 2017).

Second, service firms could develop specialized services to offer to clients abroad. For example, embodied object exports as described by Ball, Lindsay, and Rose (2008) can be used by firms such as in engineering, product design, software consultancy and market research, to export their specialized services directly to clients in different markets. Service firms could also be involved in embodied people exports where they send their staff to host markets on short-term assignments to deliver and produce professional services (Ball, Lindsay, and Rose 2008). Engineering consulting firms, for instance, usually allocate professionals to international projects in a foreign market (Krull, Smith, and Ge 2012) or a management consultancy firm could send their consultants to directly interact with the firm's international customers (Grönroos 2016). The specialized services to clients abroad delivered by experts from the home country provide a sense of credibility because these expert employees can 'offset the hesitation of foreign buyers to purchase innovative services from emerging market service providers … due to doubts regarding reliability, quality, and other desired service attributes' (Bello et al. 2016, 417). Thus, when service firms build their credibility when exchanging and interacting with clients abroad, their social capital in such interactions fosters knowledge linkages and establishes broader networks, further enabling them to identify international business opportunities and potentially expanding its growth (Ellis 2011).

Third, the internationalization of service firms could also involve cross-border partnerships and the establishment of a physical presence in foreign markets. Service firms are gradually offering new ways of service provision and collaborative partnerships with foreign partners. Online intermediaries are increasingly considered to link multiple buyers and service firms in different markets. Service firms are also pushing domestic boundaries to set up their own operations in different countries and with that there is an increasing awareness and understanding of various social, political, economic and cultural aspects. Social capital with new counterparts facilitates knowledge acquisition (Poon and Rowley 2011) with regards to the firms' involvement in foreign markets and adaptation to various political or cultural aspects to increase the firm's potential for new business opportunities and exploitation of new markets (Laursen, Masciarelli, and Prencipe 2012). Future research could, therefore, examine how service firms can build their social capital in the face of internationalization with its specific nuances of socio-political interactions in different foreign markets.

The service industry has been playing a critical role in global services and trade activities, accounting for significant levels of foreign direct investment in mergers and acquisitions in the world (UNCTAD 2014). Intense competition in domestic markets, advances in information communication technologies and the internationalization of client organizations have, however, forced many service firms to expand their business into international markets (Apfelthaler and Vaiman 2012; Krull, Smith, and Ge 2012; Grönroos 2016). Despite the expansion of many service firms into foreign markets (Abdelzaher 2012), the literature on the internationalization of service firms is surprisingly rather limited (Apfelthaler and Vaiman 2012; Krull, Smith, and Ge 2012).

Given the importance of service firms, particularly in the context of internationalization, it is important to further explore the aspect of social capital in the internationalization of service firms (Lindstrand and Hånell 2017; Suseno and Pinnington 2017a). Internationalization involves not only the provision and delivery of services in foreign markets but also requires the ability of these firms to acquire their knowledge, skills and resources and to also adapt to the various political or cultural aspects to successfully expand their services into foreign markets. Boussebaa and Morgan (2015), for example, identify the federal form and transnational form of internationalization of service firms to ensure global resource integration. By internationalizing, service firms are required to be able to integrate their resources and coordination across multiple jurisdictions (Malhotra and Morris 2009; Brock 2012). This is an aspect that is challenging and complex and yet is presently under-explored in the research. In particular, the literature on the internationalization of service firms tends to focus on developed countries and cases from emerging economies are not that extensive (Boehe 2016). This, therefore, presents an opportunity for further research to examine the role of social capital in the internationalization of service firms in emerging economies, such as in the Asia Pacific.

Social capital for service-oriented social enterprises

Social enterprises aim to address social issues or change, with Bornstein (2004, 15) highlighting that social entrepreneurs are 'the driven, creative individuals who question the status quo, exploit new opportunities, refuse to give up and remake the world for the better'. A similar definition is provided by Thompson and Doherty (2006, 362) in that social enterprises are 'organizations seeking business solutions to social problems'. Such enterprises often attempt to fill the gaps left by the private sector and government in looking for solutions to address social issues (Dacin, Dacin, and Tracey 2011).

Research has highlighted that social entrepreneurs tend to be compassionate (Miller et al. 2012). They are often individuals who desire to create social impact (Austin, Stevenson, and Wei-Skillern 2006; Montgomery and Dacin 2012; McMullen and Bergman 2017). That is, the business model of a social enterprise is about making a change in addressing a social or economic problem and creating sustainable benefits for the community/society (Mair and Martí 2006; Martin and Osberg 2007; Zahra et al. 2008; McMullen and Bergman 2017). A social entrepreneur, thus, aims to contribute to make a difference and the success of their enterprise is not only measured by profit but also in terms of the social value it creates (International Labor Organization 2017).

Social enterprises are service-oriented businesses that are built based on networks of trust for connectivity and cooperation to maintain and sustain social benefits. A lack of community solidarity and involvement makes it harder to sustain social enterprises' programmes to achieve significant impacts. McMullen and Bergman (2017) highlight that a social enterprise that is embedded within tight-knit communities may further strengthen the effects of social norms, such as reciprocity. The International Labor Organization (2017, 11) argues that the success of a social enterprise depends on the trust in the society in that 'it is challenging to identify potential social entrepreneurs where rates of trust and engagement are low'. As such, it is important for a society to have the level and extent of trust, solidarity and shared commitment for building social enterprises to address social needs. As noted by Onyx and Bullen (2000, 195), 'The development of social capital requires the active and willing engagement of citizens working together within a participative community'. Thus, social enterprises would benefit further from coordinated and trusting networks of community.

Several scholars have argued that social capital in terms of the quality of relationships between individuals and organizations as well as within a society can be found in social enterprises as these enterprises are reliant on their relational networks for coordinated actions in addressing socioeconomic issues. For example, Dees, Emerson, and Economy (2002) argued for the importance of network relationships for social entrepreneurs. Such networks are required to create innovation to resolve social problems. Oprica (2013) further outlined that social enterprises can benefit from social networks as a way of building their social capital to achieve their social entrepreneurship objective. Collaborations enable social enterprises to access and use resources, such as financial help, credibility, expertise and institutional resources, to achieve social goals (Mair and Martí 2006). Social entrepreneurs are also more likely to expand their capabilities and social reach through their social capital spanning across different networks of similar and diverse groups of actors (Dees, Emerson, and Economy 2002; Montgomery and Dacin 2012).

Existing literature has also highlighted the potential contribution of social enterprises in building social capital (Evans and Syrett 2007; Bertotti et al. 2012). As noted by Bertotti et al. (2012), some social enterprises can promote bonding and bridging social capital where people from different backgrounds can meet and share their problems. Lumpkin, Bacq, and Pidduck (2018) highlight that a community level of analysis is essential when exploring or discussing the impact of social entrepreneurship. It is, indeed, important to note that communities are the context in which social entrepreneurship change is most likely to occur. As such, the link between social entrepreneurship and social capital in the community is critical, even though it has not been extensively examined in the extant research (Lumpkin, Bacq, and Pidduck 2018). One future research direction could examine the link between social entrepreneurship and social capital in terms of improvement in sectors such as employment, health, education, welfare, environment and social equity, as well as poverty alleviation, as in the study by Alvarez and Barney (2014).

Social enterprises are growing significantly in the Asia Pacific. Here, the rise of social enterprises is mainly driven by millennial philanthropists who use advanced technologies to not only earn revenues and profits, but to try to change the world for the better. The governments of many countries, as well as corporations, are also aggressively promoting social enterprise for impact. For example, the Asia-Pacific Declaration on Social Enterprise and Impact Investment acknowledges the partnerships between governments, the private sector and civil society, including the governments of 17 countries and the British Council, to facilitate social enterprises for a sustainable future to solve social and environmental problems (The British Council 2017). However, quite surprisingly, social entrepreneurship research in the Asia Pacific is not that extensive (Sengupta and Sahay 2017) and this essentially serves as an interesting research gap to explore further.

In essence, future research may benefit by examining the link between social capital and service-oriented social enterprises particularly in the context of the Asia Pacific. There is a circular relationship between social capital and social entrepreneurship, as noted by the International Labor Organization (2017). An increased level of social capital enhances the growth of social entrepreneurship as more individuals and businesses become more tolerant of each other, are more cohesive and are more willing to work together to address social problems. Social enterprises in the community in turn enable the creation of social capital; social entrepreneurs help to facilitate the development of trust and social cohesion that is very much needed to promote collaboration and togetherness in the community/society. The application of social capital in service-oriented social enterprises, whether as a precursor to creating social enterprises or as an outcome of social enterprises, has not been extensively examined in the context of the Asia Pacific, and is, therefore, worthy of further exploration.

Public policy programmes to create social capital

Much research on social capital in the general and strategic management fields is focused on the micro aspect of examining social capital for individual and organizational benefits (e.g. Gubbins and Garavan 2015; Hollenbeck and Jamieson 2015). Social capital, however, is one of the indicators of society well-being (OECD 2001). At the lower level of analysis, individuals who are experiencing social capital in terms of having supportive and extensive personal networks are more likely to be satisfied and live longer (Elgar et al. 2011). At the higher level of analysis, social connections within the society can generate shared values for democratic participation, employment, education and even crime reduction (Deller and Deller 2010). As such, policy-makers need to consider building the interconnectedness between actors within the society for the creation of social capital. For example, relationships between industry and universities can be built and maintained further to foster innovation for the benefit of society (Jackson et al. 2017). Creating social capital is often a long-term goal and it is an iterative process of understanding and experimenting the policies that work and those that do not.

Redding and Rowley (2017) noted the importance of both human and social capital in fostering societal progress and stability in the Asian region. Social capital is built on networks of trust, and policy-makers, therefore, need to create a programme that builds trust in the community/society. One of the ways in which social capital can be built in the context of the Asia Pacific is to build community partnership as part of social and public programmes. For example, in Singapore, the government has over the years established community centres around the country's districts where members of the public can meet for exercise and shared social services, such as singing or forming a band together. In Indonesia, Park (2010) noted the emergence and active participation of Chinese civic organizations to better integrate Chinese Indonesians and build bonding social capital in the country. In Thailand, Susomrith and Suseno (2017) highlighted that social capital has been utilized by individuals and organizations particularly at the top level of the hierarchy. This then creates wealth and expands corporatist interest and network coalitions, with the government being keen to formulate and implement strategies to create social capital to bring about economic and political stability. In China, Burt and Burzynska (2017) found that brokering relationships lead to success and that trust and *guanxi* ties are important to the Chinese entrepreneurs. The Chinese Government has launched several programmes to build such ties and create a more harmonious society, including a nationwide reemployment project and community education (China Daily 2012). The Government of the Philippines has also implemented community-driven development programmes to target the poor communities in the country's provinces to empower local communities, build social capital and improve socio-economic welfare (Innovations for Poverty Action 2017). India, on the other hand, has been noted to display weak social capital which could influence the country's prosperity and growth (Shah 2012; The Times of India 2016). As such, policy-makers need to be proactive to actively promote and support a collaborative engagement process among the public.

Policy-makers need to create a regulatory environment where policies are not too rigid and obstructive in order to foster social capital in the society. Policy-makers also need to provide platforms and infrastructure that promote the exchange of information or even dialogues between societal actors to address challenges and other socioeconomic problems. These are important and interesting avenues for research and theory to explore and map.

Exploratory studies addressing the future directions on social capital research

Our collection contributes to the threefold future research directions. Table 1 illustrates this and the broader picture of the implications of social capital in service-oriented firms in terms of the three future directions: the internationalization of service firms, social capital for

Table 1. Social capital in service-oriented firms: future directions.

Topics	Study
Internationalization of service firms	Suseno
Social capital for service-oriented social enterprises	Tham et al.
	Suseno
	Seet et al.
Public policy programmes to create social capital	Suseno
	Oh et al.
	Wu et al.

service-oriented social enterprises and public policy programmes to create social capital particularly in the context of the Asia Pacific.

The works in our collection found the following. Tham et al.'s study provided a comparative case study of coffee service enterprises within the Asia Pacific. The piece by Suseno illustrated how social capital was created in Indonesia's urban communities as a result of disruptive innovation in a firm's service provision. The case further explored various government support for entrepreneurs and also examined the context of internationalization as the case firm potentially expanded to other foreign markets. Oh et al. then highlighted the use of social networking service among netizens in South Korea and how it created social capital to enable downward mobility of social elites in the country. The study by Wu et al. illustrated the role of social capital in enabling the development of technology management capability that can then subsequently facilitate new product development in service-oriented manufacturing firms in China. The findings are especially important for the implementation of public policy programmes for innovation as the new product development performance of China's service-oriented manufacturing firms has remained relatively weak. Finally, the study by Seet et al. considered the importance of social capital, the 'know-who', in a social enterprise such as a start-up accelerator in providing beneficial outcomes for entrepreneurs.

Conclusion

Social capital has become an increasingly prominent topic of research and discussion in the last few years. Notwithstanding the substantial literature on social capital, there have been fewer attempts to examine social capital in the context of service-oriented firms. Our review revealed that research on social capital mainly has focused on the egocentric or sociocentric approach of social capital and the outcomes of social capital at different levels of analysis. To advance the social capital literature, we provided a collection of works with distinct insights for empirical and practical implications of social capital in service-oriented firms in the Asia Pacific. We also provided a trio of directions for future research and theory development on social capital in terms of the internationalization of service firms, the application of social capital for service-oriented social enterprises and the provision of public policy programmes to create social capital particularly in the context of the Asia Pacific. We hope that our work and that of the others in this collection have successfully highlighted this dynamic field of research and practice on social capital in service-oriented firms in the Asia Pacific region.

Disclosure statement

No potential conflict of interest was reported by the authors.

References

Abdelzaher, D. M. 2012. "The Impact of Professional Service Firms' Expansion Challenges on Internationalization Processes and Performance." *The Service Industries Journal* 32 (10): 1721–1738.

Aldrich, D. P., and M. A. Meyer. 2015. "Social Capital and Community Resilience." *American Behavioral Scientist* 59 (2): 254–269.

Alvarez, S. A., and J. B. Barney. 2014. "Entrepreneurial Opportunities and Poverty Alleviation." *Entrepreneurship Theory and Practice* 38 (1): 159–184.

Apfelthaler, G., and V. Vaiman. 2012. "Challenges and Opportunities of Internationalization in Professional Service Industries." *The Service Industries Journal* 32 (10): 1589–1592.

Austin, J., H. Stevenson, and J. Wei-Skillern. 2006. "Social and Commercial Entrepreneurship: Same, Different, or Both?" *Entrepreneurship, Theory and Practice* 30 (1): 1–22.

Ball, D. A., V. J. Lindsay, and E. L. Rose. 2008. "Rethinking the Paradigm of Service Internationalisation: Less Resource-Intensive Market Entry Modes for Information-Intensive Soft Services." *Management International Review* 48 (4): 413–431.

Bello, D. C., L. P. Radulovich, R. Javalgi, R. F. Scherer, and J. Taylor. 2016. "Performance of Professional Service Firms from Emerging Markets: Role of Innovative Services and Firm Capabilities." *Journal of World Business* 51 (3): 413–424.

Bertotti, M., A. Harden, A. Renton, and K. Sheridan. 2012. "The Contribution of a Social Enterprise to the Building of Social Capital in a Disadvantaged Urban Area of London." *Community Development Journal* 47 (2): 168–183.

Boehe, D. M. 2016. "The Internationalization of Service Firms from Emerging Economies: An Internalization Perspective." *Long Range Planning* 49 (5): 559–569.

Bornstein, D. 2004. *How to Change the World: Social Entrepreneurs and the Power of New Ideas*. New York: Oxford University Press.

Boussebaa, M., and G. Morgan. 2015. "Internationalization of Professional Service Firms: Drivers, Forms, and Outcomes." In *The Oxford Handbook of Professional Service Firms*, edited by L. Empson, D. Muzio, J. Broschak and B. Hinings, 71–91. Oxford: Oxford University Press.

Brock, D. M. 2012. "Building Global Capabilities: A Study of Globalizing Professional Service Firms." *The Service Industries Journal* 32 (10): 1593–1607.

Burt, R. S., and K. Burzynska. 2017. "Chinese Entrepreneurs, Social Networks, and Guanxi." *Management and Organization Review* 13 (2): 221–260.

Cheung, F. S. L., H. Mirza, and W. Leung. 2008. "Client Following Revisited: A Study of Transnational Advertising Agencies in China." *International Journal of Advertising* 27 (4): 593–628.

Child, J., S. B. Rodrigues, and J. G. Frynas. 2009. "Psychic Distance, its Impact and Coping Modes." *Management International Review* 49 (2): 199–224.

China Daily. 2012. *Building the Road to Harmony Needs Social Capital*. http://europe.chinadaily.com.cn/epaper/2012-06/29/content_15535607.htm.

Contractor, F. J., S. K. Kundu, and C.-C. Hsu. 2003. "A Three-Stage Theory of international Expansion: The Link Between Multinationality and Performance in the Service Sector." *Journal of International Business Studies* 34 (1): 5–18.

Dacin, M. T., P. A. Dacin, and P. Tracey. 2011. "Social Entrepreneurship: A Critique and Future Directions." *Organization Science* 22 (5): 1203–1213.

Dees, G. J., J. Emerson, and P. Economy. 2002. *Strategic Tools for Social Entrepreneurs: Enhancing the Performance of Your Enterprising Non-profit*. New York: John Wiley & Sons Inc.

Deller, S. C., and M. A. Deller. 2010. "Rural Crime and Social Capital." *Growth and Change* 41 (2): 221–275.

Elgar, F. J., C. G. Davis, M. J. Wohl, S. J. Trites, and J. M. Zelenski. 2011. "Social Capital, Health and Life Satisfaction in 50 Countries." *Health Place* 17 (5): 1044–1053.

Ellis, P. D. 2011. "Social Ties and International Entrepreneurship: Opportunities and Constraints Affecting Firm Internationalization." *Journal of International Business Studies* 42 (1): 99–127.

Evans, M., and S. Syrett. 2007. "Generating Social Capital?." *European Urban and Regional Studies* 14 (1): 55–74.

Gallouj, F., K. M. Weber, M. Stare, and L. Rubalcaba. 2015. "The Futures of the Service Economy in Europe: A Foresight Analysis." *Technological Forecasting and Social Change* 94 (1): 80–96.

Grönroos, C. 2016. "Internationalization Strategies for Services: A Retrospective." *Journal of Services Marketing* 30 (2): 129–132.

Gubbins, C., and T. Garavan. 2015. "Social Capital Effects on the Career and Development Outcomes of HR Professionals." *Human Resource Management* 55 (2): 241–260.

Hollenbeck, J. R., and B. B. Jamieson. 2015. "Human Capital, Social Capital, and Social Network Analysis: Implications for Strategic Human Resource Management." *Academy of Management Perspectives* 29 (3): 370–385.

Innovations for Poverty Action. 2017. *Community driven development in the Philippines*. https://www.poverty-action.org/study/community-driven-development-philippines.

International Labor Organization. 2017. *Promoting Social Entrepreneurship and Social Capital*. http://www.ilo.org/wcmsp5/groups/public/–africa/–ro-addis_ababa/–sro-cairo/documents/publication/wcms_589097.pdf.

Jackson, P., R. K. Mavi, Y. Suseno, and C. Standing. 2017. "University-Industry Collaboration Within the Triple Helix of Innovation: The Importance of Mutuality." *Science and Public Policy*. doi:10.1093/scipol/scx083.

Johanson, J., and J. E. Vahlne. 2009. "The Uppsala Internationalization Process Model Revisited: From Liability of Foreignness to Liability of Outsidership." *Journal of International Business Studies* 40 (9): 1411–1431.

Krull, E., P. Smith, and G. L. Ge. 2012. "The Internationalization of Engineering Consulting from a Strategy Tripod Perspective." *The Service Industries Journal* 32 (7): 1097–1119.

Kwon, S.-W., and P. A. Adler. 2014. "Social Capital: Maturation of a Field of Research." *Academy of Management Review* 39 (4): 412–422.

Laursen, K., F. Masciarelli, and A. Prencipe. 2012. "Trapped or Spurred by the Home Region? The Effects of Potential Social Capital on Involvement in Foreign Markets for Goods and Technology." *Journal of International Business Studies* 43 (9): 783–807.

Lindstrand, A., and S. M. Hånell. 2017. "International and Market-Specific Social Capital Effects on International Opportunity Exploitation in the Internationalization Process." *Journal of World Business* 52 (5): 653–663.

Lindstrand, A., S. Melén, and E. R. Nordman. 2011. "Turning Social Capital into Business: A Study of the Internationalization of Biotech SMEs." *International Business Review* 20 (2): 194–212.

Lins, K. V., H. Servaes, and A. Tamayo. 2017. "Social Capital, Trust, and Firm Performance: The Value of Corporate Social Responsibility during the Financial Crisis." *The Journal of Finance* 72 (4): 1785–1824.

Lumpkin, G. T., S. Bacq, and R. J. Pidduck. 2018. "Where Change Happens: Community-Level Phenomena in Social Entrepreneurship Research." *Journal of Small Business Management* 56 (1): 24–50.

Malhotra, N., and T. Morris. 2009. "Heterogeneity in Professional Service Firms." *Journal of Management Studies* 46 (6): 895–922.

Mair, J., and I. Martí. 2006. "Social Entrepreneurship Research: A Source of Explanation, Prediction, and Delight." *Journal of World Business* 41 (1): 36–44.

Martin, R. L., and S. Osberg. 2007. "Social Entrepreneurship: The Case for Definition." *Stanford Social Innovation Review* 5 (2): 28–39.

McMullen, J. S., and B. J. Bergman Jr. 2017. "Social Entrepreneurship and the Development Paradox of Prosocial Motivation: A Cautionary Tale." *Strategic Entrepreneurship Journal* 11 (3): 243–270.

Meyer, K. F., M. Wright, and S. Pruthi. 2009. "Managing Knowledge in Foreign Entry Strategies: A Resource-Based Analysis." *Strategic Management Journal* 30 (5): 557–574.

Miller, T. L., M. G. Grimes, J. S. McMullen, and T. J. Vogus. 2012. "Venturing for Others with Heart and Head: How Compassion Encourages Social Entrepreneurship." *Academy of Management Review* 37 (4): 616–640.

Montgomery, A. W., and P. A. Dacin. 2012. "Collective Social Entrepreneurship: Collaboratively Shaping Social Good." *Journal of Business Ethics* 111 (3): 375–388.

Nahapiet, J., and S. Ghoshal. 1998. "Social Capital, Intellectual Capital, and the Organizational Advantage." *Academy of Management Review* 23 (2): 242–266.

OECD. 2001. *The Well-Being of Nations: The Role of Human and Social Capital*. http://www.oecd.org/site/worldforum/33703702.pdf.

Onyx, J., and P. Bullen. 2000. "Measuring Social Capital in Five Communities." *The Journal of Applied Behavioral Science* 36 (1): 23–42.

Oprica, R. 2013. "Social Networking for Social Entrepreneurship." *Procedia – Social and Behavioral Sciences* 92: 664–667.

Park, J. B. 2010. "Civic Networks and Building Social Capital in Indonesia: An Innovative Experiment by Chinese Organizations in the Post-Suharto Era." *Journal of International and Area Studies* 17 (1): 75–90.

Poon, I., and C. Rowley. 2011. "Knowledge Management." In *HRM: The Key Concepts*, edited by C. Rowley and K. Jackson, 142–146. Routledge.

Prashantham, S., and S. W. Floyd. 2012. "Routine Microprocesses and Capability Learning in International New Ventures." *Journal of International Business Studies* 43 (6): 544–562.

Redding, G., and C. Rowley. 2017. "Conclusion: The Central Role of Human and Social Capital." *Asia Pacific Business Review* 23 (2): 299–305.

Renko, M., S. K. Kundu, R. Shrader, A. L. Carsrud, and A. Parhankangas. 2016. "Liabilities, Advantages, and Buffers of Newness." *Group & Organization Management* 41 (6): 786–822.

Sengupta, S., and A. Sahay. 2017. "Social Enterpreneurship Research in Asia-Pacific: Perspectives and Opportunities." *Social Enterprise Journal* 13 (1): 17–37.

Shah, H. 2012. *Prosperity and Social Capital: Is India Missing Out?* The London School of Economics and Political Science. http://blogs.lse.ac.uk/southasia/2012/11/02/prosperity-and-social-capital-is-india-missing-out/.

Simon, G. L., and D. H. B. Welsh. 2010. "International Professional Service Firms: How Do They Affect Government Policy?" *The Service Industries Journal* 30 (1): 11–23.

Suseno, Y., and A. H. Pinnington. 2017a. "Building Social Capital and Human Capital for Internationalization: The Role of Network Ties and Knowledge Resources." *Asia Pacific Journal of Management*. https:// link.springer.com/article/10.1007/s10490-017-9541-0.

Suseno, Y., and A. H. Pinnington. 2017b. "The War for Talent: Human Capital Challenges for Professional Service Firms." *Asia Pacific Business Review* 23 (2): 205–229.

Suseno, Y., and A. H. Pinnington. 2018. "The Significance of Human Capital and Social Capital: Professional-Client Relationships in the Asia Pacific." *Asia Pacific Business Review* 24 (1): 72–89.

Susomrith, P., and Y. Suseno. 2017. "Social Capital and the Social Context of Business Networks: The Case of Thailand." In *Business Networks in East Asian Capitalism: Emerging Trends, Emerging Patterns*, edited by J. Nolan, C. Rowley and M. Warner, 269–288. Kidlington: Elsevier.

The British Council. 2017. *International Coalition to Promote Social Enterprise for Sustainable Development Across the Asia-Pacific Region*. https://www.britishcouncil.org/international-coalition-promote-social-enterprise-sustainable-development-across-asia-pacific-region.

The Times of India. 2016. *8–10% Growth Rate Must for India: Singapore Deputy PM*. https:// timesofindia.indiatimes.com/india/8-10-growth-rate-must-for-India-Singapore-deputy-PM/articleshow/53881018.cms.

Thompson, J., and B. Doherty. 2006. "The Diverse World of Social Enterprise: A Collection of Social Enterprise Stories." *International Journal of Social Economics* 33 (5/6): 361–375.

UNCTAD. 2014. *World Investment Report 2014: Investing in the SDGs: An Action Plan*. New York and Geneva: United Nations Conference on Trade and Development.

Zahra, S. A., H. N. Rawhouser, N. Bhawe, D. O. Neubaum, and J. C. Hayton. 2008. "Globalization of Social Entrepreneurship Opportunities." *Strategic Entrepreneurship Journal* 2 (2): 117–131.

Zhou, N., and M. F. Guillén. 2015. "From Home Country to Home Base: A Dynamic Approach to the Liability of Foreignness." *Strategic Management Journal* 36 (6): 907–917.

Index

For Product Safety Concerns and Information please contact our EU
representative GPSR@taylorandfrancis.com
Taylor & Francis Verlag GmbH, Kaufingerstraße 24, 80331 München, Germany